ENDORSEMENTS FOR CHARGING GRIZZLIES

Do you ever wonder the secret to a thriving marriage? Long to connect with your kids? Feel overwhelmed by your day-to-day demands? If so, take a moment to meditate on the principles of *Charging Grizzlies, Rude Neighbors* as Warren Baldwin unwraps the greatest gift anyone could ask for, wisdom!

Greg and Julie Gorman
Authors of *Two Are Better Than One ... God Has a Purpose for Your Marriage*

As a writer, Warren displays the same effective communication skills I have enjoyed in his speaking for many years. The subject matter in this new book is broad and handled in a practical and challenging way. I recommend this book without reservation."

Michael A. Christensen
Shepherd/Evangelist, Cody Church of Christ, Cody, Wyoming.

Warren Baldwin has compiled a gem within the pages of this book. In my twenty plus years working in full time ministry and teaching I have used various commentaries, reference books, and resources to teach from the book of Proverbs. This study of Proverbs has now become one of my favorites because of its rich depth, practical and applicable content, and its ease of use for teaching, counseling, or personal study.

Jon Hackett, M.S.
Strata Leadership, LLC, Trainer, Coach, and Professional Speaker

Words like practical, concise and relevant came to mind as I read. Warren's writing style appeals to wholesome common sense and character. In a world that has embellished and glorified immorality leaving young and old alike in confusion, the lessons of wisdom drawn from the Proverbs are timely and applicable. I recommend this book to teer mature alike; it is a good compass. I think that familie use this book in family devotion settings to spark thou

D1409822

in these practical Christian principles. Warren's stories are applicable and relevant in affirming the wisdom of the proverbs. This book reflects well the intent of inspiration to equip individuals, couples and children with tools to live more wholesome lives. Read it!

Bill Goben, Minister, Billings, MT

Our society is in a moral dilemma. *Charging Grizzlies* points us to a resource that can help us find our way out – the book of Proverbs. With stark clarity Warren explains the teaching of this biblical collection of wisdom, eternal truths for a world that has lost its way. Don't miss this book.

Richard Hill
Elder, Teacher, Farmer, College Roommate, and Friend

In this book, *Charging Grizzlies*, Warren Baldwin has selected key verses from Proverbs to explain with insightful and useful examples from real life situations. These eloquent examples will give the reader greater understanding of the message of Proverbs.

Dr. Benjamin M. Locklear
Mangum, OK

The section on preaching the one-sentence proverbs was very helpful because it shows how to study the proverbs and present their message to other people. It provides a simple, step-by-step way to understand the message and shape the lesson. It helps to relate the proverbs to life.

Bona Valca
Harding Student, Minister's Wife, Mom

CHARGING GRIZZLIES, RUDE NEIGHBORS

Jessica —
Proverbs — for
changing lives and families!

Warren B
Prov. 1:8
May 2018

WARREN BALDWIN

CHARGING GRIZZLIES, RUDE NEIGHBORS

AND MORE
GEMS FROM
PROVERBS

ISBN-10: 1944704442
ISBN-13: 978-1944704445

Published by Start2Finish
Fort Worth, Texas 76244
www.start2finish.org

Printed in the United States of America

Unless otherwise noted, all Scripture quotations are from HOLY BIBLE, NEW INTERNA-TIONAL VERSION®. Copyright © 1973, 1978, 1984 by International Bible Society. Used by permission of Zondervan Publishing House.

Cover Design: Josh Feit, Evangela.com

CONTENTS

Foreword   *11*

Introduction   *15*

  Who Wrote Proverbs?   15

  How Does Proverbs Produce Wisdom?   17

  Wisdom & Order   20

1 Marriage   23

  Keep Your Love at Home   23

  Wives Who Bless the Fountain   25

  Anatomy of an Affair   28

  Romance & Marriage   30

  Irreconcilable Differences   33

  A Woman Who Fears the Lord   35

  The Wife of Noble Character   37

2 Kids   41

  Learning to Make Choices   41

  Honey, Trust Me   42

  Storytelling   45

  What Our Children Should Never Hear   47

  What Our Children Should Hear   49

  Sparing the Rod   51

  Power of Example   53

  What Can I Do?   55

  Listening to Our Children   57

  No Respect for Weakness   59

  Understanding Billy   61

  Respecting Parents   63

  Children in the Checkout Line   65

3 Family   **71**

Family Conversations   71

Family Memory   73

Harming Our House   75

The Family Meal   78

4 The God We Serve   **81**

Behavior vs. Love   81

Answered Prayer   83

God Is Our Shield   85

The Lord's Discipline   87

Delighting in Mankind   89

Noble & Humble   91

Sorrow-Acre   93

5 The Disciplined Life   **97**

Two Meals   97

Work Habits   99

Fantasies   101

Easy Money   103

Discipline   105

The Simple   107

Stern Discipline   109

Worthy Goals   111

Honey   113

The Hidden Cost of Drunkenness   115

6 Setting the Example   **119**

Mentor a Youth   119

Blazing Trails   121

Rebuke   122

Personal vs. Positional Authority   124

Integrity Endures		127
Gray Hair		128
Modeling		131
Tractor Pulls		133
7	**Daily Challenges**	**135**
Industry		135
If You Would Be Happy		137
Silence in the Face of Danger		139
Defensive Control		141
Tale of Two Funerals		143
The Process of Forgiving		145
Showing Pity		147
8	**Words, Words, Words**	**151**
Tongues of Silver		151
Fitting Speech		153
Build or Destroy		155
Why the Righteous Man Escapes Trouble		157
Pleasant Words		159
Choice Morsels		162
Restraining the Tongue		164
An Apt Word		166
Strife		168
Crafting Our Worlds		170
9	**Relationships**	**173**
Listening Is Ministry		173
Aberrations of Friendship		175
Seeking Goodwill		178
Cautious in Friendship		180
A Cheerful Look		182
Problems in Community		185

Charging Grizzlies 187

Forgiveness has a face 189

Wounds From a Friend 191

Rude Neighbor 194

Friction 196

Iron Sharpens Iron 198

Absolute Surrender 200

Acting Out 201

10 Matters of the Heart 205

Do You Have the Wisdom of Solomon? 205

Land Mines 207

Pride & Quarrels 211

Listening 213

We Can Encourage 214

Is Peace Possible? 216

Judgment or Mercy? 218

Belief Aids 221

Money in the Hand 223

Ski Slopes & Pride 225

Never Satisfied 227

Life, Prosperity, & Honor 229

Suggestions for Studying Proverbs 233

How to Preach One-Sentence Proverbs 233

How to Preach Themes in Proverbs 236

How to Preach Extended Sections in Proverbs 239

Scripture Index 243

Subject Index 249

FOREWORD

Life is tough sometimes, isn't it?"

My friend was trying to read on a plane but the woman seated next to him was pretty intent on talking. He put his book down and engaged her in conversation. When she found out they were flying to the same city, she told him what motel she was staying in. She followed that with a smile and invitation to come see her.

My friend thought of his wife and kids at home. He thought of the Bible students in his classes at the university and the people in the church he served. He thought about God. How could he explain such an indiscretion to all of them? There was no way he could accept this woman's invitation. But, she was emotionally needy and he didn't want to add to her pain.

As he was struggling with how to say no in a convincing but graceful manner he noticed numerous scars on her wrists. "Life is tough sometimes, isn't it?" he asked. She followed his gaze to her wrists and said, "Oh, you have no idea how tough." With that, the conversation changed, and he was able to share some deep and important truths with her. My friend gave the woman a proverb and she ran with it, allowing it to change her thinking and her conversation.

I wonder if there isn't some connection between this story and what God intends for us to do with the proverbs. I think God would like for us to take a wise saying and run with it, allowing it to open our minds, redirect our thinking, and change our conversation.

Think of an hourglass laid on its side. Instead of the wide parts being at the top and bottom of the narrow passage way, they are to the left and right of it (and the ends of the hour glass are open, not closed). Think of the narrow part as the saying of a proverb, the wider part to the left as the story (or stories) behind the proverb, and the wider part to the right being potential future stories. Now, in your mind, or on a piece of paper, put a proverb in that narrow place, like Proverbs 15:18: "A hot-tempered man stirs up dissension, but a patient man calms a quarrel."

Over many years the Sage observed hot-tempered people pushing and prodding others into altercations, even fights. He also observed those who were more even tempered had a cooling effect on people's emotions. His years of observation led him to condense these past experiences into a succinct statement embodying multiple stories. So, the movement of the hour glass is from left to right, from the stories to the statement. It continues to move to the right, opening up into another series of future stories. Those future stories are situations of flaming emotions where people can decide if they will be hot-tempered and stir up trouble, or will exercise control and calm the situation. See Proverbs 22:24-25 to see other applications the Sage made from observing hot-tempered people.

So, a proverb is a collection of backstories condensed into a succinct statement embodying those experiences, and then projected into the future. It challenges us to apply its wisdom to those future experiences, enabling us to make better decisions than we could have otherwise.

The Sage wants us to do with the proverbs what the lady on the plane did with my friend's statement about life being tough sometimes: he wants us to run with it. What does this proverb make you think? What past stories from your own life does it call to mind? What emotions does it stimulate? Notice how the backstory flows into the condensed statement, the proverb. Think about what the proverb has to say about your personal experiences with anger. Then, continue to run with the proverb by envisioning future stories. What if your coworker explodes in anger again next week? What does the proverb teach you about new ways to respond? What does it say about the friends you associate with? Is there any way you might be drawn into their drama? Might it be better for you to find other friends?

The proverbs were written to teach us and challenge us. I have a friend who interprets the Bible by asking each passage, "If I take this text seriously, what do I have to change?" He says the answer to this question is more important than all the history and background information you can discover about the text, such as who it was written to and the situation in their world. That can be helpful to know, but what matters more is our answer to the questions, "If I take this text seriously, what do I have to change? What kind of world is God trying to create with this passage, and how do I fit in to it? What is God calling for me to be or do based on what this passage says?"

This book, *Charging Grizzlies*, is my attempt to run with the proverbs and ask the questions about what God is trying to do and how the proverbs fit into our daily life choices. Sometimes I explain what an individual proverb means, and sometimes I show how it dovetails with a real life story, either my own or another's. Both approaches are an attempt to run with the proverb, assimilating it into my life and asking what it is trying to do in or with me.

This is similar to what I tried to do in *Roaring Lions, Cracking Rocks and Other Gems from Proverbs*. Something different in this volume is introductory essays at the beginning, and essays at the end about how to study, preach, and teach proverbs in your context. I hope you find it all helpful.

Warren Baldwin

INTRODUCTION

WHO WROTE PROVERBS?

There is no way of knowing how many of the three thousand proverbs Solomon spoke made it into the book of Proverbs (1 Kings 4:32). Three passages in Proverbs refer to Solomon's contribution to the book (1:1; 10:1; 25:1), but we know other people and groups participated in writing and collecting the sayings as well. Agur contributed sayings (30:1) and King Lemuel passed on the oral teaching of his mother (31:1). Men of King Hezekiah's court copied sayings of Solomon that had been passed down but apparently had not made it into the book yet (25:1). These various contributors to the final collection of the proverbs indicate the process involved numerous personalities over a period of hundreds of years.

As many as four different groups representing four different social settings may have been involved in the production of Proverbs. One group is the Royal Court. A king could have either produced or collected wise sayings himself, like Solomon, or he could have employed the services of the wise men to do the work, like Hezekiah. Training young men in wisdom would benefit a king by producing responsible citizens and workers for the healthy functioning of society. Further, young men who performed in an exemplary manner would qualify for service in the king's court. Proverbs about kings appear in chapters 14, 16, 19, 20, 21, 22, 24, 25 and, 29. The fact that many of these proverbs present the king in a positive light indicates the king's interest in their message. "When a king sits on his throne to judge, he winnows out all evil with his eyes" (20:8) is one example.

Another suggestion is schools specializing in wisdom instruction, making teachers in these settings possible authors. Other ancient societies had such schools, so it is possible that Israel had some. There is a reference to such a school during the intertestamental period (in Sirach 51:23), but that does not establish that there were such schools during the period of the kings when the proverbs were being written and collected. There is not much evidence to support the view that wisdom schools in Israel produced Proverbs.

A third setting is the village. In ancient communities, older men would sit at the village gates hearing the concerns of the citizens and rendering judgments. It is natural to assume that these men would also talk about how to deal with problem situations relating to communal behavior such as neighborliness (27:14), friendship (27:6, 10), work ethics (10:4; 18:9), management principles (27:23) and healthy living in general (11:25, 27). Many proverbs deal with these particular issues. Related to these concerns are the numerous proverbs that reflect a rural setting. Community elders would want young farmers to know that "He who gathers crops in summer is a wise son, but he who sleeps during harvest is a disgraceful son" (10:5). Such wisdom teaching handed down by communal leaders would promote healthy social functioning.

Finally, the family is a possible setting for the production of Proverbs. Numerous times the proverbial writer says, "My son," and then appeals for a hearing, arguing for the superiority of wisdom, or offering some teaching or insight. "My son, pay attention to my wisdom, listen well to my words of insight, that you may maintain discretion and your lips may preserve knowledge" (5:1-2). This proverb is directed to a young man about to face an exciting but dangerous temptation: an immoral relationship. The writer then informs the young man of the dangers inherent in such a pursuit, followed by a convincing argument for the sanctity and beauty of a covenant relationship (marriage). Wisdom is the key to save this naive young man.

Proverbs 4:1ff presents a strong case for the family setting of Proverbs. "When I was a boy in my father's house, still tender, and an only child of my mother, he taught me ..." (4:3-4). Three generations of a family are involved in the educational process: a grandfather, a mother and father, and the son. "The explicit comments about education in the O.T. (Deut. 4:10; 5:31; 11:19) as well as the dynamics of Prov. 1-9 suggest that learning came about when a father instructed his son in a family setting" (Waltke, *Proverbs* 1:27).

The fingerprints of several individuals and groups have been left on the writing and collecting of the proverbs. Over the years these various groups could have produced the wisdom germane to their particular concerns. As the assimilators of the wisdom material became aware of other sayings, they could have easily incorporated them into the larger collection.

Because a number of individuals were involved in producing Proverbs, many writers today refer to the author of individual proverbs, and even of the book as a whole, as "the Sage." This term allows for the contributions of Solomon, Augur, Lemuel, Lemuel's mother, the men of Hezekiah's court, and any other personalities without having to discern who penned any particular saying.

Of course, we trust that working behind any individual or group was the hand of God, ultimately producing this compendium of wisdom so that we might fear the Lord (1:7) and trust in him with all of our being (3:5).

HOW DOES PROVERBS PRODUCE WISDOM?

> The proverbs of Solomon, son of David, king of Israel: for attaining wisdom and discipline; for understanding words of insight.
>
> Proverbs 1:1-2

The goal of Proverbs is to teach wisdom for life. The context to learn this wisdom is in a relationship with God ("fear of the Lord," 1:7). While someone who doesn't walk with God can still receive benefit from studying the book, the full nutritive value will be missing. Walking with

God and growing in wisdom involves trusting him with all our heart and submitting our will to his. "Lean not on your own understanding" (3:5) means that if our perspective on an issue conflicts with God's, we forego our own.

Proverbs does not give instruction on every type of wise behavior for every conceivable situation. Rather, it emphasizes the importance of learning important principles that apply in a wide variety of situations. Let's think of this in two facets.

There are many specific instructions or examples in Proverbs of how to act wisely. Instructions include working hard, saving money, showing respect, fleeing immorality, and speaking kindly.

Consider Proverbs 10:19, "When words are many, sin is not absent, but he who holds his tongue is wise." It is prudent to hold one's tongue as speaking too much is not only annoying to other people, but increases opportunity for sinning. This is an example of specific instruction.

While there are times to hold one's tongue, there are other situations where wisdom demands that we speak. We must speak to nourish others with our words (10:21), whether that be an encouraging comment (15:4, 30) or a necessary rebuke. How do we know when to remain silent or when to speak? If we decide it is time to speak, how do we know what is proper and fitting to say? This leads to another facet of proverbial instruction.

The instructions or examples in proverbs are also principles that apply to more than one situation. Remaining silent is the proper instruction for one situation but may not apply in another. To continue drawing from Proverbs 10:19 as an example, regarding who, when, and how to rebuke, we must be discerning, lest we correct a fool (mocker) and he turn on us in wrath (9:7-8a). It is the wise who benefit from correction (9:8b-9; 15:31), so that is who we want to give attention.

So how do we know when it is time to finally speak? What words do we use? To whom do we speak them? Over time and through the accumulation of proverbial instruction, insight from others, and experience (both pleasant and painful), "the lips of the righteous (learn) what is fitting" (10:32).

In one setting, we may hear a person speak foolishly and decide the timing isn't right, or the person isn't ready to listen, so we hold our words. In another setting, we might hear the same foolish words uttered by someone else, but because we know their heart is different, we speak to them.

While individual or sentence proverbs offer concrete instructions or examples of how to act, we must use prudence to know when and how those instructions apply. The greater aim of Proverbs is to teach the principles of wisdom so the student has a base from which to draw insight for new situations.

This ability of the proverbs to be deeply ingrained in us and then applied in other settings is known as its performative force. We can't just memorize a proverb and think we have it; we must be able to assess and understand the dynamics of a particular situation to know how the proverb(s) shapes our conduct. This understanding becomes the mix of wisdom and insight that forms our world outlook, ethics, and ability to discern the dynamics of new situations so we can respond appropriately (David Kelsey, *Eccentric Existence: A Theological Anthropology*, 1:223).

We all teach our children not to run in the road. We point at the street in front of our house and say, "No!" with great firmness. If they challenge us by running into or near the street, we may deliver a smack to the behind. Hopefully our command, "Do not go in the road," followed by punishment if they do, will function as proverbial wisdom to our children to steer clear of the street.

Then we take our children to grandma's house. As we are unloading items to take inside, there are a few unsupervised moments when our children can follow us into the house, or they can explore the environment away from the watchful eyes of mom and dad, including trying to cross the street. What will the children do? Did the spanking they received at home for disobedience regarding the road give them any insight and knowledge beyond our front yard? Will they apply the lessons learned at home to the street in front of grandma's house? If so, our words are functioning with performative force. The lessons learned are carried beyond the initial experience and are being applied in wider situations.

We can't expect that our command to not go in the road will last forever. Eventually, our children will have to cross a street. So, we teach them to "Stop, look and listen." If some fear of the pavement and speeding cars still resides within them, they will be careful. The initial lessons learned years ago of avoiding danger by not going in the road will still guide and guard their actions, keeping them safe.

The ultimate lesson we hope our children will learn is that they stop, look, and listen, not only at a highway, but in the presence of any potentially dangerous situation in life. A boy at school that is too debonair, a powdery substance that promises escape, a financial investment that cannot lose - these are all potentially dangerous highways. The speeding cars on this road are people, substances, and empty promises that can crush us.

The lesson learned early on about "Don't go in the street!" and was later expanded to "Stop, look, and listen," applies to more than just the street in front of our house. It applies to all the roads of life. That is the nature of a proverb. Each proverb contains a gem of wisdom that can be applied to a specific situation and context. But their real value and performative force lies in their power to ingrain themselves into our psyche and influence our thinking and ethical choices on all the highways we encounter.

WISDOM & ORDER

God created order in the world. Flowing streams, sunshine, and vegetation are all part of the peace and harmony in God's ordering of things.

When Adam and Eve selfishly ate the fruit in an attempt to be more like God, they disrupted his order. They thought only of themselves and not of the well-being of the whole creation, both present and future. Selfishness does that; it craves for the self without thought for the harm it causes others now and later. James recognizes this problem when he writes, "Where you have envy and selfish ambition, there you find disorder and every evil practice" (James 3:16). Notice the connection between selfishness and disorder.

Proverbs seeks to promote wisdom and the well-being of people.

Wise people benefit not only themselves but also those around them. To be wise in Proverbs is not to be smart, but to know how to live in harmonious and mutually beneficial relationships with others. It is to live with the intention of blessing the lives of others and enhancing their well-being. Marriages are closer, families are stronger, school and work environments are more positive, and neighborhoods are safer the more people pursue the goal of wise living and healthy relationships.

Healthy living doesn't happen accidentally. Wise people desire a godly life and they intentionally promote a beneficial order for their family and other people.

This intentionality can be seen in the Good Wife of Proverbs 31:10ff. This woman is busy! She gets up early in the morning to provide food for her family. That takes money, so she engages in business. She spins cloth, makes garments, and sells them in the market place. She intends to make money honestly, part of God's order. Her intention determines the ordering of her activity. The Good Wife is moving toward something good and her family will eat.

Her intentions provide more than the ordering of activity and the healthy functioning of her family. Her work also provides order for the larger social realm. The community benefits from her work as well. The Good Wife intends to get money for her family. Meanwhile, another person intends to buy a garment. When these two people meet at the market a fair exchange takes place: money for the garment. One now has the money to buy food and one has clothing. Both the Good Wife and her customer leave happy.

The Good Wife could have undermined this process by selfish and evil activity, such as by selling a shoddy garment. This would be a poor exchange of good money for a lesser quality item. In a more extreme case, she could have robbed the customer of her money. In this instance, there would be no exchange. If the Good Wife had acted selfishly by cheating her customer with poor quality for good money, or by theft, her evil actions would have produced disorder. Think of the hurt, anger, and pain she prevented in others by acting with good intentions and good behavior.

The Good Wife in Proverbs 31 is more than just a good wife. The

Good Wife is also a metaphor for all of us who seek godly wisdom, who seek to trust in the Lord rather than lean upon our own understanding (3:5). She is a metaphor for all of us who intend to live godly lives, and in so doing set about ordering our lives with activity that is beneficial and prosperous for everyone. Order serves the community need for well-being, and it does so with hard work, honesty, and fairness.

The Good Wife benefits not only herself, but also her family and anyone who does business with her. She enhances and enriches the well-being of everyone her life touches. When we walk in the footsteps of the Good Wife, we have the same positive affect upon others.

It is enlivening and empowering to think that today you and I actually help God in the proper ordering of his universe. When we live intentionally to enrich the lives of others, we enhance their lives and society at large benefits. When we tip a waitress generously, when we thank a neighbor for his kindness, when we buy lunch for a drifter, or when we work a full day, we promote the kind of order that benefits everyone, and we make the Good Wife proud.

CHAPTER ONE

MARRIAGE

KEEP YOUR LOVE AT HOME

Drink water from your own cistern, running water from
your own well.

Proverbs 5:15

Wisdom is a source of strength God gives a man to help him resist
sexual temptation. Wisdom includes knowing the dangers of illicit sexual relations, including the possible loss of one's family and standing in
the community (5:14). Since wisdom includes a continual striving for
character and integrity, engaging in improper relations would derail that
pursuit.

A relationship with God is another source of strength. This in itself is
a feature of wisdom (Prov. 1:7). A relationship with God, fed with Bible
study, prayer, and fellowship, strengthens one to keep all other relationships pure and holy.

Jesus is the greatest example of maintaining integrity in the midst
of situations that could offer temptations. He could move confidently
among men and women who struggled with their morals because his relationship with God provided him inner strength. He avoided the sins of
the world, while at the same time associating with people in those sins
and calling them to a higher life. He was a friend, teacher, and mentor to
an adulterous woman (John 4) and a cheating tax collector (John 19).

Jesus came to love sinners, not use them for selfish pleasure or gain.

Proverbs 5:15 begins a discussion that introduces a third source of strength for young people to avoid sexual immorality: a vibrant sexual relationship with their spouse. "Drink water from your own cistern, running water from your own well."

Metaphors have always been a popular way to communicate sensitive issues. For the wisdom writers, water was a frequent figure of speech for sexual relations. In Proverbs 9:17 water is used for sensual pleasure: "Stolen water is sweet." Because this statement is made by Woman Folly to entice young men off the path of discipline and moral behavior, we know this use of water is a reference to inappropriate sexuality.

In Song of Songs 4:15, water is used in a positive sense between a husband and wife. "You are a garden fountain, a well of flowing water streaming down from Lebanon." In the larger context, the husband is praising his wife's beauty and physical allurements, identifying and extolling various parts of her body. The wife is not shy or retiring about this attention, but glories in it. She responds with an invitation to her husband to find his refreshment in her: "Awake, north wind, and come, south wind! Blow on my garden that its fragrance may spread abroad. Let my lover come into his garden and taste its choice fruits" (Song of Songs 4:16). The metaphors for lovemaking continue in chapter five with both the husband and wife reveling in each other's attention.

The Sage promotes this same level of physical activity between the spouses and warns that the activity be exclusive to them. "Drink water from your own cistern, running water from your own well" means the husband finds his relief and pleasure in only one person: his wife. She is his only well and garden and he is to be hers. In the spirit of this passage, the New Testament asserts that the wife's body does not belong to her alone, nor does the husband's body belong to him alone, but each belongs to the other. In this exclusive relationship each gives up the claim to their own body for the benefit of their spouse. In this sexual relationship, the husband and wife will not only find pleasure and bonding, but a defense against immorality (1 Cor. 7:2-5).

We are physical beings with various bodily hungers and drives that demand relief. Sex is one such hunger, and it drives us to another person for satisfaction and companionship. This is natural and is proper and celebrated in the context of marriage. With a clear conscience and unbridled joy, a young bride and groom may enjoy the refreshing water of their own cistern.

WIVES WHO BLESS THE FOUNTAIN

> Drink water from your own cistern, running water from your own well. Should your springs overflow in the streets, your streams of water in the public squares? Let them be yours alone, never to be shared with strangers. May your fountain be blessed, and may you rejoice in the wife of your youth.
>
> Proverbs 5:15-18

While these verses speak primarily to husbands, there are implications for wives as well. A husband who cheats on his wife or fails to give her appropriate attention leaves her feeling betrayed and abandoned. In her hurt and loneliness she may seek consolation in a relationship with another man. Overflowing springs and streams of water running in the streets is a likely reference to the wife stepping out of the marital relationship in response to the husband doing so (addressed by the reference to drinking water from his own cistern or well. The cistern or well is the sexual relationship shared by a husband and wife). Solomon acknowledges that some women in a situation of betrayal by their husbands may become springs that overflow in the streets, seeking love and affirmation with another. Many women don't respond that way, however. They choose the high moral road this passage encourages.

God is concerned with developing wisdom and a moral consciousness in everyone, male and female. Proverbs is addressed primarily to young men, as can be seen in the moral instructions directed to male temptations: the lure of attractive women, voluptuous kisses, and sensuous perfume (cf. Prov. 7:10-18). Proverbs warns against the wiles of the immoral woman who draws men from the moral path (chapters 2,

5, 6, 7) and who seeks pleasure in stolen water, (a likely metaphor for immoral sexual behavior). But it also honors the wise and moral woman for building a healthy home (14:1). Also, the Wise Wife of Proverbs 31 is extolled for the selfless attention she showers upon her husband and children, something she likely would not do if her energies were spent upon a secret lover.

While Proverbs enjoins moral behavior for a man, it clearly assumes it for a woman as well. So, if a husband is unfaithful, seeking sources of sensual refreshment from a woman other than his wife, that doesn't mean the wife has to do the same. She can exercise her moral fiber and rededicate her efforts to do all she can to preserve what she can of her home.

A wife has tremendous power to nurture refreshment in the home to help prevent it from deteriorating to the point of either partner seeking affection elsewhere. She can use initiative and creativity to ensure that the springs and fountain of the home continually attract the attention of her husband.

Proverbs 7 presents us with a sexually aggressive married woman who, unfortunately, is unfaithful to her husband and is directing her energy toward an unsuspecting young male visiting the big city. She spots the boy wandering aimlessly and accosts all of his senses with her feminine appeal. She wears alluring apparel (v.10), envelops him in a passionate embrace, kisses him energetically (v.13), speaks temptingly (v.14-18), and perfumes her private chamber (and likely herself, v.17). Everything she does inflames the young man's mind and body. Yet everything she does is so wrong because she is not married to this young man. Her drive and ambition is completely misdirected because such affection is meant for her husband.

Proverbs doesn't say why this woman acts this way. It just warns young men to avoid such volatile, immoral situations. God gives men five senses to experience pleasure. When all five of them are under sensual attack at one time, it will be difficult for even the strongest, most centered of men to resist for long. The immediate response requires a family-oriented man to just run!

Let's look at Proverbs 7 from another perspective. What makes the

Proverbs 7 woman so dangerous to a man? The fact that she is offering what every male craves: a healthy, inviting, and energetic romantic encounter. And while the approach of the Proverbs 7 woman is so wrong when exercised outside of marriage, it is so right when directed toward her husband.

What man wouldn't double time it home if he knew the love of his life was waiting to embrace him offering the wiles of the Proverbs 7 woman? One of the greatest (and most exciting) weapons a husband has in his arsenal to ward off the overtures of the seductress is his wife. Wives who occasionally show their husbands the level of excitement and interest that the Proverbs 7 woman does keep the fires burning at home.

Jobs, demands of the home, and caring for energetic kids often leaves a wife and mom so exhausted she simply doesn't have the strength to give an energetic and sensuous greeting to her husband, and it is unfair to expect her to. During the years when the children are little romance can easily take a back burner. While that is understandable and sometimes unavoidable, it is also dangerous. The sizzle in a marriage may falter and die, but the need for love, acceptance, affection, and sex does not. But if a husband and wife don't find them in each other, they become easy pickings for any aggressor on the prowl. Don't let exhaustion give room to a Proverbs 7 woman claiming what is yours. And, yes, while all the adultery chapters in Proverbs hold the man accountable for his moral offenses, even when he is under assault by an aggressive pursuer, a loving wife who is equally aggressive at home can do much to assure his faithfulness.

Wives, be the spark plug sometimes. Your romantic aggression means more to your husband than he will ever tell you, largely because men don't like to talk about their feelings. But if you notice your husband smiling more, being kind and gracious in the home, telling you to go shopping while he watches the kids, and taking out the trash without being asked, you'll know why. Your initiation of a sexual encounter will make your husband feel valued, proud (in a healthy sense), wanted, and grateful to you. Conversely, never initiating can leave him feeling unwanted. Pride will keep him from saying, "I'm hurt," so he will likely mask his bruise in anger and vengeful speech and actions. He may even withdraw from you.

Julie Gorman, author of *What I Wish My Mother Had Told Me About Men*, wrote, "A man can never blame his wife for his own transgressions; ultimately God holds him accountable for his own actions. Likewise, the wife should never negate the powerful truth that she should safeguard and ferociously protect her incredible opportunity to satisfy the longings of her husband's desire for intimacy."

A man has the responsibility to maturely process disappointment and keep his pride in check. But, his wife can help him with that by occasionally providing allurement that lets him know that she values his God-given energy. Such a wife robs the Proverbs 7 woman of her effectiveness and keeps the fountain a welcoming and blessed relationship.

ANATOMY OF AN AFFAIR

> The lips of an adulteress drip honey and her speech is smoother than oil ... Keep to a path far from her, do not go near the door of her house ...
>
> Proverbs 5:3, 8

Affairs occur because husbands and wives grow apart from each other and grow closer to someone else. It is that simple. Their obedience to God, the strength of their love for each other, and the moral commitment that sustained the vow wanes, and they fall.

Hollywood frequently portrays affairs as sudden, passionate exchanges between handsome men and beautiful women that reach an intensity their marriages never can. And, sometimes that is true. Emotions often intensify in forbidden pleasures. Every kid knows the stolen cookie tastes sweeter than the one served openly on a platter (cf. Proverbs 9:17). While some affairs may occur suddenly and without warning, I don't believe that is the norm. In most cases, affairs are the result of a gradual decline in positive affection and behavior towards one's spouse, and the gradual development of those feelings and actions toward a third party.

Jerry and Lynn Jones identify six stages of development in the anatomy of an affair. The first is attraction. Attraction is the pull we feel toward the pleasantness of another's personality or the beauty of their appearance. It is the same dynamic we experienced when we were drawn to the sweetness and good looks of our future spouse. Getting married doesn't suppress the natural inclination we have to recognize such appealing features in other people. It may lie dormant for a while after our marriage while still in the ecstasy of new love, but it can and will surface again. There is nothing inherently wrong with feeling an attraction. But it becomes wrong and dangerous if we pursue it.

The second stage in the sequence of events in the anatomy of an affair is proximity, that is, being close to the person we are attracted to. Sometimes we can't help it. Our work center might be close to that person. Shoving our desk across the office and against another wall may not be an option. They may also live next door or go to church with us. We may not be able to control all situations of closeness to someone we are attracted to, but we can avoid creating opportunities for physical closeness. Whether we have any control over proximity, we can control our hearts and minds.

Interaction is the third step. If we are close to the one we are attracted to, we have opportunity to interact with them. It may be small talk and sharing a cup of coffee, something innocent in the absence of attraction. But, if we are nurturing a secret desire, then our conversation is devious.

Jerry and Lynn say there are three red flags at this stage in the development of an affair. One, are you excited at the prospect of seeing that person today? Two, do you give extra effort to look nice for them? Three, do you create opportunities to see them? Answering yes to any of these questions is a red flag. Answering yes to all three means sirens are going off. Beware!

The fourth and fifth stages, self-disclosure and equity, are interwoven. Self-disclosure is opening your heart and sharing deeper, more personal feelings. "My wife and I aren't talking much now. When I get home she gripes about how long I work, or how I don't make enough money. I just want someone to talk to sometimes." If the other person responds with warmth and understanding, and even shares personal thoughts, this is the fifth step: equity. Equity means the other person has accepted your disclosure and is now offering her own. "Oh, I understand. My husband has no idea of all the work I do around the house. I wish one time he would just ask me how my day was."

At the equity level an emotional bond is being formed. One becomes vulnerable, crossing boundary lines of appropriateness. The other perceives the depth of emotions, accepts the tender disclosure, and responds in kind. Attraction, physical closeness, and heart-felt bonding are combining to create an emotional firestorm that must be extinguished immediately, if it still can, or it will lead to the sixth and final stage in the anatomy of an affair: adultery.

The man forgets his vows, his wife, his kids. The woman forgets her vows, her husband, her kids. They make arrangements, they meet, they fall. It's not a sudden fall. It is the final act in a series of events that has progressed for weeks, months, sometimes even years. At any juncture in the process the husband or wife could have followed Solomon's advice: "Keep to a path far from her/him, do not go near the door of her/his house" (or office or motel room).

God promises that "No temptation has seized you except what is common to man. And God is faithful. He will not let you be tempted beyond what you can bear. But when you are tempted, he will also provide a way out so that you can stand up under it" (1 Cor. 10:13). We need to claim that promise when any temptation assails our heart, including the attraction of another person. Remember the warning of the Sage from many years ago, "The lips of an adulteress drip honey, and her speech is smoother than oil ... Keep to a path far from her, do not go near the door of her house ..." (Jerry and Lynn Jones, *Marriage Matters Seminars*).

ROMANCE & MARRIAGE

> Do not lust in your heart after her beauty or let her captivate you with her eyes.
>
> Proverbs 6:25

Television and Hollywood may be more influential in shaping our views of marriage today than any other single source. Drinking from the cistern of these opinion-makers means we imbibe their views on marriage, divorce, sex, romance, parenting, and other critical aspects of sexuality, family-making, and life.

For those who do not seek spiritual guidance from the Bible and fellowship in the Christian community, television and Hollywood may be their primary source for information and perceptions about marriage and family life. Not many of the examples provided are biblical or spiritual. What kind of long term influence might shows like these make on young people who do not have healthy marital and family role models in their lives to offer a balanced view of marriage, romance, and sex?

Even people who do seek genuine Christian nurturing through the Bible and church can be influenced by the glitter and glitz of the beautiful people who star in some of the popular movies and shows. I've heard young people approaching marriage compare their relationship to characters from television shows, even the soap operas. I much prefer them to say, "I want a marriage like my grandparents. They had problems, but they stuck it out and are still married after 50 years."

One of the great harms of the entertainment industry's influence on marriage is how it shapes our view of romance. Genuine romance between a man and a woman involves care, tenderness, communication, and certainly, warm feelings. Hollywood's contribution to our concept of romance is that it is also non-stop intensity and excitement. Any slacking of the intensity of feeling or excitement of physical contact necessitates finding another partner. The current partner may be a husband or wife, or could just be a boyfriend or girlfriend. Marriage really doesn't matter in the ethics of big screen entertainment.

But it does matter to God. And it does matter in the real world. Anyone who has been abandoned by their partner for a more exciting prospect has experienced the pain of our current misnomers about romance.

I'm not against the idea of intensity and excitement in a relationship that leads to marriage, and I'm certainly for them continuing in the marital union as they take on fuller expression between the husband and wife. But defining romance on the basis of intensity and excitement ignores at least three essential ingredients that enable a marriage to last. These three ingredients also allow the husband and wife to experience, over and over and in new and fresh ways, deep feelings and satisfaction that those in constant pursuit of the new and exciting will sadly miss.

The first ingredient, fidelity or faithfulness, is being emotionally and sexually committed to your spouse to the exclusion of all others. Many of the Hollywood-type romances omit this concern in the interest of finding someone more engaging or provocative.

Next is being family-oriented. Love for your spouse includes respect and honor for their parents, siblings, and extended family. It not only dishonors a boy or girl to engage sexually with them before marriage, it also dishonors their entire family. Pain and shame brought into the relationship by premature or inappropriate sex will be felt by the siblings, parents, and grandparents. Another aspect of sex being family-oriented is that it is God's means of bringing new life into the world. Sex is for pleasure, yes, but it is also for procreation, so a great deal of love and commitment must accompany sexual activity between husband and wife. There will be times (sometimes long ones) in the child-rearing years when intensity and excitement for romance has to be patient.

Finally, there is forgiveness. Romantic partners who successfully navigate the path of life together must exercise this essential ingredient for each other in generous measures. Forgiveness may prove to be the most important ingredient for success in many marriages. How many times has your spouse offended you? Then you must be ready at all times to forgive at least one more time.

Intensity and excitement likely characterized our dating years and first few years of marriage. That is good and wonderful! But for the long haul, nothing can replace fidelity, family orientation, and forgiveness. If we pursue romance to the neglect of these three big conditions of the heart, we will experience Hollywood-type romance at times, along with the infidelity and brokenness that characterize those relationships as well.

Stanley Hauerwas wrote, "Romantic love seeks intensity, not continuity" (*A Community of Character*, 192). Romance is good and wonderful, but it can't guarantee the continuity or long term commitment essential for a healthy marriage and family. Continuity comes when we remember that our spouse is God's gift to us, and when we don't allow the allure of another's beauty to excite our passions and derail our marriages (Prov. 6:25). As we practice faithfulness in our marriage, we find that the ensuing continuity has a certain magic, a romance that the quest for excitement and intensity often misses.

IRRECONCILABLE DIFFERENCES

> Better to live on a corner of the roof than share a house
> with a quarrelsome wife.
>
> Proverbs 21:9

Couples seeking a divorce often state irreconcilable differences as their reason. There are issues between them that cannot be resolved and have caused intense arguing, leading them to seek a permanent separation. Proverbs 21:9 apparently envisions such a heated scenario, with a husband seeking any means of getting away from his wife's angry demeanor, even living on the corner of a roof. But, it must be remembered that such a disposition is not the sole property of the wife, because a man can also possess such an ungodly spirit, as Proverbs 26:21 attests: "As charcoal to embers and as wood to fire, so is a quarrelsome man for kindling strife." Both a husband and wife share guilt in allowing differences to escalate to a point that dissolving the union seems the only reasonable solution.

Some irreconcilable differences are trivial. For example, it is not uncommon for people to fight and split over not getting to buy things they want, such as clothing or cars. I read about a couple divorcing because they cheered for different football teams. If this wasn't a hindrance to them getting married, why should it have been a reason for them to divorce?

Many times the issues are more serious. One of the partners might have an addiction that is disrupting the marriage and family. One might be a big spender and drives the family into debt. One partner might be very aggressive, intimidating the more subdued partner. Sometimes one is very critical of the other, making him or her feel devalued and unappreciated. These problems that seem irreconcilable are pretty serious and deeply hurt the feelings and self-esteem of the other partner.

What does it mean that the problems are irreconcilable? It means the couple has presumably worked on the problems but has not been able to achieve any kind of resolution. Talking to each other, visiting with church leaders, prayer, and even counseling has not stopped the offending behavior. One party in the marriage continues to practice their addiction, spend carelessly, be overly aggressive, or criticize too much. What is the offended party to do?

At this point some couples divorce. In fairness to people who profess irreconcilable differences, some of these people have suffered greatly. They have genuinely tried to work on their problems. They have taken inventory of their own lives and contributions to their marital problems, talked to their spouses, read books, and sought help from professionals. Still the problems persist. What else can they do? Divorce seems to be a reasonable option.

But consider two things. One, every marriage has irreconcilable differences. Every couple I have ever spoken to admits to having issues they can't resolve to the satisfaction of both parties. They learn to accept the other person, live with the inconvenience of their differences, and even learn to change their expectations so the intensity of the differences lesson. Think about it: don't you have differences with nearly every significant person in your life? Why should marriage be any different?

Secondly, no matter how stressful the differences are, God wants us to hold our marriages together. About marriage Jesus said, "... The two will become one flesh. So, they are no longer two, but one. Therefore, what God has joined together, let man not separate" (Matt. 19:6). In marriage a man and woman find a way to overcome, overlook, or even rise above their irreconcilable differences. They create a union that becomes bigger than their personal choices and desires. They live for their partner. They stay together.

Let me point out that physical or emotional abuse is in another category than differences. There are laws to protect people from abuse, even husbands and wives from each other. Even in cases of abuse, though, I've known of couples getting counseling and working their marriages out.

I've seen too many husbands and wives walk away from each other because of differences they did not believe they could survive. Yet millions of other couples survive those same difficulties. When couples divorce, then remarry, they often find the same problems they fled from in their first marriage. Differences are impossible to avoid because they are the stuff of life. The best biblical suggestion for a couple struggling with irreconcilable difference is to stay in and continue to work on your marriage. It won't be easy, but God will see you through.

A WOMAN WHO FEARS THE LORD

> Charm is deceptive, and beauty is meaningless, but a woman who fears the Lord is to be praised.
>
> Proverbs 31:30

The Proverbs 31 poem extolling the superlative qualities of the virtuous woman begins with a question: "A wife of noble character who can find?" The poem answers the question: a man fortunate enough to marry a woman who fears the Lord, devotes herself to the daily affairs of a household, nurtures her children, and brings honor to her husband.

The wife of noble character is found among the women in our church family, the women we bump into at the grocery store, and those we cheer with at Little League games. The wife of noble character is my mother, my mother-in-law, my daughters, and daughter-in-law. The wife of noble character is the woman I have celebrated life with for over thirty years.

The narrator of Proverbs 31 invests nineteen verses extolling the virtues of the Noble Wife. The praise reaches its crescendo in verses 29 and 30 when her husband offers his feelings about his beloved: "Many women do noble things, but you surpass them all. Charm is deceptive, and beauty is meaningless, but a woman who fears the Lord is to be praised."

Charm refers to the social and personal skills a woman can use to attract the attention of a man. Beauty refers to her physical allurement. Charm and beauty can be misused by a woman with devious intentions:

"Like a gold ring in a pig's snout is a beautiful woman who shows no discretion" (Prov. 11:22). The Sage is aware of this danger and spends considerable effort alerting young men to it (Prov. 2:16-19; 5:1-14; 6:23-35; and 7). Charm and beauty are neutral qualities, their merits or demerits to be determined by how they are employed. Nothing is more alluring to a spiritual young man than a woman of virtue who is also both appropriately charming and physically beautiful. Her presence is a lightning strike to his heart, emboldening him to approach her and pursue first a conversation, then a life together. Her charm and beauty enrich their romance and marital experience.

But the wise husband knows the truly enduring qualities of his wife are not the externals of charm and beauty. Charm can suffer after years of pain and disappointment; physical health and attractiveness fades for us all. Only the internal qualities of godliness endure: love, devoted service to family, care for strangers, fairness to all, and fear of the Lord.

Proverbs opens with a profound statement about the essence of our relationship with God: "The fear of the Lord is the beginning of knowledge" (Prov. 1:7). Everything else that follows in the book - the common sense, practical suggestions, and insights for life - are ultimately as shallow as charm and fleeting as beauty unless they are built upon the key foundational principle of fear of God. It is fear of the Lord that enables a relationship with him and allows our growth in wisdom and virtue.

The Noble Wife has spent a lifetime developing her relationship with God and her family. Through wisdom she has built her house (Prov. 14:1). Her charm and beauty are not devilishly employed to derail the morals and lives of young men. Rather, they are used to bring enjoyment to the life she shares with her husband. And though the physical beauty of her youth will fade with time, the love of her devoted husband will not, and he will rejoice in the wife of his youth (Prov. 5:18). And, in inexplicable ways, her charm and beauty will not fade to him, but will take on new depth and meaning.

How fitting that this book which opened with a call to fear the Lord ends with praise for one who does. A woman who fears the Lord is to be praised. She shall be praised by her family in her home, her friends at the city gate, and by God in the final gathering: "Well done, good and faithful servant."

THE WIFE OF NOBLE CHARACTER

Proverbs 31 sets the bar high for womanhood. The woman modeled here is intelligent, motivated, competent, family-oriented, spiritual, and hardworking. She is every woman's dream and every woman's nightmare. A Christian woman today can look at her life as the consummate example to emulate. She can also grow frustrated from the demands this example places on her.

The question in verse 10 may not be rhetorical: "A wife of noble character who can find?" The Sage may really wonder if such a complete personality can exist. A similar question is asked about a man in 20:6: "A faithful man who can find?" Proverbs is about developing wisdom, character, and a faith-based life (1:7), qualities that require study, discipline, mentoring, and hard work over a lifetime. Since such a level of maturity is as rare as rubies (10:b), the Sage may harbor doubts about how many men or women could attain such a level. Or, he may be prodding his readers to be grateful should they have such a noble spouse.

"Her husband has full confidence in her and lacks nothing of value" (31:11). The wife's nobility is her strength and ability to provide adequately for her family. Knowing the domestic scene is under her capable oversight, the husband makes himself vulnerable, entrusting himself to her care.

The fact that the husband lacks nothing of value demonstrates the wife's energy and productivity. Life is a battle, a constant warring against scarcity and lack, a battle to ensure that our loved ones have food to eat and clothing to wear. That sense is embodied in the statement "her husband ... lacks nothing of value." This phrase comes from a Hebrew word meaning "to plunder." It is a military term referring to "the spoils of warfare ... suggesting that the woman is a warrior in the battle of life." (Longman, Proverbs, 543). This doesn't mean that she lives in hostility with other people or that she robs people as soldiers sometimes do to defeated populations, but she recognizes that just as the first couple battled against the encroachment of weeds in their garden (literally, Gen. 3:18, 19), so she must wage war against the encroachment of debt, hunger, and desperation in her garden, her family. So she works hard, like a warrior in active combat, to provide what her family needs.

"She brings him good, not harm, all the days of his life" (v.12). The good she brings him is economic. Her head and hands are employed negotiating business deals (v.16) and making clothes for sale (v.24). But the value she brings her home is not limited to financial matters. She has a benevolent spirit (v.20), a love for her children (27-28), and a heart for God (v.30). She is a noble woman.

The Proverbs 31 Woman sets the bar high. But is it set too high? Can anyone achieve the levels of success this woman has without suffering significant burnout? Does this woman's child cry at night? Run high fevers? Question her authority? Does she ever get frustrated that her husband is sitting at the gate (v.23) instead of helping her at home? Does the fabric of her sanity ever unravel?

Questions like these cause some interpreters of Proverbs to question if the Proverbs 31 Wife is real or symbolic. Thomas McCreesh notes that this wife performs her role so well her husband has nothing to do but sit at the gate all day basking in the respect she has earned. Can she perform her role so well that the husband's contribution to the family is unnecessary?

McCreesh also notes a correspondence between the Proverbs 31 Wife and Woman Wisdom in the earlier chapters of Proverbs. In Proverbs 1, another woman, Woman Wisdom, is crying out in the streets for the simple to listen to her words of insight (v.20ff). In chapter 9 she fixes a meal in her house of wisdom for the simple to come dine, feasting on the ways of understanding (v.1ff). In opposition to her, Woman Folly has also fixed a meal, urging the simple to gorge themselves on her unhealthy banquet of stolen water and food (v.13ff).

Chapters 1 through 9 depict two women vying for the attention of the young and simple. They can dine on the wisdom and morality of Woman Wisdom (the representative of God), or they can dine on the foolishness and immorality of the pleasure served up by Woman Folly (a representative of ancient pagan idolatry). Seen in this way, chapters 10 through 30 of Proverbs is the meal that Woman Wisdom serves. The young and simple who make these chapters their meal, feasting on Woman Wisdom's insight on morality, honesty, prudence, decency, integrity, and other core values, will find themselves under Woman Wisdom's protective care. They will lack nothing of value and will be respected in the community (the city gate). Woman Wisdom thus becomes Capable Wife (or the Proverbs 31 Wife), taking care of the young and simple who have dined at her banquet. (See "Wisdom as Wife: Proverbs 31:10-31," *Revue Biblique* 92 [1985]).

Is the Proverbs 31 Woman real or symbolic? Let's turn to Ruth, the daughter-in-law of Naomi and eventual wife of Boaz, her kinsmen-redeemer, for a look at a noble woman. In Ruth 3:11 Boaz tells her, "And now, my daughter, don't be afraid. I will do for you all you ask. All my fellow townsmen know that you are a woman of noble character." How does Ruth measure up to the high standards of the wife in Proverbs 31? She was loyal to Naomi, she "plundered" (not in a negative sense of stealing, but in the positive sense of harvesting) the fields to provide food for her family, and she upheld the community standards by honoring Boaz's kinsmen-redeemer role rather than pursuing younger (or wealthier) men (Ruth 3:10).

As a real, live person, Ruth embodied many of the qualities of the Proverbs 31 Woman. Perfect? No. But certainly one who modeled the value of fearing the Lord and doing the best she could to see that her family could trust her and would praise her, because they lacked nothing of value from her hands.

CHAPTER TWO

KIDS

LEARNING TO MAKE CHOICES

> My son, do not forget my teaching, but keep my commands in your heart, for they will prolong your life many years and bring you prosperity.
>
> Proverbs 3:1-2

I thought it was funny when I told some friends my dad had been a boxer. I was with a bunch of middle school buddies in a late night brag session, and I thought this would get their attention. It did.

Dad didn't think it was nearly so funny when I told him what I did. "I know you are proud of me," he said. "But you don't have to make up stories. You don't have to make me bigger in your friends' eyes than what I really am. At your age everything a parent does is right. But when you get older, you will start to question the way your mom and I did things. You'll be free to pick the best of what we did and then come up with your own ideas. When you get married, your wife will have her own set of ideas about life, and then the two of you will work through these ideas and issues together."

"Okay," was about all I could say as I sat there wishing I hadn't told him. "I did tell them later that I was just kidding."

"That's good. But you shouldn't have made up that story at all."

Dad was doing two things. One, he was teaching me to be honest and realistic about life, our family, and our achievements. Everyone enjoys success of some kind, but we don't need to embellish those accomplishments with tall tales and outright lies. Honestly assess your life and family, take note of what is honorable and exemplary, and launch out in life on that firm foundation. Muddying the family water with falsehood clouds our vision and hampers wise decision making in the future.

Secondly, he was preparing me for the day when I would come out from under his supervision and oversight and begin making choices on my own. That is a crucial transition many parents don't anticipate and many youth are not ready for.

It is one thing to walk a straight path when parents are guarding our decisions and actions. It is quite another to be making those choices on our own away from their protective oversight. At that time we need the rock-sure foundation of family honor and ethics stamped upon our hearts to guide us. This imprint of sound teaching from mom and dad is the internal compass that guides our direction and choices. Without this compass we could veer off the path of truth, self-control, and sensible living and crash on the rocks of indiscretion.

The Sage recognized this. "Do not forget my teaching but keep my commands in your heart." The Sage was encouraging his son to think about his words, planting them deeply in the sinews of his being so he could act on them in future settings. If the wise counsel of the father is planted deeply within the son's heart, it will function like a seed, growing and expanding and taking on a life of its own. The fruit of this seed is the son dealing honestly in business, considerately with neighbors and kindly with his wife and kids.

Thank God for the training of children by their parents. It is still God's preferred method for preparing the next generation.

HONEY, TRUST ME

> Do not plot harm against your neighbor who lives trustfully near you.
>
> Proverbs 3:29

"I was about five years old when my mother took me into the back yard. She played a game with me that a lot of parents play with their children."

The woman telling me this story was about fifty years old. She was a patient in an alcohol rehabilitation program and was visiting with me to discuss issues of faith and recovery. Part of our work together was to explore how God could provide the strength she would need to become and remain sober. Another important aspect of our work was for her to identify incidents from her life that caused her pain and shame. That's what she was doing now.

"My mother took me into the back yard to play a game with me and teach a lesson about life. She taught me a lesson that was so profound it is still with me. I haven't been able to shake it in all these years. It still haunts me.

Mom lifted me up on a rock wall along the cement sidewalk. It was several feet high. Since I was a little girl the wall seemed like a mountain."

'Okay', mom said, 'Jump!'

Jump? You want me to jump? I asked mom.

'Of course I do, honey,' mom said. 'You jump and I'll catch you.'

But mom, I'm scared! I'm up high!

'I know. But I want you to learn about trust and faith. You jump and I'll catch you.'

Are you sure, mom? Will you catch me?

'Of course I'll catch you honey. You can always trust your mother!'"

She was intense, this lady. Her voice was subdued, her eyes cast down, but her pain was inescapable. I couldn't understand why the retelling of this little game was evoking such extreme emotion in the woman. She continued.

"It took considerable prompting, but I finally trusted my mother enough. I jumped."

She paused and wept silently for a moment. Then she said, "My mother was standing there with her arms out, smiling, encouraging me to jump. She promised to catch me. But when I jumped, mom lowered her arms, stepped back, and let me fall on the concrete sidewalk. As I lay there crying, my mother leaned over me and said, 'I did this to teach you a lesson. Don't ever trust anyone. They will always let you fall and you will get hurt.' Then she walked off, leaving me crying in pain. And I have been in pain ever since."

The jarring of her bones and the tearing of her knees couldn't compare to the jarring and tearing of her heart. This woman learned her lesson well, and never trusted her mother or anyone after her fateful jump. She spent her adult life yearning to be valued by someone, to be held by a man that loved her, and to be cherished, but she could never hazard the risk of trusting someone to experience love like this. The closest she came to real love was her relationship with a bottle, and it was killing her.

But something deep in her psyche convinced her that this was not the way life was supposed to be. This poor woman knew she had been violated by her own mother, and that good and pure desires and needs had been twisted by her. She wanted to experience life in a new, fresh way. She knew the first step was to seek help for her drinking, to trust that someone would care enough to struggle through the grueling process of recovery at her side. Most of us will never know the superhuman effort required for her to take that first step at a meeting and say to a stranger, "Will you help me?"

Do not plot harm against your neighbor who lives trustfully near you, or against your own spouse or children who live in your home. Trust is a key ingredient in any relationship. Violate it intensely or frequently enough, and you destroy any opportunity for happiness and a healthy relationship.

As a child, this woman was intentionally battered to discourage any faith and hope in other people. Yet we need to trust others, even with their failings, so we can enjoy connection with them. This woman is learning that, and she progressed in recovery and slowly learned to trust others, largely because she was learning about someone who would never let her fall: God.

If you experience an inability to love and trust, because arms that promised to catch you did not, take heart in another verse from Proverbs: "Trust in the Lord with all your heart" (Prov. 3:5). He will never let us fall.

STORYTELLING

> When I was a boy in my father's house, still tender, and an only child of my mother, he taught me and said, "Lay hold of my words with all your heart; keep my commands and you will live.
>
> Proverbs 4:3, 4

Loving mothers and fathers have always passed on stories of their childhood to their sons and daughters. Dinner time when I was a boy was the occasion for my parents to say, "When I was your age...." We then would be treated with stories of mom or dad's youthful exploits. We especially wanted to know what they were like when they were our age. Our sister identified most with mom; the boys with dad. We wanted to know if he had a girlfriend? Did he win all of his fistfights? Did he ever have to "visit" the principal's office?

Good dads and moms, going back even before the time of David, have taught their children and shared the stories of their faith. God told parents to capitalize on teachable moments, when relaxing at home, walking along the road, and going to bed (Deut. 6:6-9). I'll bet Solomon listened with rapt attention when his dad said, "Son, did I ever tell you about the time I fought the lion?"

A family friend asked "How and when do you choose teaching opportunities with a young child? Do you make every opportunity a teaching lesson, or does that become something they will tune out or become desensitized to?"

This is a very good question. We certainly want our children to obey us, but we don't want to overburden them with endless rules. How can we take advantage of all the teachable moments when we are together without desensitizing them? Tell a story.

Storytelling is a prized art in many cultures, especially oral cultures (an oral cultural is one that relies less on the written word or technology for communication and more on the spoken word). In an oral culture, the stories of grandma and grandpa, and even the story of how the tribe settled on this remote mountain before grandma and grandpa could remember, are passed down by older members of the family telling the stories to the younger ones. Stories passed on what was historically significant for the family and tribe.

Today we rely on books to do that for us. But we don't even rely enough on good books! Too often our attention is arrested by television. Many children today don't know the stories of Great Grandpa, Aunt Minnie, or even their own mom or dad. The connection with the people of the family's past, including their culture and values, is broken.

Family storytelling promotes healthy communication, provides life lessons, and creates connections to family and friends. Here are some good reasons to honor the ancient tradition of storytelling in your family.

One, stories bind the storyteller and those who listen. If listeners like the story, they like the person telling the story. That's important for mom and dad when the listeners are their children!

Two, storytelling develops interest and imagination. TV tends to dull the imagination. All the action is performed before the viewers' eyes. In storytelling, the listener must use his imagination to picture the characters, feel their plight, and rejoice at their deliverance or success.

Three, storytelling creates vision for a new world. The listeners get caught up in the excitement and drama the storyteller builds. They flow with the dynamic of the characters and plot. The imagination of the listeners can be challenged to envision a world where there is a land flowing with milk and honey and people are respectful of each other (which may be one reason Jesus told stories).

Four, storytelling teaches. Even without stating a point, there is always a point to a good story. In fact, when it is told well, the story is the point.

Storytelling can be done with large groups of people before a speaker standing on stage, or it can be done at a kitchen table with mom and dad regaling children with stories from their own lives. Since storytelling binds the teller and the listener together, cherish those times when you can tell those stories and the children will listen. Then, as they experience life and have a story to tell, listen with rapt interest. Children are great storytellers, too. As we listen to their stories, we reinforce that they are important to us. Not listening to them stifles communication and TV becomes an easy replacement. By listening to their stories, our children are learning the art of story, are knitting our heart to theirs, and offer hope that the art of storytelling passes on to the next generation.

WHAT OUR CHILDREN SHOULD NEVER HEAR

With their mouths the godless destroy their neighbors...
Proverbs 11:9

Tongue, mouth, speech, words and lips are interchangeable terms in Proverbs to refer to the nature, content, intent, and effect of our communication on other people. The nature of our speech is either wholesome or unwholesome, either pure or defiled. The content of our speech is either life-enhancing or life-degrading; the intent is either to enliven a heart or kill it; and the effect is joy or misery, life or death. The death may be spiritual and emotional, or it could actually be physical death. We have been shocked by the stories of teens taking their lives after being hurt by the words of classmates. The proverb is true: "The tongue has the power of life and death" (Prov. 18:21).

There are at least three things our kids should never hear from us, verbal expressions that are deadly and cruel. The first is name calling. Calling someone a degrading name plants a tag in their mind that shapes how they view themselves and impacts in a negative way how they function in life. Calling our children stupid, retarded, moronic, or a host of other equally horrible terms (some with moral connotations) shapes their view of themselves. The hurtful names we call them become the images they have of themselves which then feed the expectations of how they think they are supposed to act and perform. Exceptionally brilliant children may indeed act stupid if that is the image we plant inside them.

The second is cursing or other profane speech. This designation would include taking the Lord's name in vain. I've heard parents actually call down curses on their children in the name of God. That is ironic and wicked, since God himself chooses to send down blessings on us and our children. How arrogant to assume the place of God and issue a spiritual denunciation on someone God himself has not even announced! Included in this broad designation of cursing and profane speech would be any language that we know is not appropriate for more public settings, such as school or church. It not only damages the souls of our kids, but of us as well. "The mouth of a fool invites ruin" (Prov. 10:14) for himself and his family.

The third thing our children should never hear is fighting between the parents. It can be okay, even good, for our children to hear us have a disagreement, especially if we are discussing the issues maturely and positively. What better way to prepare them for their own adult relationships and marriage than to hear how we do it constructively? But, if the home is already characterized by name calling and perverse speech, then disagreements between the parents can be traumatizing to the children, undermining their sense of security and making them question their position in the home. What sane parents would subject their kids to this? I remember as a kid staying the night at a friend's house when, after we turned in, his parents erupted into a loud and vulgar verbal fight. I had never heard that and was scared. My friend said, "Oh that happens all the time." I was horrified at the thought of living in that kind of shouting all the time.

Through the misuse of their tongues the unrighteous destroy their neighbors. In Proverbs 11 neighbors are not just those who live next door, but anyone in close association. The unrighteous damage the hearts of co-workers, church members, and even their own families with their painful and destructive speech.

This statement appears in a larger context discussing and contrasting the net effect of a righteous and wicked lifestyle. The righteous person enhances the lives of those around him, adding joy and value to their lives. The wicked person has the opposite effect, bringing pain and wrath to those around him. The only joy the wicked person brings is in his depar-ture. "When the wicked perish, there are shouts of joy" (11:10). The righ-teous bring joy by their presence; the wicked bring joy by their absence.

The home of the wicked man or woman suffers because of the name calling, foul language, and fighting that emanates from an angry and hate-ful heart. They can remedy the situation by submitting their hearts to a thorough cleansing and curtail the abusive nature of their speech. They can then avoid hurting not just the folks who live next door, but the ones who call them mom and dad.

WHAT OUR CHILDREN SHOULD HEAR

> The wise in heart are called discerning, and gracious words promote instruction.
>
> Proverbs 16:21

Much of our children's working vocabulary will be learned by the time they are five years old. It is incredibly important that the words they hear during those first five years are healthy and wholesome, and the spirit in which they are delivered is spiritual and nurturing. Critical and nega-tive speech will plant unspiritual and self-defeating thoughts deep within their psyches, which can then shape unspiritual and self-defeating behav-ior. Every child deserves to hear at least four things during their formative years.

The first is instruction. Instruction covers all aspects of life, from dressing neatly to treating other people with respect and working hard on a job. These things cannot be left to chance. Incredibly, I encounter a number of older teens who have never had a job and have never even had occasional work, such as raking leaves, cleaning out a garage, or painting an old shed. They graduate high school or college and wonder why em-ployers aren't standing in line to give them a good job. It also doesn't help their chances of landing gainful employment if they haven't been taught to give a firm handshake, look someone in the eye, and carry on a con-versation. The list of necessary things to teach a child would also include basic instruction about God and spiritual things, good behavior, dating etiquette, maintaining moral purity, principles of a healthy and fulfilling marital life, and even parenting. Teaching teenagers about parenting may be one of the best inducements for them to date carefully and marry wisely.

Secondly, our kids deserve to hear appropriate correction. "The words of the reckless pierce like swords, but the tongue of the wise brings healing" (Prov. 12:18). Belittling a child as a means of correcting him may alter his behavior for a time, but it will likely plant hurt and resentment even more deeply. The goal of correction when children act out or misbehave is not to produce feelings of low self-worth and uselessness, but to encourage them to think about their conduct and course in life.

Appropriate correction means we address the misbehavior of the child. We want him to know he acted badly without thinking he is a bad or incorrigible child. Calling the child stupid, bad, and hopeless breaks the child down; it doesn't build him in the wholesome image of God. "The tongue of the wise brings healing," even when done as disciplinary action.

Thirdly, every child deserves words of encouragement. The world will hurt our kids enough, wounding their spirit and diminishing their sense of worth. Shelley Faust wrote, "No matter how deeply hidden, wounds left unattended do not disappear. Hurtful words become a filter through which we see and experience life if we let them" (http://isthatyoulord. blogspot.com/). We need to speak gracious words that balance the negativity of the world and clean the filters of hurtful words. We certainly don't need to join in the destruction. "Gracious words are a honeycomb, sweet to the soul and healing to the bones" (Prov. 16:24). Listening to our kids, expressing confidence in their abilities, and encouraging their attempts at new activities helps produce confidence and self-assurance in them, something they will need to live life bravely and successfully.

Finally, our kids need our help in shaping their vision for the future. When they are in middle school, we can speak about issues they will face in high school, college, and beyond. This is not an attempt to ignore the present or rush their lives. Rather, it is a way to help them think forward and envision a future that has room in it for them. We can speak to them about study programs, career choices, relationships (including marriage), and where they might like to live. Talking to our kids about their future in a positive way can help them overcome insecurities or fear and actually embrace the future with excitement.

Proverbs 13:14 says, "The teaching of the wise is a fountain of life, turning a person from the snares of death." Life is too precious to just let it happen. The lives of our children are too precious to let them grow up on their own. We must teach with great intentionality and urgency the important lessons of life and eternity. Our teaching is the fountain of life to save them from the snares of death.

SPARING THE ROD

> He who spares the rod hates his son, but he who loves him is careful to discipline him.
>
> Proverbs 13:24

Many in contemporary American culture regard spanking as an act of abuse. Sadly, our society has witnessed too many incidents of an enraged (or deranged) parent so severely abusing one of their children under the guise of discipline that the child died. Many other children have suffered permanent physical and emotional scars from abusive treatment. Such out-of-control parents may starve their children, lock them in a closet for long periods, or beat them mercilessly.

We must be careful when reading the proverbs about spanking that we do not project our contemporary perceptions back on the ancient text or the Israelite culture. The proverbs about spanking do not advocate child abuse, but careful and consistent training and molding of life.

The New English Bible reflects this perspective on Proverbs 13:24: "A father who spares the rod hates his son, but one who loves him keeps him in order." The Sage is not advocating the abuse of a child. Rather, he wants to spare him from a listless and profligate life. He wanted young people to grow up with a sense of order, purpose, and self-control. Without these inner qualities, young people would lack an orientation in life, drifting from one pursuit to another, aligning themselves with ne'er-do-wells, and even falling into a life of crime. Discipline is one very important means of saving children from such a fruitless existence.

There are actually two sides to discipline. The first is teaching and training. Children cannot know the importance of picking up their toys, speaking respectfully to an adult, not touching a hot stove, or staying out of the road unless we first teach them. Verbal instruction at this point is essential. Training is when we demonstrate for them the kind of behavior we expect. We can lead our children through the house and help them pick up their toys, take them to the closet or toy box and then put them away. After teaching the process, and repeating the experience several times, we can reasonably expect they know how. Now we need to expect them to do it. That leads to the second side of discipline.

After we teach and train our children to speak and behave in a healthy way, we now have to expect them to live up to our expectations. We also need to be aware that they will fail, sometimes because they are simply young and immature, at other times because they are willfully defiant. If our kids have cousins visiting, and they are busy playing, not putting toys away is likely a case of being excited and overlooking responsibilities. But if the parent says, "Put your toys away," and they stand there adamantly refusing to comply, that is willful disobedience and must be addressed. This is the second side of discipline: punishment.

The word "rod" in Proverbs can refer to an actual spanking or may be a metaphor referring to any form of corrective discipline, such as assigning more chores or depriving them of a desired activity. The form of corrective discipline to use will depend upon the nature of the offense as well as the frequency and severity of occurrence. One thing is certain: when children willfully disobey, the parents must invest the time and effort to discipline them, whatever form they choose to employ. Failure to discipline the child and to let recurring incidents of purposeful rebellion slide is not an act of love by the parents. Love is a concern for the child's long term well-being and necessitates discipline to break the disruptive and disobedient behavior, and for steering the child toward obedience. Sometimes that even means administering a spanking.

A spanking is effective when it hurts and gets the child's attention. An ancient Egyptian proverb says, "Boys have their ears on their backsides; they listen when they are beaten." A former pupil testified: "You caned me, and so your teaching entered my ear" (R. N. Whybray, "The Book of Proverbs" in The Cambridge Bible Commentary, 80). Whybray adds, "The point of this saying is that spoiling a child is a sign, not of parental love, but the lack of it." Spoiling means letting children have their way.

The period after the spanking is often an ideal time to go back to the first part of discipline and re-teach the principles of obedience you want your children to follow. That is love. Failing to discipline, and allowing the children to persist in disobedience is sentencing them to a life of selfish-pursuits and disorder. That is not love. To state the first part of Proverbs 13:24 in the positive: "He who uses the rod loves his son."

POWER OF EXAMPLE

> He who walks with the wise grows wise, but a companion
> of fools suffers harm.
>
> Proverbs 13:20

Jonathan remembered his father buying two raffle tickets for a new car at $2 a piece, one ticket for himself and the other for his boss. He wrote the name of his boss on the back of one of the tickets to give him later when he collected the $2.

Jonathan's family was hopeful but didn't really expect to win the vehicle. Since they didn't have a car it would be a great blessing, but the purchase of the ticket was more to support a charity than it was to win.

Hope turned to celebration when, on the day of the drawing, one of the tickets Jonathan's dad purchased was called. But celebration turned to dilemma when his dad turned the ticket over and saw it bore the name of the boss on the back. The winning ticket was the one Jonathan's dad had designated for the boss.

The family discussed the dilemma over dinner. "Dad, your boss already has a car, we don't. We need it more than he does," Jonathan reasoned with his father.

"That's true, son. But there is an ethical component here. My boss told me to buy a ticket for him and he would pay me back later. So, I bought a ticket for both of us, and penciled his name on the back. That is technically his ticket and his car."

"But you haven't given him the ticket yet. You could simply erase his name on the one and give him the other. We could get the car and no one would know."

"Yes, they would, Jonathan. We would know."

Jonathan watched with sorrow and confusion as his dad handed the boss the winning ticket for the brand new car and the boss gave him the $2. Nothing about the transaction made sense or felt fair to him. Until years later....

Jonathan wrote a tribute to his dad after he passed away, describing how the character of his father had shaped his own. Of course, he wrote about the raffle for the car. "We could have accepted the car and no one outside our family would have been the wiser for it. But we would have known, and there would always be that cloud of doubt about if we had done the right thing. If we were sneaky about this, what else would we be sneaky about in the future? What long term effect would it have on the kids? How would they remember their dad? My dad chose moral clarity over material gain and that made all the difference in my life. When I am confronted with tough ethical choices today I only have to ask, "What would my father do in this situation?" to get my answer. Always go with moral clarity and ethical integrity. Always. Winning the car would have been nice, but winning the ethical battle changed our lives." Note: I read this article about 45 years ago in Reader's Digest. Some of the details, including the name of the boy, are reconstructed as best as I can remember them. One thing I remember with certainty: the father chose ethics over winning the car.

My friend, Bill Watkins, told me about the father of a troubled college student. He was a good parent who taught his children the right way to live, and was now distressed that some of those lessons had not taken root. He told Bill, "I spent most of his childhood trying to make him a better boy. If I had it to do all over again, I would try to be a better man."

The Sage put it this way: He who walks with the wise grows wise. One of the best teaching tools God gives us for the shaping of our children's lives is the power of example. Years later our children may forget some of the lessons we taught them verbally, but they will never forget when we choose right and moral over personal gain and pleasure. Walking wisely and ethically blazes the trail for our children to walk confidently in our steps.

WHAT CAN I DO?

> The laborer's appetite works for him; his hunger drives him on.
>
> Proverbs 16:26

"What can I do? He never listens. He won't go back to school. He won't get a job that pays enough to cover his bills. He keeps getting money from his father and me. He stays out late. He borrows our car because he can't afford one, and sometimes we have to call a cab or hitch rides because he doesn't bring our own vehicle back to us!

He is so infuriating! We have two other younger children that we need to give our attention to. We rarely get to see our high school daughter or middle school son play basketball because we have to drive our oldest son to his part time job, or he has the vehicle. He is controlling our lives and I am so tired of it!! Is there anything we can do?"

"How old is your son?"

"He's only twenty-one years old, so I know he is young and going through a hard time. His father and I just think he needs time to figure out what he wants to do. But we do wish he would go back to college or get a decent job so he can buy his own car. Is there anything we can do?"

"Okay, your son is twenty-one years old, has dropped out of college, and can't or won't get a full time job. He lives at home, borrows your car, takes your money, steals your time from your other kids, and disrupts the whole family. Is that it?"

"I don't mean to make my son sound like a bad boy. He's a good boy. He's just young and confused. He's not sure what he wants to do. He's finding himself; do you know what I mean? He is so smart and talented. He could be a teacher, a doctor or a gourmet chef if he wanted to. He just can't decide what he wants to do. What do you think we should do with him?"

"Nothing."

"Nothing? You think we should do nothing? We have to do something; this is our son! How can we do nothing? That would be bad parenting. We are doing everything we can to help this boy out so he can have a good life. I give him money, I drive him around town, and I let him borrow my car. We fixed an apartment for him over the garage because he wasn't making enough money to get a place of his own. But we are getting tired. Surely there is something we can do?"

"Actually, there is something you can do. Nothing. The best thing you can do for an intelligent, twenty-one year old man who is too directionless or under-motivated to get a real job is nothing. Don't give him money. Don't provide his living quarters. Don't loan him your car or drive him around town. Don't give him food. And do not miss another ball game of your younger children because of this man. Do nothing for him."

"I cannot believe you would suggest that we just abandon our son. You call yourself a minister? Doesn't the Bible say to help those who need help? Our son just needs some help, that's all. If you can't give any better advice than this, I don't think I want to hear anything else from you. We are through."

"The laborer's appetite works for him; his hunger drives him on." What would happen if mom and dad cut some of the strings attached to this young man? How long would it take before his appetite worked for him and provided the motivation he needed to get serious about life?

LISTENING TO OUR CHILDREN

> He who answers before listening - that is his shame and
> folly.
>
> Proverbs 18:13

Nathan swatted his son, Caleb, after the fifth time he got up and said, "Dad, I want a drink." Bed time should not be this difficult. When a parent puts a child to bed, the child should stay. If the child willfully disobeys, as Nathan's four-year old son clearly seemed to be doing, stern measures were necessary.

But when his son got up the sixth time, an inner sense told Nathan there was something else going on. He looked down at his pajama clad son, not even reaching up to dad's waist. Nathan wondered what his son was thinking. So, he dropped to a knee, threw his arm around his little boy, and said, "Come here son." Caleb was not responsive to his dad's hug. He stood stiff and rigid. Something was up.

"I can see you don't want to go bed," Nathan told his boy, "but I'm telling you that even if you don't want to, I sure do love you, and I'm really glad that I get to be your Dad."

The boy cried at this warm response from his dad, and he melted into his strong arms. In the security of this protective embrace, the son was free to spill his heart: "Daddy, every night a wolf chases me."

Nathan suddenly felt smaller than his son. Yes, you sometimes have to spank children when they are willfully disobedient. You have to confront their rebellion and teach them to respect the rules of the home. If you don't, their rebellion may never end, and can spill over into their relations at school, sports teams, and marriage and family. Rebellion and defiance must be faced head on and dealt with firmly by mom and dad. That is an important principle to parenting. But, it is not the only principle. Another equally important principle, perhaps even more important, is for mom and dad to listen.

"He who answers before listening - that is his shame and folly." It is important for owners and managers of companies to listen to their employees. No, not turn over the reins of leadership, but listen. What is it like working on the floor? Is it productive? Is it safe? Are there better ways of doing things? Managers who listen and incorporate what they learn into future decisions and practices help their companies be more profitable, safe, and enjoyable to work in.

It is important for church leaders to listen to their members. Ministers, elders, and deacons may know the Bible and church policy, but do they know the needs of their people? What families are struggling with marital turmoil? With disobedient children? With financial stresses? With moral lapses? With spiritual direction? No matter how well church leaders know the Bible and church policy, if they don't listen to their members, and learn from them, they will not be able to help them. Their knowledge will fail them and their ministry will fall flat.

And for all these reasons it is also important for parents to listen to their children, as Nathan did. Sometimes children refuse to go to bed as an act of willful disobedience and parents need to respond to that. But even then they need to listen, because sometimes their apparently bad behavior may not stem from rebellion, but from fear. And a mom or dad will only know that if they are tuned in to their children, looking for clues, listening for what is not being said, and being sensitive to their needs.

"Daddy, every night a wolf chases me."

"Well boy," Nathan told his son, "tonight when he comes after you, pick up a big stick and tell him, 'Now look here, wolf, you'd better leave or I'm going to bonk you right on the nose. And if I can't whip you, my Dad is right behind me, and he'll come and beat you up.'"

Caleb's tears dried, he smiled and fell asleep in two minutes. The next morning when his dad asked how he slept, the four year-old answered, "Fine. I beat him up. I beat the wolf up." Nathan later wrote, "What are parents for? Part of their job is to take on monsters so the kids can feel safe, knowing that they don't have to face the wolves on their own" (Nathan Ingram, *Christ at the Coffee Shop*, 7-9). Amen, Nathan. You learned that because you listened.

NO RESPECT FOR WEAKNESS

Discipline your son, for in that there is hope; do not be a
willing party to his death.

Proverbs 19:18

Why do kids pick on classmates who are the least able to defend
themselves? Why do bullies harass kids who are smaller and weaker than
themselves? Because the bullies know they won't be hurt in retaliation by
the kids they are agitating. But I think this is only partially true.

I was standing next to a hog farmer when he placed a young piglet
into a pen. Since the farmer couldn't reach all the way over the fence and
place the piglet on its feet, there was a small drop to the ground for the
young hog.

Other piglets survived the drop over the fence, but this one got its
leg caught underneath its body and got hurt. It began to squeal, attracting
the attention of the other piglets. Immediately the injured piglet was sur-
rounded by his peers, but not for care and support. The other little hogs
could tell from his whine that their friend was injured, and they came over
to attack him. They chewed on his ears, his legs, and his tail. He was already partly lame and couldn't move well, so when the other pigs boxed
him in, he could not move at all.

The squeals of the injured piglet became unbearable. But, that did
not evoke any sympathy from the other residents of the pen. Instead, even
more came running over to harass and further injure the little guy. Not
until my friend climbed into the pen and drove the attackers off did the
lame pig receive any relief. After a few minutes his leg was fine and he
resumed walking without squealing. The other piglets looked at him for a
moment, saw he was fine, and left him alone.

I think what happened in the hog pen that day helps us understand
why kids at school pick on other children they deem defenseless: we don't
respect weakness. I'm not saying it should be this way, but that it is a realistic explanation for the way things are. It is not until we are taught to respect others and show concern for the weak that we treat others according

to their needs. Attaining such a perspective is a process that takes many years to achieve.

I think this lack of respect for weakness explains more than the behavior of hogs in a pen and kids in school. It explains the struggle that exists in the home between parents and their children.

Children do not respect weakness in their parents any more than they do in their peer group. Every encounter with classmates and parents or any authority figure is potentially a test of wills to see which participant has the will to win. For example, a parent may tell a child to pick up his socks. When the child refuses, the parent tells him again. The parent knows it is important training for a child to learn to clean up after himself, so he stays with it, urging the child, pleading, eventually even threatening the child with all kinds of horrible things if he doesn't pick up the socks.

Meanwhile, the child goes on playing with his toys or watching TV, blissfully ignoring mom or dad. Do you know what the child is thinking? "Mom and dad are weak. They won't do anything to me. All their attempts to get me to obey are just squealing because they have no power in this home. I took it from them. They are weak, and I don't respect weakness." All that has to happen for the child to prove his point is to wait a little longer, and very often, mom or dad will just reach down and pick up the socks themselves. Score one for the child.

What I saw in the pigpen that day was chaos; chaos produced by lack of respect for a fellow resident of the pen. What I see in some homes is chaos; chaos produced by lack of respect for parental authority in the home. Only the intervention of my friend saved the life of the injured pig and restored order. Only the intervention of parents with a strong resolve will restore order in the home and preserve the lives of the children.

Discipline your son, for in that there is hope for proper respect in the home and order in the life of your child. Simply put, parents have to desist from squealing (begging and bribing the kids to obey), and with strength of character and determination, prevail against the challenges to their authority.

UNDERSTANDING BILLY

> Folly is bound up in the heart of a child, but the rod of discipline will drive it far from him.
>
> Proverbs 22:15

"You just have to understand Billy. He doesn't intend to be mean or destructive when he throws rocks at cars, pushes smaller children down, and talks back to adults. He has always been like this and doesn't mean anything by it. He just has a lot of energy and a mischievous spirit. But people don't even try to understand him. It really isn't fair to Billy."

Every community has a Billy, and with him there is a very concerned parent who works hard to make everyone around Billy overlook his misbehavior and accept him as he is. This parent darts from church to school to the baseball field to the Cub Scout meeting trying to convince the minsters, teachers, coaches, and den leaders that the problems they have with Billy really aren't the fault of Billy. The problem is their lack of understanding and intolerance.

It is easy to be sympathetic with Billy's parents, and it is natural to assume they have insight into the son's psychological make-up that accounts for the boy's disrespect for adults and lack of regard for his peers. Maybe if we observe the boy long enough, we will pick up the psychological cues, and understand and be able to help others tolerate Billy's misbehavior, and maybe even help Billy better adjust.

And maybe not.

Billy's main problem is not that other people don't understand him sufficiently, but that he is not given correction when his behavior deserves it. His parents may be sincere and well-intentioned in their attempts to shield him from accountability and punishment. But, they are also shielding him from learning about how he should conduct himself within community standards. They are also subjecting him to a lifetime of frustration, because not every community will be willing or able to bend its standards to accommodate Billy's inappropriate behavior.

Sadly, Billy misbehaves and no one in his life expects him to do better. Instead, they expect everyone to accept Billy as he is, without administering any corrective measures.

Rather than everyone else having to understand Billy, he needs to understand the adults in his world. If he is an eleven-year-old boy in a classroom, Cub Scout den, or baseball team, he needs to understand that the adults are in charge, and he needs to behave. If he doesn't, he can expect some kind of discipline.

Firstly, to expect adults and other children to just understand and accept a disrespectful and disobedient child is unfair to the adults and the other kids. Further, it is terribly unfair and destructive for the disobedient child. For the rest of us to understand Billy and overlook his poor behavior means we need to honor Billy as the center of the universe. Do school systems and community athletic programs need to revise their rules to accommodate a little boy who has no regard for anyone? Must everyone else's feelings and rights be set aside in the interest of the child who has never been expected to behave? This is a recipe for future criminal behavior on the part of children unfortunate enough to be raised in such circumstances.

Secondly, for the rest of us to have to understand and accept aberrant behavior means Billy will always be right, no matter how disorderly he acts. If he trips another child, sasses the teacher, disrupts a Bible class, mocks his teammates, or organizes a gang of other badly behaved children to vandalize school property, it simply isn't Billy's fault. When Billy's behavior is wrong, every other social system and eventually, the police department and judicial system is out of line. Everyone else is at fault except the one person who misbehaved.

Finally, to force everyone else to understand and comply with Billy's bad behavior guarantees that Billy will never grow up. He will never mature and assume his place in life as a responsible adult. He will always expect everyone to overlook his offensive speech and actions. After all, ever since he was a small child his parents lectured everyone in his life that, "Billy isn't a bad boy even when he does bad things. You just have to understand him." Being raised with that kind of overprotective care ensures that Billy will be frozen in his delinquent behavior, even as an adult.

Billy's parents are wrong. Instead of trying to get everyone else in his world to understand Billy, they need to make their son understand the world. Their goal is to help Billy mature as a man and become like the responsible adults in his life. To do that, he must learn to understand the adult world or he will never progress into it.

For too long society has been trying to understand Billy instead of loving him enough to make him behave. That has to change for Billy's sake. "Folly is bound up in the heart of a child, but the rod of discipline will drive it far from him."

RESPECTING PARENTS

> Listen to your father, who gave you life, and do not despise your mother when she is old.
>
> Proverbs 23:22

It disturbs me to hear a child yell at his parents, call them names, tell them to "shut up," and even slap them. But I do see and hear these things on occasion.

Parents who tolerate this kind of disrespectful behavior from their children are not only hurting the children, they are unraveling the fabric of their family and all of society. Churches, schools, the work place, and even society at large must practice respect for one another and for the leaders within these communities if they are going to function in a way that is healthy and beneficial for the members. Training for that kind of respect begins at home, where it is taught by the parents and appropriated by the children. Children must be taught to honor mom and dad.

Why should children be respectful toward their parents? There are at least three reasons. One, the parents have earned it. The Sage says, "Listen to your father, who gave you life, and do not despise your mother when she is old" (Prov. 23:22). This verse has a parallel structure where the second part builds on the first. Part one emphasizes listening to your father who gave you life, and part two emphasizes loving your mother when she is old. The second part builds upon the first, meaning that mom deserves respect because she, too, gave you life. You wouldn't have a life if it wasn't for the love of your father and the mother who birthed you.

The phrase "do not despise your mother" has an interesting parallel to Genesis 25:34 where it says that "Esau despised his birthright." That doesn't necessarily mean he hated it, but that he didn't regard it with proper honor. Because he didn't honor his birthright, he traded it for a measly bowl of beans. What a tragic loss. The injunction to not despise our mother doesn't just mean we shouldn't hate her. That is obvious. It also means we should not ignore her instruction, her role in the family, or her needs. Nor should we treat lightly her exalted position as the matriarch of the family. Mom deserves to be listened to and respected.

Mothers and fathers spend years investing their time, energy, and love into the lives of their children. The Bible honors that great work and says the children should as well. It is not just a coincidence that the command to respect parents is one of the Ten Commandments (Ex. 20:12; Lev. 19:3). Honor for parents is indispensable to the foundation of a well-ordered society.

Secondly, children need to honor their parents because it is right. Respect is like the concrete in a wall. Concrete is hard and firm so it can uphold the building. Remove the firmness from the concrete and the walls will collapse, crushing everyone inside the structure.

In the same way, remove respect from a child's relationship with his parents and the walls of the family will collapse. Children will not listen to and obey their parents if they don't respect them. If they don't listen to their parents, then their leading counsel becomes the immature reasoning of their own minds or that of their friends. It is only through giving their ears and hearts to their parents that children learn wisdom and proper behavior and can hope for a meaningful and prosperous life (Prov. 3:1-2).

Finally, children need to honor their parents because it is biblical. "Honor your father and your mother" (Ex. 20:12). God emphasizes the importance of respecting parents when he ties it to his own personality. After saying in Leviticus 19:3 that "Each of you must respect his mother and father," he adds "I am the Lord your God." There shouldn't be any doubt about how seriously God regards this command. In fact, in ancient Israel a son who showed flagrant disrespect for his parents could be stoned (Deut. 21:18-21).

Our children will not naturally or automatically show us respect. They will not show politeness in speech nor decorum in behavior unless we teach them. Their natural inclination will be to do their own thing, disobey us, talk back, yell and scream, throw a temper tantrum, or even slap us. Some parents laugh when their children do these things. Perhaps they are embarrassed when it is done in front of others and laughter is an easy way to dismiss the situation. Or, the parents may even think it is cute when coming from a tiny child. "Do you see how mad he is?" and then they laugh. But if we tolerate that behavior, we are teaching our own little kids that they do not need to respect us. We are teaching them that our ideas, our values, and our rules as the parents do not matter and they can do whatever they want, including jumping on the sofa and making faces at mom when they are four, to drinking and robbing from the neighbors at fourteen. Remember the stern warning from Proverbs that "a child left to himself, (that is, untrained and undisciplined), disgraces his mother" (Prov. 29:15).

We do our children an immense favor when we teach them to respect us. Respecting us means they listen to us and obey us in everything. It also means they don't talk back or speak in harsh tones. Further, when we practice corrective discipline when they disobey, even when they are very young, we are reinforcing the rules of the home at an age that will shape and mold their will in a healthy way.

Respect will continue to be an issue in families even as children grow up and leave home. But if we can at least build a healthy base when they are 18 months to three years old, it makes the teenage years a whole lot more enjoyable.

CHILDREN IN THE CHECKOUT LINE

> Discipline your children, and they will give you peace;
> they will bring you the delights you desire.
>
> Proverbs 29:17

Discipline and gratitude are first learned in the little experiences of life. Both of these dispositions are major building blocks of character, and without them we will live shiftless and selfish lives. With them, we will experience healthier relationships and be more likely to achieve significant accomplishments. A trip to the grocery store with children is a good example for how to develop, or undermine, discipline and gratitude.

Children are notorious for wanting, even demanding, a treat in a store, especially in the checkout line. Marketing experts have determined the best items to place in this part of the store: snacks and glitzy magazines. If you haven't had lunch yet, the beef jerky and chocolate bars call out your name, begging to be lifted off the shelf and placed in the cart. If you have a long wait, the urge to thumb through one of the magazines to view pictures of a movie or read "How to Have the Best Marriage Ever in Only Five Minutes" is nearly irresistible. But, it takes longer than five minutes to read the article, so you have to place it in the cart to read later with your candy bar and beef sticks.

This urge to purchase items at the last moment is heightened many times for the children at your side or in the cart. The chocolate screams for their attention! Plus, there may be other children already nibbling on the bars their kind parents are purchasing for them. "Why can't we have one?"

Children learn very quickly that moms and dads become instantly vulnerable in public places. They become embarrassed at the children's incessant demands and loud crying. The parents can be intimidated and will often give in and make the purchases just to quiet the children.

Two destructive traits are being developed in children who incessantly, even rudely, demand and receive a treat every time they go to a store. The first trait is instant gratification. They see and they want, now. It does not matter that mom is buying healthy ingredients to provide a nutritious dinner in two hours. That healthy meal later simply does not provide the allure of a sugar high now. So, if mom or dad won't give in now, the children will have to turn it up a notch and begin yelling and screaming.

The second unwholesome trait being developed is manipulation. Children learn mom and dad's pressure points early on. A public place is one such pressure point. No parent wants other people to see their screaming, out-of-control child. They fear the child's poor behavior reflects more on their failure to properly parent than it does on the child's infantile behavior. To avoid creating that impression in people, they will do anything to still the child, including giving in to their manipulative demands. Even as mom and dad place the candy in the cart, they know they are being railroaded through intimidation, but they feel powerless to do anything else. Score another victory for the kids.

How do you deal with such belligerent behavior in public places? As much as you may want to spank the child there in the aisle or checkout line, public perspectives on that today could get you jailed for child abuse. Are there other options?

We need to realize that our offspring are not the only children to make demands for treats in a store. It is quite normal, and is one facet of the power games children play. These power games can begin as early as twelve to fifteen months and can seem to intensify with age. They definitely can intensify if the children score some early victories and learn how to successfully maneuver on the battle ground of parent-children relations. James Dobson wrote that the power play of a very small child may not be a conscious function yet, but it eventually will be, and that "a strong-willed child of three or older is inclined to challenge his mom and dad whenever he believes he can win. He will carefully choose the weapons and select the turf on which the contest will be staged" (James Dobson, *Parenting Isn't for Cowards*, p.96). In our example, the battle ground is any public place, and the weapons are explosive vocal chords.

If the child's object is to win through intimidation and manipulation, the parents' objective must be to intentionally frustrate their child's goal. Every little boy and girl must learn that they cannot get whatever they want, whenever they want, through selfish and rude demands. That creates a level of expectation that cannot be met, and will lead to disappointment, frustration, and anger when future wants are not met. Better to allow the child to learn early on with the little things (like candy at the checkout line) that our whims are not always satisfied, and to be grateful for the blessings that we do receive.

So, what can a mom and dad do when their children initiate military action to defeat their parents' resolve so the parents emerge victorious in the contest of wills? First, we must resolve to never let them win. Refuse to give in. They can scream at will, but it will not affect your decision.

Doesn't that seem unfair, though, to other customers in the store? Yes. No one likes the nerve-shattering shrieks of angry kids, whether others or their own. But that itself isn't reason to give in. If we are afraid other people will think of us as ineffective parents because we let the kids scream, they will certainly think that if they see us purchasing candy for them as a bribe.

It usually takes only a couple of trips to a public place for small children to learn that not even the presence of other people will make mom and dad cower and seek peace through appeasement.

This process can be hastened in older children who are throwing a public tantrum by whispering in their ear, "Just wait until we get home." For this to be effective with the kids, we must have an established track record of consistent discipline and punishment, or they will just dismiss it as an empty threat. If we have a track record of threatening punishment but not delivering, our kids will learn quickly that we are not honest and they have nothing to fear from continued disruptive and disobedient behavior.

A very effective approach to quiet the persistent and relentless voice is to remove another item from the cart you may have already placed in there for the child. You can say, "Okay, since you can't be thankful for what we have already gotten you, and you insist on getting even more, not only will you not get this candy bar, but we are going to put the ice cream back as well, and you will get nothing." Then do it. Counselor John Rosemond tells of a mother backtracking to several stores to return items she purchased for a daughter after she exhausted her mom by demanding even more. Never again did the mother have to face such an intense test of wills from her daughter in a store (Rosemond, *A Family of Value*, 206).

My wife has used this approach on occasion with amazing results. When our kids were arguing over what movies to rent from the video store, and they would not stop, she told them to put the movies back and we wouldn't get any. Earnest apologies followed immediately, but Cheryl held her ground: no movies. The next trip to the video store was much more peaceful, even enjoyable, and the kids found ways to compromise and agree on a selection.

Saying "no" to our children does not hurt them. It teaches them discipline and encourages them to be grateful for what they already have. Giving them more and more does not enhance discipline and thankfulness; it sets unrealistic expectations that anything they want is simply theirs for the asking or demanding.

The promise of Proverbs 29:17, "Discipline your children, and they will give you peace; they will bring you the delights you desire," is true only if we discipline them consistently and fairly. We will have peace and rest after they have experienced discipline, not before.

CHAPTER THREE

FAMILY

FAMILY CONVERSATIONS

> When I was a boy in my father's house, still tender, and an
> only child of my mother, he taught me and said, 'lay hold
> of my words with all your heart; keep my commands and
> you will live.
>
> Proverbs 4:3-4

Every family should have a night or two a week at home, relaxing, walking, talking, and just hanging out together. One reason for such family time is to reestablish personal and family identity. You may be a nurse, teacher, policeman, doctor, minister, or salesman by trade, but you are a mom or dad by divine calling. Frequent nights at home will remind you of that and help you with your focus.

Secondly, such calm nights are healing and refreshing. The tensions of work, finances, and economic worries are refocused and alleviated when a family experiences health and enjoyment together.

A third reason for regular family time is so that our kids can get to know us. Being with us gives them the opportunity to read between the lines of our rules, such as, "Don't do that again!" or "You'd better not!" to see what our real value system is. They learn our weaknesses and our strengths. They learn to love us even with our faults.

Finally, family time is important because it can also be story time.

Our children need to hear about our childhood. They will delight with stories of how we collected bugs, dumped ice cream on Grandma's new carpet, snored in church, and got spanked for misbehavior. These are cute tales of our innocence that make us real to our children. They enable our kids to see us as the human beings we are. I'm sure some of the lessons Solomon learned from his father, King David, were the great stories of his life (Prov. 4:3-4).

Our kids need to hear of our early struggles with growing up. They'll want to know how we related to our parents, teachers at school, and brothers and sisters. Don't forget the heart-felt stories. Remember how disappointed you were when you didn't get the date you longed for? Remember, too, how disappointed you were at the date you did get? Storytelling lets our kids know that their generation is not the first to deal with those unnerving boy-girl issues.

Our kids need to hear how we resisted peer pressure and refused to go to drinking parties. Did that hurt us? Did we occasionally feel left out? Sure, but we survived, and if our kids will exercise some courage and restraint with their peer group, they will survive, too.

It is important for our children to hear about our early commitment to purity until marriage and how we struggled with temptation. Hearing our success stories can embolden them to live spiritually and purely.

It could also be helpful for them to hear our stories of failure. No, we weren't perfect. Sometimes we may have let our guard down and embarrassed ourselves, disappointed our parents, and even got into trouble with the law. But, we had loving parents who stood by us, a loving church that embraced us, and a loving Savior who forgave us. With this support structure we were able to survive our own misdeeds. Let's let our kids know that they have that same support structure in their lives. Knowing they can be forgiven may save their lives someday.

These conversations don't go on in all homes. One reason is parents don't know how to initiate the storytelling. Parents, relax. Initiating story telling can be as simple as saying, "Hey kids, I just remembered a story I want to tell you before I forget." The response of the children, especially the younger ones, will be, "Tell us!" Another reason is because some parents don't understand the value of storytelling. They don't realize that the ethical outlook and moral fiber of their children is largely formed by interaction with the significant people in their lives, and that includes their parents. Finally, some parents simply don't take the time. They may be fulfilling the demands of their career and neglect the divine calling God has given them to be a mom or dad.

Jesus used storytelling to attract an audience, hold attention, and eventually transform the world. We might find that storytelling can do the same thing for our families.

FAMILY MEMORY

> The memory of the righteous will be a blessing.
>
> Proverbs 10:7a

Favorite photographs of my wife and three kids adorn my desk and office. A favorite photo with my wife is one of us sitting together at an Optimist Club banquet shortly after we were married. Another is of Cheryl sitting at the kitchen table of the apartment we rented from Tom Olbricht in Abilene, Texas when I was taking a graduate class at ACU. My favorite shot of Wes is when he was five years old and we had just moved to Cody, Wyoming. He was dressed up in a western hat, boots, and belt. He was a young cowboy. We held Jenny's second birthday at her grandparents' house in Marianna, Florida. She was sitting on a bench outside and turned to face me. Her hair was curly and her grin mischievous. This picture of Jenny stands out for me. I was assembling an entertainment center when three year-old Kristin climbed up onto one of shelves and just sat there like she was the only entertainment we needed. I made sure to snap a photo of that.

All of these pictures provide vivid recall for me of special times, unforgettable expressions, and extreme joy. These pictures remind me of special times that make me proud to be a husband and father.

But there are some special times and moments when my camera wasn't working, or I wasn't fast enough and I missed a shot that might have vied for "favorite" status. My camera was set wrong when Jenny went running by during her first half-marathon. My video camera was off when Kristin made the shot of a lifetime.

Kristin, a high school sophomore, was playing against a girl about six inches taller. She made up for the size miss-match by playing very aggressively. She was lucky that a pushing foul against the other girl didn't get called by the refs. But the other girl wasn't going to let it go un-avenged.

Kristin got the ball and made a fast break for our goal. As she was going up for the shot, the other girl pushed her. Kristin hit the floor hard and slid off the court into the wall. Her basket was good and so was her free throw. As we were cheering it suddenly hit me; I had turned the recorder off. I missed the picture or video of the season, maybe of her high school career. It was quite a game, and I almost had the best part of it on video. Almost.

I'll always regret that I missed that play. I'd love to load it onto my computer and send it to family and friends. But all I'll ever be able to do is explain the great play.

That might be okay, even good. I love photographs and video of special moments. I have albums full of pictures and drawers full of videos. Photographs of family adorn my desk, shelves, and walls. They provide vivid recall of family occasions I want to remember.

But memory has special value in itself. Even without the picture or video, special moments burn themselves into our hearts and minds. Those moments live in vivid color, expression, and animation. The emotions surrounding the occasion are so vibrant they carry us back in time, and we relive the drama and the feelings. As we recall the moment with our loved ones, we re-experience the time again. The sharing of the memory and the reliving of the emotions draw us together.

It really isn't the photograph or the video that does this for us; it is the power of memory. Special times are enjoyed in our community (family and close friends), and our recall of these times, complete with conversation and emotions, keeps these memories alive and fresh. Thus, they keep our community alive and fresh.

The photographs and videos may provide stimulus to recall, but they are not the memory. The memory lives in our hearts and minds.

I'm sure I'll always remember that I missed some incredible shots and footage. But I'll never forget the people or the events that made the moments so memorable.

Take the time today to really watch your spouse and your kids. Listen to what they have to say. Take joy in your time with them. A special moment may happen at any time. Ultimately, you don't need a camera to capture the occasion. You just need a heart filled with love.

HARMING OUR HOUSE

> He who brings trouble on his family will inherit only the wind, and the fool will be servant to the wise.
>
> Proverbs 11:29

An occasional night playing cards with the guys seemed like an innocent way to relax from his stressful job, Stuart reasoned. Before he and Candy married, playing cards was one activity he and his buddies enjoyed together. Other activities included basketball, hunting, betting on sporting events, and even occasional trips to Vegas to hit the machines. Drinking was a regular feature of many of these events, but it was never a serious problem.

Since getting married, Stuart had given up many of these activities in the interest of investing time at home with his wife and now with his two kids. The occasional card game with low gambling stakes and a few drinks seemed pretty innocent to him.

But Candy still complained about it. "It's not that I object to you having some time with guy friends," Candy explained to her husband. "It is that I don't trust some of your old buddies. I realize you have changed and matured, but they haven't. I don't like the drinking, pornography, girlfriends, and vile humor. I don't trust them, and I'm afraid of their influence on you and eventually on the kids."

Stuart sighed. He really didn't seem to understand why his connection to his old gang could be so worrisome to Candy, and how that could subtly undermine her trust in him.

Stuart did not mean to cause any stress or problems for his family. Yet, even though he acted innocently and naively, his wife still thought he brought harm to them. Trust was undermined through his connections to friends that Stuart had to admit were a bit irresponsible and undisciplined. Even though Stuart was innocent of the more offensive behavior of his friends, his wife was still concerned that he was bringing trouble to his family.

There are numerous ways we bring trouble into our homes and threaten its existence. One way is through the pursuit of pleasure. God is certainly not against our having a good time! Jesus himself enjoyed a good meal and the presence of friends. He knew the value of a good time. But pleasure that draws us away from the values of the home is foolishness. "He who loves pleasure will become poor; whoever loves wine and oil will never be rich." (Prov. 21:17) Pleasure that is too expensive or leans toward the immoral is dangerous territory.

Stuart flirted with pleasure that was potentially both expensive and immoral. His wife's concern with the influence of friends who gambled, used porn, and pursued unhealthy relationships with women was well grounded. What if one of the friends started an X rated movie or invited some of their girls over after the card game? Would Stuart's moral fiber hold? What if one of his kids walked into the room? Should Stuart object to such behavior in his presence? Quietly leave? Pleasure is fine, but it must be of a quality and standard that supports the fabric of the family. This is one way we can bring trouble into our homes. Another is being careless with money, as Barbara's story shows.

Barbara liked nice things but was never able to afford them until she married Ken, a successful retailer. On their first date at an expensive restaurant Ken told her, "Don't even look at the prices. Get whatever you want." He had no idea about the level of expectation he created in his future wife.

Barbara and Ken married after a brief romance. Ken was thirty-two and was ready to settle down and begin a family. When Barbara said they would need to do some things to the house, Ken turned the reins of interior design and other domestic matters over to Barbara, which she gladly accepted.

Several rooms in the house were redecorated, refurnished, and even re-carpeted. Ken didn't seem to mind the new painting on the walls, but he did ask his new bride to go easy on the check book. "Once all this is done, I'll be able to slow down," Barbara said with a smile.

But when the first baby came, and then the second and more expenses piled up, Ken sensed things were out of control. He had to draw money out of a savings account on several occasions to cover checks Barbara wrote. Then he discovered she had received two credit cards he didn't know about and they were maxed out. When he tried to talk to Barbara, she always seemed nervous and preoccupied. But when he finally stood firm and said, "We have to talk!" Barbara knew there was trouble.

The problem with money is never the money but our attitude toward it. It is love of money that leads to all kinds of evil (1 Tim. 6:10). That evil may be spending foolishly so we get into debt we can't recover from (22:7) or hoarding it rather than sharing with others in need (11:24). Laziness (24:33-34), big plans but no work (14:23), and chasing fantasies (28:19) all lead to financial destitution.

A misuse of the tongue is another one of the major causes of offense in the home. Sins of the tongue pierce healthy relationships like a sword, and they include lying, stirring up dissension, quarreling, gossip, mocking speech, and endless harping or criticism. But a sin of the tongue need not be this sinister. A major offense is speaking endlessly and carelessly. "Reckless words pierce like a sword, but the tongue of the wise brings healing" (12:18). Though not intended to hurt and maim, reckless words do have that destructive result because "the speaker is one who is thoughtless and rambles on" (Murphy, 91).

One man hurt his family through humor. Through tears his teen daughter said, "I know dad loves me, but his constant ridiculing of me in front of others embarrasses me. I'm afraid to bring anyone home because of him. Some of the kids think he is funny and repeat what he says at school. That hurts." This dad epitomizes the truism that reckless words pierce like a sword. He doesn't filter or temper the abundance of words, so he inevitably utters some that stress relationships. If nothing else, the weight of his over-abundance of words is enough to strain the seams of a relationship. Restraint is an indication of wisdom: "When words are many, sin is not absent, but he who holds his tongue is wise" (Prov. 10:19). Exercising discipline with one's speech protects the home from damage.

Stuart, Barbara, or the dad never meant to cause any stress or problems for their families. Yet, even though they all acted innocently and naively, they still brought harm to their families. They showed a lack of consideration, undermined trust, and hurt feelings. The wise who listen to the voices of family members who love them, who feast on Proverbs, and who reflect upon their behavior can stem the tide of hurtful behavior, heal the wounds, and bring great blessing to their families.

THE FAMILY MEAL

> Better a dry crust with peace and quiet than a house full
> of feasting with strife.
>
> Proverbs 17:1

> When Jesus was at the table with them, he took bread,
> gave thanks, broke it and began to give it to them. Then
> their eyes were opened and they recognized him ...
>
> Luke 24:30-31

Something good happens when people who care about each other sit down to a meal together. A powerfully positive dynamic is created when family and friends place their feet under the same table for food and fellowship. This is especially true when the gathering is dad, mom, and the children. Consider these four suggestions.

One, communication. Real communication is more than the canned phrases and responses we toss out as we hurry past each other. "How are you doing?" "Fine." "Good." "And you?" "Fine." "Good." "Later." "Yup. Later."

Real communication occurs after we work through these often sterile niceties and discuss matters of real importance. That can happen at meal time, when we are gathered around the table with the tv off and cell phones in another room. "Dad, I saw a guy bully a smaller kid at school today. I wanted to step in and stop him, but I was afraid. Do you think that is bad? How do I get over that fear?" Those kinds of questions only come after we have had time to relax and be vulnerable in front of other people we trust. They aren't asked in the hurried moment, or in between logins to our Facebook or Twitter accounts. They come after we have invested time and conversation with each other.

Two, instruction. Our children's primary source of information, instruction, and character development is mom and dad. They move in our shadows and under our influence from the moment of their birth until they leave for college, and even long after that. Regular and consistent meal time together is an incredibly ripe opportunity for healthy and positive instruction to take place. Deuteronomy 6 says we are to teach and impress our kids with the commandments of God in numerous life situations, including when we sit down together (vss 6-7). Sit down to what? Most likely a meal. Something happens when we are chewing on our food and on our thoughts in close proximity. One of the children asks a serious question and mom and dad get to give serious and reflective answers. If the question is tough enough, the conversation can continue the next night, even the night after. And in this warm environment ears are opened and hearts are receptive in ways they are not when we are hurrying past each other in the hallway.

Three, communication and instruction leads to another good thing happening, and that is the development of the children's ability to think and process information in a healthy way. Our advice and counsel to our children will likely differ from what they hear from the television shows or their peers. They now have our views in their minds on various topics, such as manners, work, sex, parenting, and family life. In one ear they hear the voices from the sitcoms or some recording artist. It may not be what we want them to hear. But, in the other ear there are the echoes of last night's conversation at the dinner table, with mom and dad presenting a very different view about how to handle their bodies, approach marriage, and prepare for parenthood. Blessed are the children that have that echo from their parents to balance what they hear from their peers and the entertainment industry. Mealtime, with communication, instruction, and learning how to think and process information, helps our children mature into solid young people with a strong sense of their own identity and ethical system. When they go to college they won't have to spend several years floundering in uncertainty and dangerous behavior in search of themselves.

Finally, number four, mealtime as a family generally promotes better nutrition and thus healthier bodies. Fast food is convenient to our schedules, but may not be so convenient to our arteries. When mom or dad fix the food from scratch, with healthy ingredients, it fuels good conversation, good instruction, and good thinking, and also provides good fuel for the body of the children. You really can't beat several nights a week of dad, mom, and the kids sitting around a table with good food and good company. The family meal is one of life's great joys and one of God's great blessings for our lives.

CHAPTER FOUR

THE GOD WE SERVE

BEHAVIOR VS. LOVE

He mocks proud mockers but gives grace to the humble.
Proverbs 3:34

Moral sin horrified Sarah's parents. They had seen the lives of numerous young people in their church and community severely disrupted by moral indiscretion. When Sarah was a young girl, they determined to raise her with such moral conditioning that she would never make a misstep herself and experience such fallout.

Sarah's ethical training was exemplary. Her parents modeled modesty and purity. They taught their daughter that her body was the temple of God's spirit and should be kept pure (1 Cor. 6:18-20). They showed her the passages about God judging and punishing adultery and fornication (1 Cor. 6:9-10; Rev. 21:8). They didn't let her dance or date until she was sixteen, and then closely monitored the boys who came calling. They built such a wall of ethical conditioning, biblical teaching, and parental control around Sarah that there was no way she would fall victim to inappropriate behavior.

But she did.

Explanations for why people act out escape us. Sure we know that sometimes it is curiosity, peer pressure, pleasure seeking, naiveté, spiritual ignorance, or even rebellion. But how do you explain Sarah's case? She was a sweet, innocent girl. She was protected and monitored. She knew all the right answers to questions about behavior and deportment. How could she act out and swap her moral upbringing and standing for fleeting pleasure?

Sarah's parents were horrified. After drilling her for answers and berating her for misbehavior, they cried at their own failure.

For her part Sarah felt doomed. She wondered herself why she acted out. She loved her parents and respected their lifestyle. She wanted to be a good girl, marry a Christian man, and teach a children's class at church, just like her mother. She envisioned hosting youth parties at her house and driving kids to area church events. Sarah sighed. It was all over now. She sinned big. She defied her parents' instructions. Sarah could reach only one conclusion about her role in her moral sin: she was a bad person.

Bible verses she didn't think of that fateful night now flooded her mind. "The wicked will not inherit the kingdom of God." "The body is not meant for sexual immorality." "Flee from sexual immorality." "The sexually immoral will (not) inherit the kingdom of God." "The sexually immoral ... their place will be in the fiery lake ..." That last one filled Sarah with indescribable horror.

Sarah didn't make the distinction in her mind between committing a sin and being committed to sin. She couldn't. This significant nuance had never been explained to her. In her youth and immaturity, Sarah could only conclude that she was a lost sinner. Since that was her mental image now, that is the role she began to play. Sarah's uncharacteristic moral lapse became routine. Sarah the good little girl became Sarah the moral wretch.

What a tragic and unnecessary set of circumstances. If only her well-intentioned parents had added a few other theological gems in her training program. One, only Jesus lived a sinless life. Two, we are all sinners, all of us, even Sarah's parents. Three, we all need grace and mercy for salvation. Four, God gives us that mercy through Jesus, even when our lives are steeped in sin and filth (Rom. 5:8). Five, we can never get so low that the grace and mercy of God cannot reach us and save us. Never ever.

How sad that some people think they are so bad that God cannot save them. Don't we realize it is because we have acted badly that Jesus died? It is not because of my righteousness that Jesus extends his hand to me; it is because of my sin. That's how much he loves me and you.

Serena Woods made a profound statement about this in *Grace is for Sinners*. She writes, "If that group (a family or church) had any kind of working knowledge of who God is or taught less behavior lessons and more love lessons, then the standard wouldn't be what a person does, the standard would be how a person loves" (p.127). If we only teach behavior but not love and forgiveness, we do not prepare our kids for when they do a very human thing: sin.

Sarah sinned. And because most of her instruction had been about proper conduct, she thought she was incurably stained and soiled when she fell from her lofty position of pure behavior. Since she was ruined now, why try to live better in the future? By her own reasoning, her sin would always have a stranglehold on her mental image of herself, impelling her to further acts of destructive behavior.

Sarah's great hope is that a beloved brother or sister will greet her with a warm embrace, look into her grief-stricken eyes, and say, "Sarah, God loves you. This church loves you. You sinned. So has everyone here. It is for this very reason that Jesus is here for you today. God delights in giving grace to the humble. You have been humbled by your sin. Now, cry out and God will hear you. Remember, 'The Lord is far from the wicked but he hears the prayer of the righteous' (Prov. 15:29). You aren't wicked because you fail; you are only wicked if you reject God and choose to wallow in rebellion. You have a righteous heart. Pray, and God will hear."

I hope all of our kids, in all of our families and in all of our churches, know that God loves them. It is important that we teach our kids to behave well; it is incredibly important that we teach them how much God loves them when they don't act so well. And I hope that someone tells Sarah, and she will hear.

ANSWERED PRAYER

> The Lord is far from the wicked but he hears the prayer
> of the righteous.
>
> Proverbs 15:29

A great challenge for Christians is to believe that God really hears our prayers and responds to them. We have the assurance from Proverbs that God hears the prayer of the righteous, and we have that thought continued repeatedly in the New Testament. One of the great exhortations to communicate with God is in Philippians 4:6 &7: "Do not be anxious about anything, but in everything, by prayer and petition, with thanksgiving, present your requests to God. And the peace of God, which transcends all understanding, will guard your hearts and your minds in Christ Jesus." Will we believe these promises?

Shirley does. Years ago Shirley was born into a home with an alcoholic father. He abused his family and used God's name in curses. Shirley's mother wasn't a Christian either, but she was a good woman and realized that this environment was not good for her children. To get help with her kids she sent them to a local church. Here her two children learned about Jesus and learned to pray.

Shirley was still a young girl trapped in poverty and an abusive, alcoholic household. Her parents divorced. What could Shirley do?

She prayed. Shirley prayed for a Christian stepfather who would be good to his family and take care of them. God heard that prayer and answered it. Shirley's mother married a Christian man and became a Christian herself.

Next, Shirley prayed that someday God would bring a Christian man into her life. She knew she wanted to have a Christian home and that she would need a Christian man to help her with that. So, long before she was even married Shirley prayed for that godly man to come along.

Here is a young girl from a background of alcoholism, poverty and a broken family praying, "God, please bring a good Christian man into my life to marry. I want to have a godly home with peace and love, and I need a Christian man for that." Do you think God would hear a prayer like that and answer it?

In college, Shirley began dating a young man and several years later she married him. You may recognize her name today as Shirley Dobson. That's right, Shirley Dobson, the wife of James Dobson, the head of Focus on the Family (James Dobson, *When God Doesn't Make Sense*, 132-33).

I can only imagine the anxiety, fear, and longing that filled this young girl's heart as she heard the angry rampages of a drunken father. But through her church, Shirley learned about Jesus and prayer. She prayed that God would help her provide a better home environment for her own family, and God heard that prayer. Shirley has experienced the peace that passes understanding.

We can, too. "Do not be anxious about anything, but in everything, by prayer and petition, with thanksgiving, present your requests to God. And the peace of God, which transcends all understanding, will guard your hearts and your minds in Christ Jesus" (Philippians 4:6-7).

GOD IS OUR SHIELD

> He (God) holds victory in store for the upright, he is a shield to those whose walk is blameless, for he guards the course of the just and protects the way of his faithful ones.
>
> Proverbs 2:7-8

Proverbs 2 has three parts to it. In part one the Sage, (a common reference for the authors of Proverbs), encourages young people to seek wisdom and a relationship with God. In part two, he encourages the development of moral sensitivity, or a conscience. In part three he encourages wise choices in our selection of friends, with the promise that with wise choices we will avoid evil and will be rewarded by God.

How many of us consistently do all of these good things? Attaining wisdom is a life-long pursuit. It involves hard work and consistent effort. It means we have to think, ask hard questions, study, and always be open to learning. Sometimes it is exhausting, and when we fail, it can be so frustrating. And we often stumble and fall. The truth is, we sometimes pick the wrong friends, make bad choices, and get ourselves into trouble.

If we are not careful, we can despair of ever living the righteous life that God wants us to lead. To avoid that despair, we must distinguish between a righteous and a perfect life. A righteous life does not mean one never fails. Rather, it is a life lived in the direction God wants it to go, being molded and shaped by God's spirit and truth. To be righteous means we try to live as God wants us to, being shaped by the Bible and making ethical choices. For example, if we have the opportunity to make a lot of money fast, but illegally, we will choose not to. Making money illegally or immorally is against God, so the righteous person won't do it.

A young man was arrested for dealing illegal drugs. At the time of his arrest, he had several thousand dollars stashed away. After his release from custody and a stint at rehabilitation, he was going to go back to his stash and get it for himself. But while he was in rehab, he began to realize that the money he had hidden was illegal and immoral. He made that money selling drugs to other children. His conscience began to develop to the point that he didn't feel it was the right thing, the Christian thing, to enjoy the money that he had obtained immorally. He decided to let the money go, along with the friends and lifestyle from his drug-using and drug-selling days. "Plus," he told me, "I'm afraid that if I go back and get it, then I'll be drawn right back into that lifestyle." That was a righteous decision.

Making righteous decisions is not easy. But there is good news for those trying to live righteously: we are never fully alone. Even if we stand alone, even if we stand apart from friends or classmates because we have different interests than they do, we are never truly alone. God holds victory in store for the upright; he is a shield to those whose walk is blameless. We have God as our shield to help and protect us when we seek to live righteously.

In ancient times, warriors would carry a shield into battle. Defensively a shield protected a soldier from arrows or swords. He could hide behind his shield and protect his body from being hit. Offensively a soldier could use it to push against an enemy line or even strike an enemy soldier. It was an indispensable part of a soldier's equipment.

This piece of military equipment is used as a metaphor for the kind of protection God offers us. God will protect us against attacks from enemies, and he will go ahead of us to strike at the temptation waiting to engulf us.

Interestingly, the word used for shield actually means resource, defined as "an inner power that helps one escape a fix." (Michael Fox, "Proverbs" in *Anchor Bible Commentary*, 1:114). God is our resource to protect us and guide us as we seek to live righteously. He guards the course of the just and protects the way of his faithful ones.

How is God a shield or resource for us against evil companions or temptation to sin? First, God promises that he will never allow us to be tempted above what we can bear (1 Cor.10:13). Secondly, the wise counsel of parents and spiritual friends is a valuable ally in finding the strength to do what is right (Prov. 27:9-20). Thirdly, having the Word of God in our hearts and trusting it above our own opinions is one of the greatest resources God gives us to shield us on the path of righteousness (Prov. 3:1,5). Praise be to God that with these protections in place, he holds victory in store for us!

THE LORD'S DISCIPLINE

> My son, do not despise the Lord's discipline and do not resent his rebuke, because the Lord disciplines those he loves, as a father the son he delights in.
>
> Proverbs 3:11, 12

"It's hard for me to spank him," the young father said to a friend about his son, "because I love him so much and don't want to hurt him."

"He won't mind hurting you," the friend replied. "If you don't discipline him, teaching him to respect your authority by obeying you, one day he will hurt you badly when his behavior gets out of control." The friend was trying to communicate to the young father that the incentive to discipline does not come from anger, but from love. Instruction and punishment, the two sides of discipline, are designed to shape the course of our children's lives.

Why does the Lord discipline us? One, it could simply be to punish the evil doer. Sodom and Gomorrah suffered a hardship from which they were never permitted to learn their lesson. They were punished.

Two, hardship or discipline is often administered to encourage our return to God if we have strayed. In each of the instances of God sending suffering in Amos 4, he says, "Yet you have not returned to me." God's clear intent in these passages is that suffering would cause people to reflect upon sin and waywardness and find their way back to God.

Three, God may send discipline to make us stronger. The testing of faith can produce perseverance in the heart of the faithful, leading to greater maturity (James 1:2-4). Challenges accost those who live in Christ. Sometimes those challenges come from our own undeveloped and immature character, and sometimes they come from evil sources outside us. Each time we resist strengthens our fiber and matures us.

How does the Lord discipline? One method is through hardship. God has used hunger, drought/thirst, a poor harvest, plagues, and defeat to discipline his people. Each of these measures is described in Amos 4. In each instance God takes credit for the hardship: I gave you empty stomachs, I withheld rain, I struck your crops, I sent plagues, I overthrew your cities. God leaves no doubt that he can and will engineer hardships for discipline.

A second approach is through natural consequence. God may choose to let events run their course as a teaching method. After David's betrayal, he experienced a general disruption in the affairs of his home. One son abused a half-sister. That son was killed by the half-sister's brother. This same son drove David from his kingdom and died in the rebellion. Did God engineer these events? Possibly. Or it could be that they were a natural consequence of order and respect breaking down in the home. Cause and effect is a major teaching tool in proverbial wisdom. Suffering the natural consequences of poor decisions can train us to think and act with greater care in the future.

Natural consequences can be seen in Proverbs 3. The Sage warns us to acknowledge God, not be wise in our own eyes, and honor God with our wealth (vs. 6-7, 9). The promise for obedience is that we will enjoy health in our bodies and abundance in the harvest of our labor (vs. 8 & 10). Then the Sage says to not despise the Lord's discipline, but understand that he loves us.

The natural consequence of trusting and walking in God's will is that good results will flow from good decisions, while bad results will flow from rebellion against God and refusing to walk in his paths. But the bad consequences, no matter how severe or inconvenient, are a form of God's discipline and rebuke. If we can embrace that discipline and learn from it, we can be the blessed man of verse 13 who finds wisdom.

Fathers discipline their children because they love them (Hebrews 12:7). Refusing to discipline results in ill-trained children and chaotic homes. Sometimes the courts have to step in and provide the discipline the home did not. This can be a form of God's rebuke, and whether it is by natural consequence or his direct operation, God's rebuke should not be resented but embraced.

DELIGHTING IN MANKIND

> I was the craftsman at his side. I was filled with delight day after day, rejoicing always in his presence, rejoicing in his whole world and delighting in mankind.
>
> Proverbs 8:30-31

Bob and Pam refused to abort their baby. They would trust God's will in the matter of this child, not that of their doctors. After the birth of her fourth child, Pam contracted a parasite. When her health weakened, doctors advised her not to have any more children. She didn't plan to, but God had a different plan, Pam says. She became pregnant with her fifth child.

Pam's doctor recommended an abortion, but Pam and her husband adamantly refused. They were missionaries in the Philippines and believed fervently that God had a plan for their lives, whether they could see it or not. They maintained their faith several months later when the doctor told her the fetus was dead and would need to be removed. Bob and Pam refused again. It wasn't until her seventh month that another doctor examined her and determined that the baby was alive. Pam delivered a healthy baby boy in August 1988, and she named him Tim.

Bob and Pam refused the medical advice they received because it countered what they knew about God's will. God is the author of human life (Gen. 1:26, 27). His personality puts an imprint upon us that deems us valuable above all human means to evaluate and calculate. Our stock soars off the charts. Even when the market plummets, our value soars. Every one of us bears the image of the Creator and the stamp of his approval.

The passage in Proverbs reveals something of the heart of God toward his creation. Not only does God create life, but he also delights in the life he has created. Wisdom personified does the speaking in Proverbs 8. Wisdom says that she was the craftsman at God's side working as his instrument in creation. She says she rejoices in the world and delights in mankind. Since God is the author behind creation and Wisdom, I think it is safe to say that God himself delights in mankind. God delights in us because he is the Father and we are his offspring.

That is why we honor life. To honor means we respect, value, and exalt life. Nowhere in this sense of honor can we justify ending the life of the unborn. Even if baby Tim was going to be handicapped or deformed because of his mother's weakened condition, Bob and Pam could not bring themselves to function as God and decide to terminate his life. They would honor God, and in honoring God they would honor the life of their unborn child.

But what if the baby had indeed been handicapped, either mentally or physically? Would the decision to abort the baby have been better than to bring it to life outside the womb? I would counter that question with another: "Who are we to decide?" God placed eternal value on human life when he said we are made in his image. That value is not determined by height, strength, looks, athletic ability, or academic achievement. It is determined simply by God's delight in his creation.

Bruce Waltke wrote "Though humankind in its weakness is far removed from the heavenly realm where God and wisdom soar, yet the person in the street is the object of Wisdom's delight ..." (*Proverbs*, 1:422). Human weakness sometimes results in human tragedy and misfortune. That is sad, but does not in any way offset the value God has created within us.

Let me tell you a little more about this baby born in the Philippines years ago. He was home schooled through high school and upon graduation went to college at the University of Florida where he was a very good student. One of his interests was football, not just watching it, but playing it. In fact, he was the quarterback for the University of Florida Gators and later played in the NFL. You might recognize him as Tim Tebow (Pat Shannan, *American Free Press*, Sept. 7, 2009).

Not every baby saved from the abortionist's knife will grow up to become a star athlete, a renowned scientist, or a Pulitzer prize-winning author. But every child allowed to come to full term receives something even greater than any of these other accomplishments: he is a being that God delights in.

NOBLE & HUMBLE

> The fear of the LORD teaches a man wisdom, and humility comes before honor.
>
> Proverbs 15:33

Most of us are comfortable with people who are like us. From social groupings in a community to the high school cafeteria, you will notice that people of similar educational levels, income, political views, and social strata tend to gravitate toward each other. Rare is the person who can move with comfort and ease among the various groups.

Jesus was a person who could do that. He was comfortable with saint or sinner. He could speak with ease to the educated head of the synagogue or to the disfellowshipped sinner who was cast out of that religious setting. He could dine with the Rabbis or the Reprobates.

Jesus was himself in any setting. He could lovingly rebuke a sinner and tell her not to sin anymore, or he could rebuke a preacher and tell him he was a hypocrite. He could engage a Pharisee wanting to know more about his work and mission, and he could engage a tax collector or a broken woman who needed his work and mission.

Many of us adapt our speech and behavior to fit different groups. We have regular speech and religious speech; regular behavior and religious behavior. A youth group member suggested a certain movie to watch. Another teen said it was too sensuous and wouldn't be appropriate to watch with a church youth group; he would save it to watch with his worldly friends. I was at first appalled at the brazen inconsistency in his behavior; today I marvel at his honesty about it. Many adults do the same as this teenager, but with less honesty.

Jesus didn't fit speech or behavior to a certain group; he was always the same. "I am the light of the world. Whoever follows me will never walk in darkness, but will have the light of life" (John 8:12). "I have come that they may have life, and have it to the full" (John 10:10). Jesus was always the same because he had integrity. In every setting he was the light; he was the offer of abundant life; he was the door; he was the good shepherd. With saint or sinner, royalty or commoner, Jesus was the same.

Jesus was the same because he knew his purpose. God sent him to redeem a fallen world. Though Jesus walked the path of man, enduring all of his struggles and temptations, Jesus would never give in. Too much was at stake. Nothing less than the redemption of the world weighed upon his shoulders.

Jesus could move with ease among different groups of people because he was so committed to the purpose God had for him. Leadership and power might tempt him, but that was not God's call for him, so he never gave in. Jesus could enjoy the food and laughter of the tax collector and social outcast crowd without joining in their misbehavior. He could endure a social gathering with the religious mighty but not join in their treachery or their harsh judgments of the common man. He was tempted in all points as they were, yet without sin.

His incredible inner strength with all people and situations came from remembering his purpose for all people. He belonged to everybody, yet would be controlled by no one. Thus he could walk among the various groups of Israel, offering comfort, sharing the Word, healing, forgiving, and teaching, and he gained an audience.

Jesus "was to be all his life one of those men of the people whose natural nobility allows them to meet all men as equals" (Daniel-Rops, *Jesus and His Times*, 113). He was the Son of God, yet he could and did meet all men as equals. He condescended to the lowly and the upper crust, and met them where they were, on their terms, and made his offer of life.

As I study Jesus' life and consider the impact it makes on us, I'm struck by his nobility and humility. The confidence in his purpose and the flawlessness of his life produced his nobility; his love for people and willingness to meet them anywhere gave him his humility. As we attempt to walk in his footsteps, I pray we can do so with the same nobility and humility that he did. We carry on his mission of extending ourselves in the name of the Father to a fallen world. Nothing less than the redemption of the world is at stake. Let's pray that God makes us fit for the task.

SORROW-ACRE

> The righteous care about justice for the poor, but the wicked have no such concern.
>
> Proverbs 29:7

In Denmark, long ago, a young boy named Goske was accused of burning down the barn of the lord of the estate. No one saw him commit the arson, but two witnesses claimed to have seen him in the area. The boy's mother, a peasant widow, offered up desperate cries and pleas for Goske, her only son. Still, the boy was taken into custody. Whether innocent or guilty, Goske would be made an example to the other peasants.

It is a heavy responsibility to preside over a large estate. There is the upkeep of the expansive home and outbuildings, farming operations, financial accounting, care of the peasants who live on and work the land, and civil engagements with those of equal social standing. It was the responsibility of the lord of the estate to decide what to do with a young arsonist.

The boy could be sent to prison. He could be forced into the military. He could also be pardoned if the landowner so decreed. This very situation may have been occupying the lord's mind as he was riding among his rye fields, taking note of those ready to be harvested, when a peasant woman begged his attention. It was the widow Anne-Marie, the mother of Goske, the accused arsonist. "Please help my son, my only son" she cried!

"Here is what I can do for you," the wealthy landowner replied. "This field of rye takes three men one day to cut. If you can harvest this field by yourself, in one day, I shall release your son back to you. If you fail, you will never see him again." So moved was she by the lord's offer she kissed his riding boot.

Sunrise saw Anne-Marie swinging the scythe against the stalks of rye. Onward she moved, never stopping, never pausing, through the morning hours, the early afternoon hours, and into the evening. Exhaustion began to set in. She stumbled. Someone offered her water. In sympathy someone cut a stalk of rye. "No! No one may help her! She must cut the rye herself!" bellowed the lord of the estate.

Through it all the landowner watched. "Let her have her son back," his nephew implored. "Hasn't she done enough?"

"No," said the rich man. "The role of gods is not to interfere with the tragedies of man. As owners of this estate, we play the role of gods in the lives of our servants. We will watch, but we will not interfere. She knows the arrangement. If she cuts the field, her son is returned. If she fails, she will never see him again."

So Anne-Marie pressed on. Townspeople came to watch. The lord ordered Goske released from prison so he could observe his mother's work and feel the full weight of his crime. He followed behind her, stricken with guilt at the slavery imposed upon his mother for his sake, yet powerless to help her.

Finally, the last stalk of rye was struck. Anne-Marie sunk to her knees. Her arms dropped. Women bystanders cried. Her son knelt beside her. The lord stepped forward. "Your son is free, Anne-Marie. You have done a good day's work," he said.

Anne-Marie collapsed into the arms of Goske. She breathed her last in the embrace of the son she died to save. The lord commemorated her sacrifice by placing a stone in the field which the peasants named, "Sorrow-Acre" (Isak Dinesen, *Winter's Tales*).

At another time and in another place, yet another plot of ground was named to symbolize the deaths that occurred there. It was called Golgotha or The Place of the Skull (Matt. 27:33; Luke 23:33). Here there was no pompous lord standing aloof, unmoved by the suffering of his servants. No, in this field the Lord intervened in the tragedy of the peasants by sending his own son to die for their desperate plight. "For the Son of Man did not come to be served, but to serve, and to give his life as a ransom for many" (Mark 10:45).

CHAPTER FIVE

THE DISCIPLINED LIFE

TWO MEALS

> Wisdom has built her house; she has hewn out its seven pillars. She has prepared her meat and mixed her wine; she has also set her table. She has sent out her maids, and she calls from the highest point of the city. 'Let all who are simple come in here!' she says to those who lack judgment. Come, eat my food and drink the wine I have mixed.
>
> Proverbs 9:1-5

Food serves our bodies and our relationships. The nutritional value of the food sustains our bodies and gives them strength. The relationship value of food sustains our bond with family and friends when we dine together. Mealtime provides opportunity for being vulnerable, sharing stories, enjoying fellowship, healing past wounds, and eagerly anticipating future banquets together.

So important is the function of sharing a meal together to build and sustain relationships that the Bible draws upon the experience to illustrate higher realities beyond the meal itself. Proverbs 9:1-6 is an example of that.

Two meals are served in Proverbs 9. The first by an industrious host commonly referred to as Woman Wisdom. This woman built a house requiring seven pillars, indicating it is wide and spacious, thus able to accommodate many guests. She set a luxurious table of meat and wine. Meat was a special treat for many ancient people, and the wine was mixed, meaning she probably added special spices to create a unique and satisfying flavor. After the meal was ready, Woman Wisdom sent her servants out to the highest point of the city to cry out, "Let all who are simple come in here ... Come, eat my food and drink the wine I have mixed." Those who attend this banquet will find nourishment for their bodies, but they will find even more. The fellowship value of this meal means that those who dine will "walk in the way of understanding."

Meanwhile, another woman in Proverbs 9 is inviting guests in to her meal as well. This hostess is known as Woman Folly. Unlike Woman Wisdom, the second lady is not industrious with her house or her meal. In fact, she is loud, undisciplined, and foolish. Instead of working hard she sits in the doorway of her house and calls out to those passing by, "Let all who are simple come in here!" She invites the same people Woman Wisdom does! In fact, they both offer their invitations at the highest point of the city, a place of great significance, and they invite the same people, those who are simple and gullible. But whereas the first lady serves fine meat and wine, the second serves stolen water and food. "Stolen water is sweet," she says, "food eaten in secret is delicious." The enticing element of this second meal is not the nutritional value of the food, but the excitement of the erotic and forbidden nature of the meal. It is secretive, and those who dine here do not nourish their bodies, but revel in pleasures that are improper. In fact, any pleasures experienced by those who fill themselves on this meal will be short lived. "Little do they know that the dead are there, that her guests are in the depths of the grave" (Prov. 9:13-18).

Obviously, something is taking place here that is larger than the meal itself. The Sage is using food and meal as a metaphor for paths of life. Woman Wisdom, the grand and industrious lady who serves a fine meal and whose diners become wise, is issuing her call from God. She is inviting the simple to come follow the ways of divine wisdom and godly ethics. She calls the gullible to leave the world and enter relationship with God.

Woman Folly, on the other hand, represents any competing thought, personality, or system to the great God of heaven. Like Woman Wisdom, Woman Folly is positioned at the highest point of the city, the place where temples were built in ancient society. Whereas Woman Wisdom represents God, Woman Folly represents the false idols and religions that plagued Israel. Today, she represents anything that calls us away from godly living with its promise of sweet, forbidden drink and pleasure.

God has served a meal, rich, succulent, hearty, and nutritious. It feeds more than our bodies; it feeds our lives, character, and souls. In the immediate context, the meal is the wisdom of Proverbs. In the larger context, the meal is the whole Bible, from which we learn of the invitation to salvation in Jesus and a relationship with God.

The Father calls us. "Come, eat my food and drink the wine I have fixed. Leave your simple ways and you will live; walk in the way of understanding" (Prov. 9:5-6). Dinner is served. Will you come?

WORK HABITS

> Lazy hands make a man poor, but diligent hands bring wealth.
>
> Proverbs 10:4

"A man makes the habits and then the habits make the man." I heard this saying repeatedly for the three summers I worked for The Southwestern Book Company based in Franklin, Tennessee. Every aspect of our sales career was submitted to scrutiny and evaluation based on this saying. Are you getting up early? Eating breakfast? In the field before 8 a.m.? Making thirty presentations a day? Closing the sale? Explaining delivery procedures? Staying positive? Reading worthwhile material? Seeing the good in your co-workers and customers? Making everyone's day brighter because they met you?

At the time many of these behaviors seemed rather trivial. But there was a point to every one of them. Initially, all of the college sales staff had to force themselves to follow proper protocol, maintain a healthy attitude, and warmly greet everyone around us. We endured long hours in the heat, humidity, and rain. Rejection, loneliness, and even desperation were constant companions as we worked far from home. Failure frequently loomed before us, making ugly faces and discouraging us even more. But there was always someone to remind us, "A man makes the habits and then the habits make the man. If you quit now, will quitting become a habit for you? Will you quit college? Your marriage? Your career? Your kids? Stick to the basic habits of success, gut it out through the summer, and you'll develop the necessary inner ingredients to succeed at whatever you do."

Fortunate are the kids with parents who teach them principles of hard work, commitment, and endurance. What I learned with Southwestern was but a reinforcement of these principles that were practiced in our home. Mom and dad talked to us about how our appearance, attitudes and behavior would be perceived by future bosses. "If you want a good job in the future, get ready for it now" was the message. The wakeup call at 4:30 a.m. to milk cows had a purpose beyond the immediate task: it was training for future work.

Sadly, many kids never learn that the habits they are developing now are making them the men and women they are going to be in the future. Sleeping late, a slovenly appearance, crude talk, and failure to turn school work in on time is not preparing them for gainful employment in the marketplace. They are learning habits that are deadly to any kind of well-paying job and satisfying career.

Also, youth that never do any kind of work before high school graduation often do not develop career building skills, development of diligence, and appreciation for the character it takes to survive in the work place. I like going into a grocery store and seeing high school students stocking the shelves, running the cash register, and carrying out groceries. They may be using their money to buy a car, go to college, or pay for a wedding. But even more, they are building character and developing habits for future success.

An attorney for a large firm told me that when they hire new attorneys they ask what the prospective new lawyers did during their high school and college years. The partners in the firm want to hear that they worked in a fast food restaurant, mowed lawns, or washed cars for extra money. They don't want to hear that their college was financed totally by parents so they could sleep late and watch a lot of TV during school breaks. Many of these students, the attorney told me, do not know how to work hard once they get a job. But kids who had to scrape and scrap for every dollar in menial jobs will appreciate the opportunity and work hard when they land a job with an office.

Success, career satisfaction, and wealth-building do not happen automatically, haphazardly, or accidentally. They occur because a serious, sober-minded young man or woman thinks about their lives, develops healthy habits, and works hard over the long haul. Diligent hands and worthy habits are the seeds of success. If developed by age thirteen or fourteen, they will be producing beautiful fruit by age thirty and forty. That fruit will be a job you like and income you can live on. Lazy hands make a man poor, but diligent hands bring wealth.

FANTASIES

> He who works his land will have abundant food, but he
> who chases fantasies lacks judgment.
> Proverbs 12:11

Farming is hard work. It is hard on the body and can be hard on the emotions. The whole of a farmer's being is involved in the labor. It takes three important ingredients for a farmer to be able to endure during those early spring and summer days while waiting on the crop.

First, farmers need to work hard. They must prepare the ground by tilling it and fertilizing it so they can plant the seed. The work is still far from over as they must continue to water the crop and manually pull the weeds or spray them with poisons. Then there is the work of harvesting, storing, and transporting the crop. There are days when a farmer's body cries out for rest and relief, but if there is work to do, there is no time for rest.

Second, farmers need faith. Their whole future is tied up in the little bitty seeds they put in the ground. They have to trust that with the proper soil preparation, fertilization, watering and weeding, the seed will grow and produce a crop that they can eat and sell. The failure of that seed to do its job would be catastrophic for the farmer.

Third, farmers need patience. It can be challenging to faith to get up every morning and look over the fields to see if the rows are taking on a green tint yet. That thin, dim hue of green means the bean or melon plants are finally starting to pop out of the soil. They continue to watch and water, weed and wait. Months pass. The farmer has spent thousands of dollars and must still hold on in faith that it will pay off. That takes tremendous patience.

If the farmers do their work and practice great faith and patience, they can expect a crop. "He who works his land will have abundant food." Proverbs promises stability and reward for those who, over time, practice hard work and diligence in any honorable trade. "The Lord does not let the righteous go hungry but he thwarts the craving of the wicked. Lazy hands make a man poor, but diligent hands bring wealth" (Prov. 10:3-4). But not everybody is hardworking and diligent. As Proverbs 12:11 says, some people are prone to chasing fantasies.

The idea of "chasing fantasies" means to pursue "worthless things" (Waltke, "Proverbs" in NICOT, 1:528). Worthless things could refer to any hope for profit or gain that is attained by means other than hard work and diligence. Think of risky ventures, gambling, or the multitude of get-rich-quick schemes available through the internet now. All of these attempts at wealth-building bypass the critical building blocks for God-ordained profit: hard work, faith, and patience. Some people, no doubt, will be successful in some of these ventures. Many people though, will lose time, money, and possibly even self-confidence.

I remember receiving an offer from an acquaintance to try out a new business opportunity. It sounded good, but I didn't know if I had the personality to pull it off. I went to a banker friend and asked, "Will you look at this and tell me what you think?" A few days later she told me, "This business might work for some people, but I don't think it will for you. It would take a considerable degree of business persona that you don't have. I don't think you could make it work." Ouch. I listened to her advice on that venture, but not on one or two others. I lost time and money.

Some attempts at wealth-building are based on craftiness and convincing people that, "This business will make you a million dollars in no time!" There are some businesses that have done that, and the right person at the right time can make it work. But any business that requires a great deal of arm-twisting and convincing to get you to sign up is probably a good business to stay away from. Proverbs says, "A good man obtains favor from the Lord, but the Lord condemns a crafty man" (Prov. 12:2).

The man who chases fantasies lacks judgment and comes to poverty (Prov. 28:19). The man or woman who gets up every morning ready to shoulder a full day of work and is careful with their income will receive favor from the Lord in the form of plenty to eat and money for the bills.

EASY MONEY

> Dishonest money dwindles away, but he who gathers money little by little makes it grow.
>
> Proverbs 13:11

I cringe every time I hear state officials say, "We are going to start a lottery. This is an opportunity for people in our state to make a lot of money. The real bonus is that the money we raise will go toward education so our children will benefit."

I wonder if the sales pitch is true. Yes, some people will make a lot of money, millions of dollars in fact, but many more will lose money. People who can barely afford groceries will spend their entire paychecks on lottery tickets, hoping beyond reason that this time they will strike it rich.

Will education really receive that much more money from the lottery system? Or will the state simply withhold the funding they previously spent so there really isn't any gain?

Lottery systems work because they appeal to our lust for more, and at a rapid pace. The most successful and wealthy business people I know do not buy lottery tickets. They know that real wealth comes by "gathering money little by little."

The New International Version says that "dishonest money dwindles away." The term "dishonest money" can also be translated as "wealth gotten by unsound means" or money attained in "haste." This verse certainly condemns acquiring money in any illegal manner. People can lie, cheat, steal, or use intimidation to get more money. The Bible clearly condemns these methods.

The emphasis in this verse isn't just against illegal means of acquiring wealth; it is against any means that seeks to attain wealth without a significant investment of one's time and labor. Wealth attained by unsound means could be money made through gambling. It is legal in many states, but it can produce far more debtors than it does millionaires. I have seen families destroyed through gambling addiction. One woman robbed her family's retirement account of $100,000 and lost it all in gaming machines. She cried as she told me, "My husband says he forgives me, but he still had me arrested. How could he do that? Has he really forgiven me?" This woman's insatiable lust for more, more, more reduced her family's financial assets, endangered her life with her husband and two little girls, and threatened to land her in jail.

Proverbs 20:21 says, "An inheritance quickly gained at the beginning will not be blessed at the end." The discipline a person exercises to save money also allows that person to hold on to the money and not lose it in speculative ventures or foolish spending. A person who receives a lot of money at one time, with no exercise of discipline, often does not have the strength or wisdom to keep it. It dwindles away and becomes a curse, not a blessing.

Very few worthwhile things are attainable in an instant. A professional baseball career, a business, a medical practice, a healthy family, a strong church, and a substantial retirement account take years and years of hard work, dependable performance, and continued learning and improvement. None of them happen overnight. There is no such thing as instant success in any of these fields.

Godly people seek success with godly character. Such character includes hard work, patience, and faith. They realize all they do is to the glory of God, so they try to conduct their business, finances, and family in a way that brings God glory. These people God will bless with fruit for their labor.

DISCIPLINE

He who ignores discipline comes to poverty and shame.

Proverbs 13:18

The New York Mets were a new and struggling team in the late 1960s when a young pitcher led them from a joke in the league to the World Series Champions in 1969. That pitcher was Tom Seaver. For nine years in a row, he struck out 200 or more batters. He became one of the first pitchers to win a Cy Young Award with less than twenty victories. The victories he did achieve were not from the stellar defense behind him, but from his finesse as a pitcher.

What made Tom Seaver such a great player? It was more than just his love for the game. Tom was a disciplined athlete all year. Many baseball players go to spring training to get in shape. Tom Seaver went to spring training already in shape. He would exercise and watch his diet all year. He was careful about eating cake in December, lest it affect his weight and health in March.

That might seem a bit extreme, but that is the kind of commitment one of the greatest athletes in the game gave his craft. That is why people today still know the name Tom Seaver.

"He who ignores discipline comes to poverty and shame." Discipline is "the ability to control oneself and focus on the important tasks at hand, even if other behaviors would be more pleasurable" (Tremper Longman, "Proverbs" in Baker Commentary, 289). Discipline is saying "Yes" to responsibility and hard work, sacrifice, and devotion. It is saying "No" to distractions and trivia, time wasting and fun.

Trivia and fun are not wrong in themselves, but a steady diet of either does not make a person spiritually, emotionally, or financially fit. Too much trivia and fun become expensive time and energy wasters. How many people with wonderful intentions and bold plans for their lives lose their momentum in meaningless distractions?

Ryan was one of the smartest kids in our junior high. He would get his homework done in class while the teacher was explaining it to the rest of us. He promoted with one of the highest grade point averages. But something happened to Ryan. In high school he had one of the lowest GPAs. He wasn't involved in any school activities. He barely made it through school.

"What happened, Ryan," I asked him. "How did your performance drop so much from eighth grade?"

Ryan smiled and said, "I learned that if you do good, then people expect you to always do good. If you make A's, then they are disappointed if you make a B. It takes a lot of hard work to live up to their expectations. But, if you make D's and then make a C, people are proud of you!" Ryan, one of the smartest kids in our school, frittered his time away in laziness and lack of discipline, squandering a promising academic career.

There are three things that help us achieve a disciplined life:

1. Remember that everything we do contributes to the success or failure of what we really want. A piece of cake, an extra hour of TV time and sleeping late may seem insignificant, but they may also undermine our higher goals and aspirations.

2. Remember that every minute we have is a gift of God. Once that minute clicks away it is gone, never to be retrieved. Do you use your minutes in a day in worthwhile activities? (Eph. 5:15-16).

3. Remember that everything we do as Christians, we do in the name of the Lord Jesus. "Whatever you do, work at it with all your heart, as working for the Lord, not for men" (Col. 3:23; cf. 3:17). The minutes really don't belong to us; they belong to God, and should be rendered to him by worthwhile activities.

Discipline isn't fun, but neither are lost dreams, shame, or poverty. Painful words you never want to say are, "If only I hadn't wasted that time and energy." Poverty and shame are overcome by making a series of small but consequential decisions to live life wisely and purposefully today.

THE SIMPLE

> The simple inherit folly, but the prudent are crowned with knowledge.
>
> Proverbs 14:18

Two things that separate the simple from the fool are time and training. (Willingness to submit to discipline and rebuke is a difference as well, but that topic is for another chapter). If the simple person does not receive training, over time he will slide into foolishness.

The simple man is untrained to think carefully and critically. He tends to think for the moment and not long term. Planning ahead means finding out who is hosting the weekend parties. Planning and preparing for college, marriage, or a career is as foreign as studying Greek or Hebrew.

The simple man is not yet a fool, but he is traveling on that highway if he is not receiving training and guidance. A fool does what is right in his own eyes (12:15), and trusts in himself (28:26). Even worse, he actually despises wisdom and correction (1:7; 22). A fool lacks self-discipline, evidenced by his inability to control his tongue (10:14), and anger (29:11). Foolishness is a progressive ailment, leading one to not only enjoy his wicked behavior (10:23), but to refuse to turn from it (13:19). This cavalier attitude about life diminishes the spiritual nature of a fool so that he cannot take his own sin seriously (14:9). The fool ultimately destroys himself (1:32).

To be simple is to be gullible or naive. "A simple man believes anything" (Prov. 14:15). This gullibility is due to lack of training, either because of youth or limited exposure to wise teaching and discipline. The remedy for simplicity is to be instructed in the ways of Proverbs. "You who are simple, gain prudence; you who are foolish, gain understanding" (Prov. 8:5).

Those of us who are parents hope our children will pick up some wisdom as they pass through our homes, and we routinely do things to ensure that happens, such as teaching them and offering discipline or en-couragement as situations warrant. Following are four ideas to add to our arsenal for helping our children grow through a period of youthful naiveté to become serious and sober minded.

One, we can teach them to think critically. To think critically does not mean to be negative or judgmental. Rather, it means to evaluate the information we receive from others and weigh what they say. Our kids will be subjected to people trying to sell them things they don't need and join things they don't need to be in. We can equip them to ask, "Is this true? Does it sound reasonable? Is the risk worth it? Will it enhance or diminish my esteem and reputation?" The fool lacks the ability to ask and evaluate such questions, and he lacks the humility to ask advice.

Two, we can teach them to question what they hear. A good teacher doesn't just answer questions; she raises new ones. The idea that educa-tion is simply the imparting of information is false. That is indoctrination, not education. A student who leaves a class having been spoon fed the teacher's conclusions and convictions may never grow out from under-neath the perceptions and prejudices of that teacher. A good teacher defi-nitely shares her convictions and gives persuasive reasons why she holds them. But she also equips her students to think on their own, to investi-gate leads, and to study all the available evidence (even that which seems to be contradictory to her own position), and to make decisions on their own. Such a young person is prepared to face additional intellectual chal-lenges and meet them with confidence.

Three, we help our kids overcome being simple by encouraging them to think ahead. "The wisdom of the prudent is to give thought to their ways" (Prov. 14:8). The wise look to the future and ask, "Where is my behavior headed? Will it prepare me for a healthy marriage and a stable career? Or will my behavior lessen my ability to function as a devoted spouse and capable employee or employer?" We can help even young children project themselves into the future by asking them questions. What would you like to be when you grow up? Where would you like to go to college? Cheryl and I wanted our kids to go to a Christian college, so we talked to them about that when they were still very little, and we took them on frequent visits to Christian schools. That set the direction of their thinking very early.

Finally, we help our children grow with wisdom when we let them solve their own problems. Many parents want to rush in and fix everything in their kids' lives. I've seen the parents of fifth grade girls actually enter into the arguments with their daughters' friends, accusing, name calling, and belittling other fifth graders. They are not helping their children, but are subjecting them to a lifetime of preteen mental dysfunction. They hinder the ability of their kids to become wise and think like adults.

One elementary school I know provides problem solving situations for their students, teaching them to think creatively for solutions.

When my siblings and I would approach dad with a problem, either a broken toy or a tense situation, he would often ask, "What do you think you should do?" He would often help us, but only after making us to think first. Sometimes he would even ask, "What would you do if I was dead and you couldn't ask me? Try doing that and see if it works."

It isn't shameful to be simple; we all start out that way because we are young and untaught. What is a shame is to remain simple and progress into the trap of foolish dispositions and behavior. The simple inherit folly, but the prudent are crowned with knowledge and healthy living.

STERN DISCIPLINE

> Stern discipline awaits him who leaves the path; he who
> hates correction will die.
>
> Proverbs 15:10

"I don't know why they have me in here. It seems the police and courts could use their money more wisely than arresting a guy like me. I've never hurt anybody."

That conversation took place inside a drug and alcohol rehab center. The patient was a twenty-eight-year-old male who was recently arrested for driving under the influence of alcohol. Not only was he drunk behind the wheel of a vehicle, but he had crashed into a light pole.

"Well, you were driving drunk," I said. "And you could have hurt people."

"Yeah, but I didn't. I never have, not even in my other wrecks."

"Other wrecks?" I asked. "Tell me about them."

"Well, I've totaled three pickups, but only two of them were mine. One of them was a company vehicle. But even in all those wrecks, I never hit anyone. The cops need to just leave me alone."

I sat there in silence, stunned by the words of this young man. He totaled three vehicles while driving under the influence and didn't think he had a problem? What was I supposed to say to that?

"Stern discipline awaits him who leaves the path; he who hates correction will die." The path in Proverbs is the way of righteousness. "In the way of righteousness there is life; along that path is immortality." (Prov. 12:28) To be righteous means to be in relationship with God, to walk in the path of godly ethics, and to live in harmony with brothers. It means being open to God's leading in your life.

To leave that path, Proverbs 15:10 says, is to invite stern judgment upon our lives. The Pharisees in John 8:44 certainly received that judgment from Jesus. They didn't believe him to be the son of God, they discouraged others from believing in him, and they even conspired to kill him. So Jesus told them, "You belong to your father, the devil." That's pretty stern, and God can be pretty stern in his discipline of us if that is what it takes to get our attention and soften our hearts.

Proverbs 15:10 can also be translated as, "Discipline is evil for the one who leaves the path." That is, the one who leaves the path of righteousness can not only expect stern judgment, but any judgment he receives he will regard as evil. In the mind of this corrupt person, any correction of his faults is seen as wrong or evil.

That is what was happening in the counseling session that day. A man arrested three times for DUI and guilty of wrecking three vehicles is sitting under judgment. It is a stern judgment. He was sentenced to a rehab program and was facing possible time in jail. Yet, as he sat under judgment, not only did he perceive it to be stern, but evil. The police, the judge, and even those of us in the counseling program were evil. We were interfering with his pursuit of pleasure, and we were bad. "Discipline is evil for the one who leaves the path."

The purpose of discipline is to save life. It is meant to arrest our attention and shock us to the reality of our situation: we have misbehaved or left the path, and we are in spiritual danger.

I had to help the man in the counseling session see that the discipline he was under was not evil, but was meant to alert him to the danger he was in. He had a debilitating addiction; he lost control, and he could hurt someone very badly. Further, he was blind to his own condition, even maligning those who were trying to help him.

"You know, you are actually pretty lucky," I told the man.

"How is that?" he asked skeptically.

"Well, the police arrested you, put you in jail, and you are pretty safe from harm. But suppose instead of a light pole you had hit a young family, and a man's wife and three kids were killed or seriously hurt by you. Who do you think would treat you better, the police, or that angry husband and father? To my way of thinking, the police and judge have done you a favor. You hurt a man's family and you don't want him getting his hands on you. You better be thankful for the police."

The man sat there quietly. After a few moments he said, "I never thought of it like that." And suddenly the rehab program took on a whole different perspective.

We can't always expect rapid change in someone who is sitting under judgment. It certainly didn't happen in John 8. Jesus told the Jewish leaders they were under stern judgment for not believing in him. Then, by the end of the chapter, those same men are picking up stones to kill him (v.59). Instead of seeing Jesus as trying to save their lives, they saw Jesus as evil. That is how people who have left the path respond to discipline.

WORTHY GOALS

Finish your outdoor work and get your fields ready; after

that, build your house.

Proverbs 24:27

What will our lives be like in five years? Ten? Twenty? The ability to look ahead and make plans is a sign of maturity.

Most people want good things out of life. But, unfortunately, sometimes we fail to adequately plan for what we would like and thus fail to make steady progress toward their attainment. No one plans on a career at home after high school graduation, but that does happen sometimes. The good things in life most of us desire are a happy family, a peaceful neighborhood, and a job that provides enough income to support the family. Nearly everyone living in a country with any economic opportunity can achieve such goals. But they won't just happen. We have to work and plan for them to happen. We have to make such achievements part of our goals.

Does that mean we have to plan to have a happy, close-knit family? Absolutely. Just like we plan on career goals, such as playing professional football, going to medical school, or graduating with a mechanics certificate, we have to plan the other aspects of our lives as well, such as family life and spiritual growth. Nothing worthwhile just happens. We have to plan and work for any good thing in life and for that, we have to have worthy goals.

Two things make goals worthy. One, they must be consistent with our internal ethic. If we are Christians, and plan to open the largest gambling casino in Las Vegas, either our ethic or our goal will suffer. The Christian ethic is about responsible use of money, purity, and sobriety. A gambling casino is about taking money and wrecking sobriety. How can a Christian operate a business that can undermine the faithful walk of another believer? Either our casino dreams will have to be abandoned or our Christian ethic is skewed.

Secondly, for goals to be worthy, they must push us to become better people. An athlete who dreams of running a marathon manages her diet, sleep, and running schedule. She becomes healthier for the experience. Someone striving for spiritual growth manages his prayer, Bible reading, and relationships. He becomes spiritually healthier while striving toward his goal.

The pursuit of any goal that requires us to abandon the morals and ethics our parents and church have taught us has to be critically evaluated with some tough questions. What is this goal asking of me? What does it reveal about me? Am I greedy, and is my financial goal revealing that? Am I power hungry, and that is the real reason I want to climb to the top? Am I lazy, and I think a manager's job will allow me to relax while others work (not realizing that a manager's job, done well, may actually require more work)?

Proverbs 24:27 offers sound advice on planning for the future: "Finish your outdoor work and get your fields ready; after that, build your house." This proverb grew out of agricultural experience. Imagine homesteaders settling new ground. They cut down the trees, saw the lumber, and build the house. They are ready to settle in for the winter. But when they open the pantry door, they notice that no food has been prepared for the long winter.

The writer of this proverb probably observed some people getting their priorities and goals out of order. They had been so concerned about a nice residence that they hadn't made sure they had the proper income or food supply from the farm to survive. So he counsels us to live temporarily in any shelter we can, get the fields ready so we'll have food and income, and then build the house.

That is a good paradigm for all of life. Work on the important matters first. Make sure our internal ethic is solid. Seek God, worship, and fellowship with people of high character. Then work toward goals that enhance our character and make us better people. Follow these two things, and our career and social goals will fall into place.

HONEY

> He who is full loathes honey, but to the hungry even what
> is bitter tastes sweet.
>
> Proverbs 27:7

"If you gave me a steak right now I wouldn't eat it. It doesn't even sound good." The friend who told me that was a farmer and loved good food, especially beef. I couldn't imagine feeling that way about a good steak

He was in a hospital bed recovering from open-heart surgery when he told me how he felt. His body had suffered from blocked arteries and was recovering from major intrusion to repair them. At that time his favorite food didn't sound appealing.

Proverbs 27:7 addresses two states of stress upon the body: one that is over-sated and one that is starved. Both conditions are unhealthy and affect the mind and appetite.

In the first, a man has gorged himself and food has lost all appeal. He seems to be beyond simply eating to satisfaction. Normally in Proverbs, honey is depicted as being sweet and desirable. The Sage even has to warn a man not to over indulge in this delicacy: "If you find honey, eat just enough— too much of it and you will vomit" (Proverbs 27:16). That which is pleasurable and desirable can become distasteful and nauseating if moderation is ignored. That is how my friend was feeling after his surgery. His mind and body, in a sick and weakened state, recoiled at the thought of normally enticing food.

The second unhealthy state Proverbs 27:7 addresses is one deprived of food. Hunger is so advanced that even undesirable food sounds satisfying. Bitter food was eaten as an act of discipline in remembrance of God's great deeds. It was a means of depriving the body of enjoyment in honor of something greater. People normally don't eat bitter food because it does not pleasure the taste buds. But to the man long deprived of food, whose body is wracked with hunger, even something bitter to calm the pains would be welcome.

The Sage may be addressing the simple matter of over-eating or starvation in respect to food, but it is possible he has other issues in mind. Food, hunger, and gluttony may be metaphors for other important matters pertaining to the body and life.

Proverbs teaches the wisdom of working hard to earn a living, but also warns about the tug of material acquisition on our hearts. The lure of money and things can overwhelm our senses and judgment, leading us to steal to get more, or to harm our families in our greed. Neither poverty nor excess in money and things is a healthy state. Moderation is key.

Personal relationships must also be approached with sane and judicious perspective. One may live so selfishly and arrogantly as to kill goodwill, or may seek so hard to make friends that motives are questioned and advances rebuffed. Such a person can come across as insincere. As with food and money, moderation is key. What is desirable is personal integrity that neither diminishes the worth of another through inconsiderate treatment nor reduces one's own standing through desperate attempts to connect.

The metaphor of honey can also apply to sexual relations. Proverbs extols the virtues and joys of marital relations, but gives harsh warning, even threat, of the dangers that ensue if one indulges outside the appropriate bounds. It also warns that withholding romance from one's partner, starving the companionship of intimacy, can so sicken the relationship that it overflows the marital boundaries (5:15-18).

The metaphor of honey, hunger, and gluttony touch not only upon matters of food, but upon other critical concerns for life: money, friendship, and sexual relations. Moderation, appropriateness, and moral undergirding are all necessary ingredients to ensure that we avoid physical and spiritual illness. They also promote health to our lives and bodies so we can enjoy these great gifts of God.

THE HIDDEN COST OF DRUNKENNESS

> The prudent see danger and take refuge, but the simple
> keep going and suffer for it.
>
> Proverbs 27:12

Getting drunk is expensive in several ways. It is expensive for an individual who gets in trouble and loses a job, loses standing in the community, and even family. One man in a treatment program for the eleventh time told me, "This is the last one. Either I successfully overcome my drinking and stay sober, or it's over." His eleventh program. Tens of thousands of dollars were spent trying to help him get sober, and it hadn't worked yet. "I've lost all credibility with my family. My only hope at having a shred of relationship with any of them is for it to work this time. I have to quit drinking. This program has to work this time, or I'm done." This man paid a high cost for all his years of drinking.

Drinking is expensive for a family. Of course it is expensive financially. One friend who quit drinking told me he was saving $400 a month. Justin never realized he was spending that much until he quit. He'd get paid on Friday, stop at a bar on the way home, and celebrate his paycheck and good feeling with everyone in the bar. "Next round's on me," he'd proudly bellow. He didn't realize until much later just how much his proud spirit had cost him: five thousand dollars a year, twenty-five thousand dollars over a five year period. But he wasn't just robbing his own piggy bank; he was robbing from his family. His poor wife had to struggle to pay the rent, keep the car running, and buy food. Her husband's drinking rendered her stressed and fearful, damaged her self-esteem, and filled her with anger.

Justin's financial expenditure on alcohol was low compared to some other guys I know. Stan spent up to $250,000 on his twenty-year love affair with booze. Not all of it was spent on drink; a lot was spent on medical care, wrecked vehicles, and court fees associated with his love. He was forty years old and could have had a beautiful log cabin in the mountains paid for with cash. Instead, he was broke and alone. His drinking cost him more than money; it cost him his family. His wife and five kids couldn't take his addiction anymore and they kicked him out. You see, drunkenness can become expensive for the whole family. None of his five kids ever received a dime from their dad for college, for a down payment on a vehicle, or even for a high school graduation gift.

Finally, drinking can be very expensive for the whole country. According to the Centers for Disease Control and Prevention, drinking costs this country $223 billion a year through excessive alcohol consumption. Part of this figure includes lost productivity at work (employees missing work or showing up with hangovers), health care, accidents, and legal costs all related to drinking. Consider also that approximately 79,000 Americans are killed each year in alcohol-related accidents and you can see that the awful toll is far more than financial.

Fortunately, Justin realized that his drinking was killing him financially, relationally, spiritually, and physically. In his late thirties he sought help through a counseling program and AA and quit. His family life changed dramatically. He raced home with his check on payday and proudly handed it to his wife, giving her complete charge of everything to do with the money. She allocated him a small sum each week for lunches and that's all he saw. And he never complained. He was so happy and grateful to have a devoted wife who stuck with him and allowed him to continue as a dad to their two little girls.

The story wasn't as happy for Stan. He didn't read the early warning signs of distress in the faces of his wife and kids, or he didn't care, and he kept on drinking. Stan kept on drinking until his whole family hated him and didn't want to ever see him again. That's pretty expensive. My friend didn't see the danger in something that for a time brought him so much pleasure, and in the end, it bit him like snake and poisoned him like viper (Prov. 23:31-32).

CHAPTER SIX

SETTING THE EXAMPLE

MENTOR A YOUTH

> For these commands are a lamp, this teaching is a light,
> and the corrections of discipline are the way to life.
>
> Proverbs 6:23

Years ago if you wanted to be a silversmith or cabinet maker, you hired yourself out to a master in these trades. You became indentured to this person for several years. Nearly every aspect of your life was under the scrutiny and supervision of the person to whom you were indentured.

There were drawbacks to such an arrangement, such as a lack of freedom. But there were benefits as well. You not only learned the skills of your trade, but as you observed the master at work, you learned money management, office administration, and social and business skills.

I frequently hear bosses complain that new employees do not understand even basic skills of graciousness and service to their companies' customers. They may understand spreadsheets and data processing, but don't know how to say "Thank you," or "I'll do that for you."

Many people are never taught the basic essentials of life. Some schools try to compensate for that by offering "Life Skills" classes. But is there another way to impart these necessary ingredients for life? Yes, through a process called mentoring.

Mentoring is simply taking other people under your influence, teaching them, and then modeling what you teach. Think of a young person in your community, church, or extended family that you would like to influence for good. How can you do that? Here are four basic elements of mentoring.

1. Take the young person on visits to church members, shut-ins, retirees, and the aged. While there you might sweep their sidewalk, rake leaves, or take out the trash. The people you visit will appreciate it, and the youth will learn to think of and serve others from your example.

2. Talk to the young person about the future. What are their goals and aspirations? They may never have thought of this before. Stir their imagination. Ask, "Where do you see yourself in five years?" They likely won't know. Just get them thinking and wondering, and help them set some goals. Show them how to make wise choices today so they can reach their goals tomorrow.

3. Teach about life. Teach them about Christ, money, moral issues, the Bible, politics, and history. Talk informally about a host of subjects. The youth will learn to engage new ideas, think, and respond intelligently.

4. Train them to train. Take another youth with you, younger than the one you are mentoring. Teach the one you are mentoring principles of mentoring the younger youth. This keeps the process moving.

You do not have to have exceptional abilities or advanced training to spend time with a young person and pass on important principles of life. You just have to have a little more experience at living and a heart for young people. With qualities like these, almost everyone can be a mentor.

The teaching of Proverbs, the messages, and training are a lamp and light to help young people make the proper corrections to successfully navigate life. All of us can have a hand in positively shaping someone's future.

BLAZING TRAILS

> The memory of the righteous will be a blessing, but the
> name of the wicked will rot.
>
> Proverbs 10:7

In Louis L'Amour westerns, a cowboy will frequently blaze a trail into some remote portion of the Rocky Mountains. He fancies himself a trail blazer, a pioneer, a first-timer to the region. Then the cowboy stumbles upon a trail and discovers others preceded him here. Was it Indians or other Europeans who left their tracks behind for another to follow? The cowboy doesn't know, but some earlier race of people traversed these hills and left their imprint.

Most of us live with the awareness that our names will not live on in the history books. Future generations of high school students will not read about a major battle we won, trade reform we initiated, or a cure for cancer we developed. Most of us will pass with little or no ripple made in the water.

Do our lives even matter? Yes. "The memory of the righteous will be a blessing" (Prov. 10:7).

Every generation needs outstanding characters who leave their mark in a big way and make it to the history books. They inspire the rest of us to push further and work harder for a better society.

But realize that the outstanding characters who make the headlines for winning elections or setting home run records are not necessarily the ones who provide health to a culture or make society work. These people generally aren't the ones who milk the cows, deliver the mail, set the power poles, or pave the streets. They alone don't raise a generation of children, teach values, and instill morals. This kind of rank and file work is done by rank and file people.

The health of a society is not measured by the few who garner the most attention. It is measured by the mothers and fathers who crawl on the floor with their babies to bond with them, who answer their unlimited questions, and who set their course in life. The greatness of a society is measured by grandmothers and grandfathers who take their grandchildren fishing, tell stories of the old days, and bake homemade cookies.

When my grandmother was in her eighties, she would call to talk to our kids, her great-grandchildren. "I don't want them to forget me," she would say. My grandmother wanted to live on in the memory of her family. She does. As a mother, grandmother, and great-grandmother, she loved and nurtured her offspring. She taught them about God and Jesus. She modeled the Savior in her life. She left her imprint. She blazed a trail that her offspring could follow even years after she left for her reward. The memory of this righteous woman is a blessing. And the memory of your life, lived well, will be a blessing for those who follow.

The memory of the righteous will be a blessing. The righteous are those who live the values of God in their lives. They live in relationship with God, their neighbors, their spouses, and their children. The righteous model Jesus. Every life they touch is made richer for their presence in it.

When the righteous die, their names will not be enshrined in the history books for coaching Little League or delivering Girl Scout cookies. But God has his own book in which he records the names of the righteous, the Lamb's book of life (Rev. 21:27).

REBUKE

> A rebuke impresses a man of discernment more than a hundred lashes a fool.
>
> Proverbs 17:10

When a friend of mine would discipline his kids or his dogs he would say, "You've got to get their attention." He usually said that after a smack to his kids or a kick to the dogs. "You've got to get their attention and then they'll listen to you." His kids were grown, so I never actually saw him smack them physically, but I did see him do it verbally, even as adults. I did see him kick his dogs when they came up to greet him. A brusque "Get out of the way!" would follow his flying foot. He got their attention, but I don't know if that really helped the dogs understand anything except that my friend could be a mean guy.

I'm not for abuse, and this verse in Proverbs does not condone abuse. But it does suggest that sometimes it takes confrontational methods to get someone's attention about an important issue of life. Even with severe confrontational methods, some people still will not learn.

Take the fool, for example. One hundred lashes will not get his attention. A fool is someone who does not listen, does not learn, and does not change offensive, immoral, or criminal behavior. He keeps acting like a fool no matter what consequences he faces. Fine him $1,000 and he thinks, "That's not so bad." Send him to jail for six months at his next offense and he thinks, "Hey, that wasn't bad either! Three square meals a day and free medical care!" On subsequent trips to prison, he begins to think of it as home.

Strike that man with 100 lashes, Proverbs says, and he will never see the error of his ways. His hard heart, his bold arrogance, and his selfish bent keep him plodding along the path of foolish and dangerous choices.

Not so the man of discernment. To be discerning means to be wise, or to have understanding. The wise person listens to the advice of others, he learns from his mistakes, and he learns from the mistakes of others. The wise man will even listen to correction, or rebuke. The fool remains unchanged after 100 painful lashes, but the man of wisdom only needs a corrective word and he will change his behavior.

What is the nature of a rebuke that the wise man will heed it? First, it gets his attention. Like a kick to a dog, a rebuke shocks one's system. It says, "Something is wrong, pay attention!" The wise man will.

Secondly, a rebuke educates. Since the wise are eager to learn and grow, they will not miss this opportunity to see if they do need to change their ways. The rebuke may be a kind admonishment from a spouse or friend, or it may even be nasty and unnecessary criticism from an envious co-worker. In either case, the wise man will consider the merits of the charges and will make appropriate changes to his life.

Finally, a rebuke shapes life. A tree left to itself may grow crooked and warped. I've staked several trees to encourage them to grow straight. That is what rebuke does to the wise. It gets attention and educates, and in the process, it encourages growth that is straight, holy, and godly.

Jesus met a man who was proud of having kept the commandments his whole life. "You are still missing something," Jesus told the man. "Sell your possessions and give them to the poor." The man walked away sorrowfully, not swayed by the loving rebuke he received. We don't have the words of rebuke Jesus spoke to another man, but we do have a record of his response. He gave half his possessions to the poor and made proper restitution. Zacchaeus honored the rebuke he received from Jesus and earned this commendation from him: "Today salvation has come to this house" (Luke 17:9).

In whatever form rebuke may present itself to you today, receive it with discernment. It may contain the words of life.

PERSONAL VS. POSITIONAL AUTHORITY

> The righteous man leads a blameless life; blessed are his children after him.
>
> Proverbs 20:7

Politics is the exercise of power in diplomatic, nonviolent means. It is the attempt to influence or rule another person's thought and actions. Four methods are typically used by those seeking to control another person. The first, and most benign, is persuasion. Persuasion can be used with good intentions to accomplish noble ends. But in the arsenal of political intrigue, if used effectively, it can induce someone to make decisions or act in ways contrary to their own best interests. The second method is misinformation, a sanitized term for lying. Someone seeking to exercise power over another decides what information to withhold and what to reveal to lead them to a desired decision. Thirdly, there is an appeal to positional authority. In this method, the one seeking power uses his real (or imagined) position in the organization to intimidate others to acquiesce to his desires. Finally, there is intimidation through threat of force or painful consequences, if the subject does not submit to the dictates of the one using political machinations.

All of these methods result in the manipulation of the subject to get him to act along lines prescribed by the politician/manipulator. These methods are not the exclusive domain of power seekers in government, but can be found in a company, a church, and even the home.

Even if the intentions and goals of a manipulator are worthy, his methods are questionable, even detestable. They result in the demeaning and dehumanizing of the people being controlled and manipulated. The result is not respect for the politician and a harmonious relationship between the ruled and the ruler, but suspicion of, and resentment for, the one exercising power. This approach may work for a while, but any system so run by selfish, manipulative measures will ultimately suffer the loss of trust from the members.

The ultimate means of guiding the thought and behavior of another person is through the integrity and depth of character of the one doing the influencing. A person who has the best interests of others at heart, who practices what he preaches, who makes allowances for the failings of others, who recognizes and openly confesses his own misdeeds, and who admits areas in which he lacks knowledge and skill, invites the admiration of others. This person is a leader with integrity, and he commands the respectful attention of other people without having to demand it.

There are two kinds of leaders: one who makes a claim to positional authority and one who leads by personal authority. One claiming positional authority appeals to his standing over others and resorts to intimidation and manipulation. He talks down to his subjects and treats them as subordinates. He may even make demands on others, something he feels qualified to do because of his high standing.

One exercising personal authority treats others with respect and dignity, even those below him on an organizational chart. He listens to the concerns of others, offers advice, sets a good example, and if he is in a position to make the final decision about a group action, does so with the good of the whole organization in mind. His own personal desires are subordinated to what is best for the whole.

If I were to host a football clinic, I could promote myself in the paper as an expert in the art of quarterbacking. If I could design a convincing ad, I might be able to get you to part with $50 to attend my clinic. In truth, I have never quarterbacked a football game except in backyard games, but I now claim the positional authority of an expert, and I even have the newspaper ad to prove it. While I am expounding on how qualified I am to run this clinic and teach you how to be a quarterback, two guys show up at the other end of the field and begin tossing a football. In a few minutes a murmur runs through my crowd of attendees: "Look at them! Isn't that Peyton? And Eli? What are we doing here listening to this guy? Let's go watch them." In an instant, and without ever having to make an appeal to it, the personal authority of the Manning brothers, based on their high level of athletic performance and integrity, supersedes that of my positional authority. Character and integrity of performance trump appeals to position.

The implications of this are tremendous for those who would lead others. Whether it is in government, business, the church, or home, nothing can replace the authority of men and women who lead with consistently high performance and personal integrity. People with skill and integrity attract the respectful admiration of others and encourage them to think and act in higher, nobler ways, and they do so without impersonal demands based on positional authority.

Proverbs recognizes just how imperative this personal authority by integrity is for the home. "The righteous man leads a blameless life; blessed are his children after him." Parents are the leaders of their home and often times must appeal to their position as the adults when making critical decisions. Their ultimate power resides not in their position, but in their character. The blameless life of the righteous mom and dad is the ultimate influence upon the future character, thinking, and decision-making of their children. The spiritual faithfulness and family health of their children in adulthood is not the result of the parents exercising political control or manipulation, but of providing a powerful example of personal authority demonstrated by the consistent goodness and high quality of their own lives. That is the greatest blessing they can bestow upon their children's lives and eternity.

INTEGRITY ENDURES

> The glory of young men is their strength, gray hair the splendor of the old.
>
> Proverbs 20:29

Gray hair should be respected. The ancient perspective on gray hair, as reflected in Proverbs, is that it means someone has lived long and accumulated wisdom along the way. Growing old means we lose physical strength and endurance, but it also means we gain something of greater value: knowledge and insight about life and godly living. That is wisdom.

Young men are known for their physical prowess, ability, and toughness. This is nowhere better observed than in the game of football. Young men in peak physical condition test their skill and strength like warriors in battle. I marvel at the hits receivers, linemen, and quarterbacks receive, and still they bounce back up to resume play. The glory of these young men is certainly in their strength and perseverance.

Danny Wuerffel is one man who tested his physical aptitude on the football field, and he did so with remarkable ability. He led his Florida team to three SEC championships and won the Heisman Trophy his senior year. Although never becoming a star at the next level of play, he did make it to the National Football League. Danny could glory in his strength.

But his physical ability and toughness is only part of the story of Danny Wuerffel's glory. Danny was invited by the Playboy organization to be a member of their all-America College preseason football team and a chance to be their Athlete of the Year. This honor would come with an all-expense-paid trip to a fancy resort and a photo-shoot with other college players named to the team.

While Danny may have regarded this invitation as an honor, he didn't accept it. Commenting on his decision to decline the offer Danny said, "It didn't take any thought at all. That's not the type of person I'd want to portray myself as." He added, "My commitment is to represent God in all I do."

While the glory of a young man may be his physical conditioning and ability, there is a deeper strength that shines even brighter and lasts much longer: his character. Long after Danny has put down the football to pursue other interests in life, the story of his decision and the glory of his character lives on. I don't remember his passing and touchdown statistics, but I do remember that he looked at an attractive offer, an opportunity for recognition and pleasure, and said, "No. That kind of attention in that kind of an environment is not what my life is about."

Young men need physical endurance to be healthy and to perform demanding tasks, especially if their work is in athletics or manual labor. But they need more than just the toning of their bodies to successfully perform at life. They need the toning of their hearts. Through instruction at home and church, they need their hearts developed to love God and pursue his way for their lives. The heart is the wellspring of life (Prov. 4:23). Through consistent teaching it can provide a lifetime of wholesome thoughts, pure behavior, and moral fortitude. But if it is not painstakingly nurtured and cared for, instead of being moral and upright, the wellspring of the heart can become stagnant, even putrid and unholy. Instead of pursuing a life of moral integrity, a man can become lost in the abundance of unwholesome sensual pleasures. Mouths that erupt with vulgarity and unclean speech, eyes that are given to pornography, and behavior that is indecent, all point to a wellspring that is becoming polluted.

That's why role models like Danny Wuerffel are so valuable and why so many more are needed. He showed that physical strength and athletic achievement is not the ultimate glory for a young man. No, the real strength that matters is character. When a young man or woman with character gets gray hair, everyone will know it is a glorious crown of honor and splendor (Prov. 16:31).

GRAY HAIR

> Gray hair is a crown of splendor; it is attained by a righteous life.
>
> Proverbs 16:31

Sore back. Creaky knees. Bulging waistline. Weak eyes. Declining strength. Gray hair. All these signs indicate that time has worked its ravaging affect upon our bodies. Proper diet and exercise can alleviate some of the devastating effects, but only for so long. The click of the clock cannot be denied, and our bodies age, weaken, and deteriorate.

We live in a culture that reacts in horror to aging bodies. We have creams and surgeries to cover the effects of time. Age spots, gray hair, and sagging skin are covered, dyed, and Botoxed in a vain attempt to fool Father Time and grant us a few more years of youth. But we know we don't really fool time, and we don't even fool ourselves. Though we try to postpone the truth, we all must one day acknowledge and accept that the longer we live, the older we get and our bodies show the visible effects of aging.

Depressing, isn't it? In our society, it is because we idolize youth. Young bodies have strength, beauty, and sensual appeal. Young bodies play sports and model clothing. Young bodies are in demand in the business, athletic, and fashion industries. Have you ever seen an ad seeking a tired, worn out body to quarterback a pro team or wear the new spring fashions at a clothing show? If we buy into society's reverence for youth and vitality, depression can become our companion when the mirror reveals the truth cosmetics ultimately fail to hide: we are getting old.

But this news wasn't depressing in the days of the Sage. The writer of Proverbs lived in a time when age was respected. He approached life from the premise that only the wise could successfully navigate the trials of life to old age. The Sage wrote, "My son, do not forget my teaching, but keep my commands in your heart, for they will prolong your life many years and bring you prosperity" (Prov. 3:1-2). Fools lived life dangerously and carelessly, thus threatening quality of life and length of years. But the wise person knew how to avoid foolish behavior and thus lived longer. In the era of Solomon and the other wisdom writers, if you met a man or woman with wrinkled skin, failing eyes, and graying hair, you felt respect for them, because you knew they had wisdom. Strength and vigor bowed in humble obeisance to experience and wisdom.

Some societies still regard old age with respect and admiration. U.S.

Army Staff Sergeant Todd Sowerby was in northern Iraq helping evacuate displaced Kurds during the first Gulf War. When the helicopter landed, a U.S. officer announced, "Children will be the first to board and evacuate." His announcement was met with disapproval by the Kurdish leaders. "You don't want your children rescued first?" an incredulous officer asked them. "Why not?"

"Because," a Kurdish leader answered, "It takes nine months to replace a child, but it takes years to replace our elders. The elders keep our culture, beliefs, and traditions alive and pass that on to the youth. Without the elders, we lose our identity."

We might conclude that the Kurds have a twisted view of values. But they would argue with us. Community wisdom, common sense, and moral absolutes reside in the minds and lives of the old people. Their standards and ideals preserved their lives through the years and sustained the health and continuity of the community. Only the salvation and presence of the old people could guarantee the survival of the community because they alone knew how to successfully live life and lead the tribe. The strength and energy of youth can build houses, plant trees, and populate new life; but wisdom and experience keep everyone living together in faithfulness to the community's history and ongoing narrative.

Gray hair is not a cause for shame. "Gray hair is a crown of splendor; it is attained by a righteous life" (Prov. 16:31). I'm sure even in ancient times, when advanced years were revered, an older man or woman who felt age creep in and youth slip away reflected nostalgically upon their younger days of energy, strength, and beauty. They missed those days. And that is why these proverbs about the glory of gray hair were written, to remind them that what they gained was of greater value than what they lost.

Wouldn't you like to see society return to a position of respect for the aged? Don't you think the aged should wear their years with dignity and pride? They have earned those wrinkles and gray hair in the crucible of life. They are crowned with splendor.

(Thanks to Chuck Hacker for the story about U.S. Army Staff Sergeant Todd Sowerby and the Kurds).

MODELING

> Train up a child in the way he should go, and when he is
> old he will not depart from it.
>
> Proverbs 22:6

There are several steps we can take to help someone do better at a task or function.

One, we can criticize them. Tell them what they are doing wrong. If you can do it sensitively enough so that the person will listen, they might apply what you are saying and improve. A lot hinges on how you perform your criticism, though.

Factors in your criticism being heard are: your relationship to the one you are criticizing, your attitude, your tone of voice, your track record in criticizing in general and this person in particular, the quality of your own performance, and the disposition of the one being criticized.

Criticism is easy to perform, making it an easy choice for the one 'helping' another. It requires nothing of the one doing the critical evaluation and everything of those being criticized. Those being criticized must be humble, patient, and willing to learn, and they have to overlook what may be a critical spirit in the one criticizing them. Too much subjection to criticism without corresponding praise and compliments could leave the one being criticized hurt and angry.

Even under optimum conditions, criticism rarely achieves its desired results of helping someone. Too many factors have to line up just right. Granted, there are times when it is appropriate to deliver criticism and rebuke (Prov. 27:5). But because criticism is too often the easy way, it is too often the least effective way of helping someone to change and grow.

Secondly, we can teach and encourage them. Whether it is planting a garden, tying shoes, or performing surgery, people must be taught how to do their task. Teaching is indispensable.

Encouraging is so closely related to teaching I couldn't separate the two. I think we need to teach in an encouraging way, not in a way that is condescending or demeaning to the one we are trying to help.

Even after someone is taught a task, it may take a lot of trial and error to actually perform well. During that time we may be tempted to criticize. It is essential that we continue to teach and encourage.

Everyone likes to be told they are doing something right. If one of my catchers misses three pitches but catches the fourth, I have to focus on the one right thing he did, compliment him, and encourage him or her to keep up the good work. Frequently, when a young athlete does something right, even after a whole series of flops, they'll look over to the coaches for affirmation. They need it. "Look coach, I got it!"

Like criticizing, teaching and encouraging must be done in the right spirit and at the right time and by the right person for it to be received.

Thirdly, we can be a model for them. One of the best ways to promote another person's positive change and growth is through modeling. Modeling is doing and living what you are trying to affect in another person.

The ideal teacher of pitchers would be another pitcher; the appropriate trainer of preachers would be another preacher. Do you want a jack hammer operator training your dentist or a butcher mentoring your heart surgeon?

A person who can perform a task is best suited to reach out to others and show them how they can perform it as well. They will have to teach and encourage, and they may even have occasion to criticize and rebuke. But their real power comes from modeling appropriate attitudes and behavior. I'm glad other dentists trained my dentist and doctors trained my doctors.

There are some critical areas in life where there can be no substitutes for competent models. Medicine, ethical living, parenting, family life, and the Christian walk cannot survive without dedicated individuals of high integrity who provide sterling examples we can emulate.

Do you have any good models to follow? Are you a good model for someone else? Can you say, like the Apostle Paul, "Follow my example, as I follow the example of Christ?" (1 Cor. 11:1).

TRACTOR PULLS

> I applied my heart to what I observed and learned a les-
> son from what I saw.
>
> Proverbs 24:32

I saw my first tractor pull at age twelve. It was amazing. Even though I didn't understand the purpose of it, (and I'm not sure I do now), it was exciting for a kid to see these huge rigs pull the tremendous weights dragging behind them.

Kids have a natural curious and creative bent if they don't watch too much TV. We didn't have a television, so we had to use our own curiosity and creativity at times to entertain ourselves. The tractor pull provided us with some exciting incentive.

When we got home, my brothers and I schemed about how we might have our own tractor pull. We got one of those red wagons that all kids used to have, and we loaded it with rocks. Then, we got our little's sisters three-wheel tricycle and hitched the wagon to it with a rope. We put some slack in the rope and sped off on the tricycle. When the tricycle hit the end of the rope, we could feel the wagon give a little with the load. Whoever pulled the wagon the farthest won.

We had a blast. Then the tricycle wouldn't work anymore. The wheels on the bike wouldn't move when we turned the pedals. So, we moved on to tying our bicycles to the load of rock. Dad later confirmed that we had stripped the gears on our little sister's tricycle and strongly recommended we quit pulling with our bikes or they would be ruined, too. Our home-made tractor pull was over.

Kids imitate what they see. We didn't have to have a tractor to stage our own version of a tractor pull. We could devise our own show with makeshift equipment. The fact that it failed at the end (and ruined our sister's tricycle) didn't diminish the success of little kids stepping out and trying something on their own.

One of the primary methods of learning that God built into the fabric of our being is to watch other people and see how they do things. From listening and watching other people, we learn how to tie shoes, cook dinner, button a shirt, and say "thank you." From other people we learn how to be gracious, offer help, go to church, and give up our seat to an older person. But our lessons don't end with these good things. From listening to and watching other people, we also learn how to lie, smoke a cigarette, deceive our parents, and be a bully.

Imitation is one of the most potent forms of learning, either for good or bad. Kids fortunate enough to be exposed to healthy and loving adults have good models to imitate. Children exposed to adults who are angry, hostile, unspiritual, and foul will invariably pick up some of these unholy traits.

Adults possess tremendous power within their being to shape the lives of young people in their orbit of life. If you are a parent, teacher, coach, or church-goer, your life is on display to a lot of younger people. If you are a Christian, you are a living prototype of what it is to model Jesus, the fruit of the Spirit, and holy attitudes. You are salt, a city on a hill, and a lamp on a stand (Matt. 5:13-16).

The tractor pull was not the last thing I imitated in my life. Since then I have consciously imitated a number of good men who powerfully modeled being a husband, father, and preacher in a way I wanted to duplicate in my own life. Even though I have not always lived up to their standards, that does not diminish the value of their examples or the process of learning from others. Imitating is not limited to children with a tricycle. Imitating is something even adults can practice to improve their lives.

There is a child or young person out there ready for your example on how to live. There is also an older person out there modeling a good life for you to copy. Let's just make sure the example we set and follow is consistent with God's will and purpose.

CHAPTER SEVEN

DAILY CHALLENGES

INDUSTRY

> Lazy hands make a man poor, but diligent hands bring wealth.
>
> Proverbs 10:4

Proverbs 10:4 appears in a block of four verses that address wealth, but money is not the primary issue in these verses. What appears more important to Solomon than wealth itself is the attitude, or the character, of a person in relation to wealth. People can be wise or foolish in regard to their money.

A foolish or evil man, for example, pursues "ill-gotten treasures" (v.2). The KJV translates this phrase as "treasures of wickedness," probably indicating that the money was acquired in illegal or unethical ways. Also, the foolish man is lazy (v.4), sleeps during the harvest and thus loses an important form of wealth: food (v.5).

The wise or righteous man, on the other hand, is blessed of God (v.3) so he does not go hungry. He is diligent at his work, justly earning his wealth (v.4). Further, he is present and hard at work during the harvest time (v.5).

Now, as in the time of Solomon, money is a critical concern. If you notice how many references to money there are in the Bible, you can't help but conclude that money is important to God. But what is even more important to God is one's character. That really seems to be the most important consideration in this section about money: one's character in relation to the pursuit and use of money.

The proverbs focus on the subject of wealth. They are relatively strict character-consequence scenarios: one's character will generate certain consequences. Evil behavior produces evil consequences. The righteous one prospers. (Dave Bland, "Proverbs" in *College Press NIV Commentary*, 112).

We may be thinking, "What about the criminals who pursue 'ill-gotten treasures' but never get caught, like the drug lords, who make millions a year and are never shut down? What happened to character being rewarded and wickedness punished?"

It is important to realize that the proverbs operate as generalities. As a general rule, good character is rewarded by God and the community. It may be rewarded with a good reputation or financial gain. An honest businesswoman is one who can be trusted. Other godly people will want to do business with her because they can trust her to fulfill a contract and pay her bills. Sending their business to the honest business woman brings her financial gain. This is an act-consequence understanding of a good person's behavior: good actions (honesty, hard work, thrift) result in good consequences (a good name, sufficient income).

But, the Proverbs also operate with a character-consequence understanding. Character runs deeper than just one's actions and is the catalyst for those actions. Character means you have the healthy internal dispositions that determine your external actions. It means you will also continue to do the right things, as best you are able, without the expectation of reward to follow. You do the good because it is good.

People with good character and work ethic may not see financial reward. The Bible does not shy away from a fact we have all observed, that unrighteous people can prosper. Proverbs 13:23 says injustice can sweep away a poor person's financial gain. Ecclesiastes 5:8-9 recognizes that those with political clout can abuse innocent citizens. Also, dishonest people may besmirch a good person's name.

We can't count on good behavior always producing the kind of results we would like. But, if we are moral and upright simply for recognition or financial reward, our motives would not be character-based.

What is the motive for being and doing good, for living a godly life? Character: being good simply because it is the right thing to do, because it is the God-like thing to do. That is how Jesus lived. Being and doing good didn't bring Jesus any financial achievement, but his "diligent hands" did bring another reward—the approval of his Father, something we are all looking for.

IF YOU WOULD BE HAPPY

> The prospect of the righteous is joy, but the hopes of the wicked come to nothing.
>
>   Proverbs 10:28

Happiness depends upon so many variables that at any point in a day we may be happy or unhappy. Breakfast served hot and on time can make us happy, but cold eggs can make us miserable. What are the ingredients that make for happiness? It depends as much on the individual you ask as on the circumstances of the day.

For some people, happiness means a trouble-free environment. I gravitate toward this one. I like to be able to work trouble-free on a task. That means no computer glitches (like my printer locking up—a frequent occurrence), no telemarketer calls, and no sudden remembrance of an errand I need to run that takes me away from my job. Give me a few uninterrupted hours to work on a lesson or an article and I'm happy! Of course, that doesn't always happen.

For many of us happiness is found in things going well in our lives. If our health is sound, we make enough money, we get time off to visit family, and our various relationships are intact, we are happy. Sure, tires will still go flat and shingles will need replacing, but as long as the general direction of life is working out, we are happy.

But where should our happiness be found? Even if our environment is not trouble-free, life-situations are not working out, and the rest of the world is not doing everything it can to secure our happiness, can we still be happy?

Happiness can be a very selfish thing. For some people happiness is found in things always going their way. It is possible to become so spoiled by things or attention that over time we begin to believe that the world owes us happiness. We may think we are owed money, pleasure, and recognition by others and if we don't get them we become unhappy, critical, and judgmental. The basis of such judgment is, "You are not making me happy!" When that is our disposition, we don't see that we owe anything of ourselves to our own happiness or that of others.

Believers can look for happiness in three areas. First, happiness is found in our relationship with God. We can have peace of mind in knowing that no matter what "slings and arrows of outrageous fortune" assail us, we have eternal security. Paul drew on this relationship when he wrote from prison, "I have learned to be content whatever the circumstances" (Phil. 4:11). His relationship with God was so real to him that it overshadowed whatever misery his prison environment might have caused him.

Secondly, we can find happiness in the blessings we have received from God. Do we have everything we want? Probably not. Hopefully not. If we received everything we want, we would be hopelessly spoiled. Truth is, we probably already have more than we need. Epicurus, an ancient Greek philosopher, said, "If thou wilt make a man happy, add not unto his riches, but take away from his desires." (William DeWitt Hyde, *The Five Great Philosophies of Life*, 4). We may indeed find it easier to limit our expectations than to satisfy a growing list of desires. Remember again Paul's statement about being content in any circumstance.

Thirdly, happiness is found in pursuing goals that are worthy of our best efforts. Pouring energy into our family, church, friendships, ministry, service in the community, study, Bible knowledge, or missions are efforts worthy of all the time, money, and effort we can put into them. It is hard to wallow in our own difficulties when we see some of the problems our neighbors have to bear. If we get involved in service to them, we find happiness in being used for another's good.

Happiness is a by-product of a life lived in relationship with God, gratitude for our blessings, and service to others. When happiness is made the goal, we are bound to be disappointed. Happiness is often something we find when we are looking for something else of even greater importance.

SILENCE IN THE FACE OF DANGER

> If you falter in times of trouble, how small is your strength! Rescue those being led away to death; hold back those staggering toward slaughter. If you say, 'But we knew nothing about this,' does not he who weighs the heart perceive it? Does not he who guards your life know it? Will he not repay each person according to what he has done?
>
> Proverbs 24:10-12

Kitty Genovese was returning home from work in Queens, New York at 3:20 a.m. She was walking to the door of her apartment building when she noticed a man at the other end of the parking lot. She turned away to avoid him, but the man came after Kitty and attacked her with a knife. Kitty, age twenty-eight, cried out, "Oh, my God, he stabbed me. Please help me! Please help me!" Her screams woke people up in the surrounding apartments. Lights came on, windows opened, and one man even yelled, "Let that girl alone!"

The assailant left and the windows closed and lights went out. But then the attacker returned and stabbed Kitty again. When she screamed, "I'm dying! I'm dying!" the lights came back on and the assailant left the scene. Kitty managed to make it into her apartment building where she collapsed on the floor at the foot of her stairs. Yet again the assailant returned, and this time he finished killing the young woman.

There were three separate attacks against Kitty Genovese over a thirty-five minute period. Scores of neighbors heard her screams and at least thirty actually witnessed one of the attacks. Yet other than one man yelling at the murderer during the first assault, not one witness intervened against the attacker, came to the woman's aid, or even called the police. Only after the third attack were police summoned, and when they arrived Kitty had already died.

"If you falter in times of trouble, how small is your strength! Rescue those being led away to death; hold back, or defend, those staggering toward slaughter. If you say, 'But we knew nothing about this,' does not he who weighs the heart perceive your denial?"

In commenting on the evil perpetrated against Kitty Genovese, Cornelius Plantinga wrote, "To shut one's eyes to an injustice, to look the other way, to pretend ignorance of evil—to do these things is to connive. We generally think of connivance as a case of active conspiracy, but it needn't be and often isn't" (Not the Way it is Supposed to Be: A Breviary of Sin, 182-84). Abstaining from actively harming others doesn't mean we are necessarily free from guilt in any injury they receive. We implicate ourselves by our refusal to come to their aid, to defend them, and at the least, to speak out in their behalf.

When asked why they didn't help the screaming woman below their apartment windows, neighbors of Kitty offered such excuses as they didn't want to get involved, they were too tired, or they didn't know why. "Does not he who weighs the heart perceive it? Does not he who guards your life know it? Will he not repay each person according to what he has done?"

"Those in a position to help in difficult, dangerous circumstances are tempted to deny reality ... Some people think that any potential danger to self or family frees them from moral obligation to do good. This view, in thought and deed, entails the moral and spiritual collapse of a society. It stands under the judgment of the One who sees through human self-deception and denial of reality" (Raymond C. Van Leeuwen, "Proverbs" in New Interpreter's Bible, 5:214).

The one who walks the path of godly righteousness cannot content himself with the thought that he has not actively harmed others. Willfully turning a blind eye to abuse, murder, gossip, slander, character assassination, or any other evil perpetrated against innocent people is to connive in their harm as surely as the ones actively engaged in the violence. To seek the righteousness of God means we cry out for justice, rebuke the evil, and offer assistance to the hurt and injured. Doing so may mean we place ourselves in harm's way. But it may also mean we will never be more like Jesus than when we do.

DEFENSIVE CONTROL

> A fool gives full vent to his anger, but a wise man keeps himself under control.
>
> Proverbs 29:11

The feeling of being in control makes me feel safe. I have been in a couple of situations where I felt out of control and I was nervous, scared, even defensive.

I felt out of control the night my car broke down outside of Waco, Texas. A man stopped some distance away and walked up to me with a hand behind his back. I appreciated what at first looked like a good Samaritan stopping to help, but the hand concealed behind him told a different story.

As the man drew closer and his hand was still held behind his back, my sense of being out of control escalated. Did he have a knife? A gun? My mind raced from feeling vulnerable and defenseless to self-protection; I would strike before the man could pull the weapon and attack me. Rather than running I squared myself to face him and begin my assault before he could make the first move.

This was a desperate time. I was a teenager away from home in an unfamiliar environment. Worse, I was under attack, at least I thought so, and I was scared. I felt so out of control of the situation and circumstances that my mind raced to emergency measures to protect myself. That is normal. People do that physically and they do that emotionally.

There are people who because of hurt and pain in their lives look at everyone as strangers with their arms behind their backs. Co-workers, church members, neighbors, and even close family look like potential armed bandits ready to attack and maim. Their emotional defense systems scream, "Lack of control! Lack of control!" They imagine great emotional pain being thrust at them like a knife, so they ready themselves into defensive positions, just like I did that night many years ago.

What is the nature of the attack they fear? Being emotionally manipulated, laughed at, scorned, used, and discarded. They may sense a lack of respect in a friend, creating an emotional jolt that takes them back to a time when someone else didn't respect them, fed them an insincere line, and abused them. In nanoseconds they sense a wave crashing over them, a wave of feeling vulnerable, used, dirty, and humiliated. No one likes these feelings, so when a person feels them coming on their emotional defense system kicks in.

My defensive posture on the side of the road was to block a knife thrust and to counter with a fist, a physical maneuver for a perceived physical attack. The person fearing emotional assault does something similar, but it isn't physical in nature. Since their fear is emotionally based, they seek to defend using tactics that will strike at the emotions of another. They may curse, make mocking comments, yell, ignore you, or be overtly rude. To defend against possible future intrusions into their lives, they may spread lies and gossip.

Yes, their behavior is sinful and destroys any hope of community. Colossians 3 makes it very clear that such behavior has no place in the life of a Christian. "Rid yourselves," Paul says, "of all such things as these: anger, rage, malice, slander, and filthy language from your lips" (v.8). Some people engage in these behaviors out of pure meanness and worldliness. But there are some who do it out of a sense of survival. Because of earlier situations in their lives that made them feel weak and scared, and may have actually been dangerous and painful, they feel the need to protect themselves against any possible future assaults. They protect themselves from being hurt by hurting others first.

That is what I planned to do on a Waco highway many years ago. Fortunately, as the man got within striking distance, he lowered his hand from behind his back where had been scratching an itch. All of my apprehension and violent plans eased. The man was a Good Samaritan. I hope that the person suffering fear and turmoil and who resorts to anger and verbal weapons to cause other people emotional pain will realize that most of the people they encounter are not devious criminals out to hurt them. Some people? Sure. Most people? No. We have to learn to let go of our false sense of control, because we do it so poorly, and trust the Spirit of Christ to mature and strengthen us within, giving us the genuine control of the righteous person. It takes a lot of work and it is a long journey, but God can help us get there with his power in our lives.

TALE OF TWO FUNERALS

> The father of a righteous man has great joy.
>
> Proverbs 23:24

He was somewhere in his early sixties, still living at home with his mother. He was unemployed, and depended on his mother's graciousness to have something to eat at night. He drank. That was pretty much his life. Sadly, his mother enabled this man's dysfunctional behavior. She permitted his behavior, coddled him, and supported his addiction.

No more than fifteen people were present at his funeral. It wasn't because the weather was bad or no one knew him. The man spent his whole life in this little community. The reason so few people showed up is that people did know him, but didn't regard his life as one worth honoring.

Why do we have funeral services? There are at least two reasons. One, we want to support the family members and close friends of the deceased. They are grieving and we want them to know we care. Maybe our expressions of concern will touch their heart and strengthen their resolve to go on. The second reason we have funerals is to honor the deceased. Our presence at the funeral indicates that we feel the life of the deceased is worth remembering. We listen to the stories of the life this person lived. We laugh and cry at the pictures in the PowerPoint presentation. We nod our heads when the preacher says, "This man or woman lived a life worth remembering. We honor the one who has gone on."

People did not attend the man's funeral because not many people felt his life was worth honoring. It was very sad.

Contrast his life and funeral with that of a fifteen-year-old's funeral a few years later. This lad lived a short but good life, even though not everything in his life was good. His dad left the family in pursuit of alcohol. His mom had to carry on with two pre-teen boys and a limited income. It was tough. The boy was hurt and needed his dad. Men from church stepped in and helped, encouraging and mentoring him.

Everyone who spent time with this young man loved him. He was very personable and friendly. He asked questions. He was forward enough that he would ask to come back to your house. No one would tell him no, and everyone was glad to have him. It is not only the father of a righteous young man who takes delight in him; it is the whole community. This was a great kid.

Then a tragic accident claimed his life at age fifteen, and the whole community mourned. Five hundred people showed up for his funeral, cramming into a room without air conditioning in the summertime to support the mom and little brother and to honor the life of the boy. His life was very short, but it was well lived, even under trying conditions.

After I performed the funeral of the older man, I went home empty and sad. I told my wife that I did not want my life to end like this man's—unacknowledged.

After I performed the boy's funeral, I sat in a chair on my front porch and cried. The loss of this boy not only hurt the community, it broke my heart. But thoughts of this boy had a positive twist as well: I want to have my life to count like the life of this teen. I hope to touch as many people in a meaningful way.

In my heart, I still grieve for what must have been the emptiness of the man. I also still grieve for my young friend who would be thirty years old today. But I also feel joy at the quality of his life and look forward to seeing him again. Occasionally I say, "I'll see you on the other side, Cole." The father of a righteous man, and the friend of a righteous boy, has great joy and expectation.

THE PROCESS OF FORGIVING

A man's wisdom gives him patience; it is to his glory to overlook an offense.

Proverbs 19:11

Forgiveness is not something that happens automatically or easily. This is especially true if what you must forgive is something very personal and painful.

Colossians 3:12-13 says, "As God's chosen people, holy and dearly loved, clothe yourselves with compassion, kindness, humility, gentleness, and patience. Bear with each other and forgive whatever grievances you may have against one another. Forgive as the Lord forgave you." The means by which we can be kind, gentle, and forgiving is stated in verse 14: "And over all these virtues put on love, which binds them all together in perfect unity."

Jesus said, "If you do not forgive men their sins, our Father will not forgive your sins" (Matt. 6:15). One apostle listening to these words was a bit slow in getting the message of forgiveness. He later asked Jesus, "Lord, how many times shall I forgive my brother when he sins against me? Up to seven times?" Jesus answered, 'I tell you, not seven times, but seventy-seven times" (or seventy times seven times; Matt. 18:21-22).

These verses provide pointed teaching about forgiving people who have hurt us and people at whom we are angry. Forgive, Jesus said, and don't even keep track of the number of times you do it. Forgive, Paul said, because God has given you the love required to do it.

I believe that. But I still believe that forgiveness is not always automatic or easy. If it was, the Bible wouldn't say so much about how and why we must forgive. If forgiveness was automatic or easy, we would just do it.

I think forgiveness is a process that sometimes takes months, even years, if the offense against us is serious enough. If you have been slandered, abused, or violently mistreated, forgiveness may be a long process. If the offense was vicious enough, forgiveness may even be a life-long process. That is okay, so long as you keep working at it.

The first step in the process of forgiveness is feeling hurt. If you have been badly mistreated and are hurt, face it and admit it. Stuffing the feeling or ignoring it will not help you or the situation. Stuffed feelings are still there, pressed deeply into the heart and psyche, breeding ugly thoughts and revenge. Instead, honestly and openly admit, "I have been hurt." Your emotions may swing from just wanting to forget it to feeling numb, to crying, and even to revenge. Own those feelings.

The second step is anger, sometimes even hate, if the offense is serious enough. During this phase we may feel anger, rage, and even a hunger for revenge. We may want to retaliate and hurt the person who hurt us with as much or more severity. We all know what the Bible says about hate. It says, "Don't do it!" We know it is wrong to hate, so when we feel hate we tend to deny it. Don't. Again, if we are feeling this emotion, the proper response is not to stuff it deep inside, where it will smolder and erupt violently later on. The thing to do is diffuse it through acknowledging the presence of hate and confessing it.

After acknowledging and confessing our hurt and hatred, we can move on to the third step in the process of forgiving: healing. Healing means we have worked through the hurt and hate, and we experience a lessening of the negative emotions. We can actually begin to pray for the one who hurt us. We can move from wishing harm to wishing well for the person.

Finally, we can begin again. Beginning again means we can enter into and enjoy relationship again. In many cases it means we can function again with the one who offended us. It means we can look objectively at the conflict and even take responsibility for our part in it. Beginning again is refreshing (The above four points are from Lewis B. Smedes, *Forgive & Forget: Healing the Hurts We Don't Deserve*).

How can we possibly work through the pain of hurt and hate to healing and beginning again? Remember Colossians 3:14: "And over all these virtues put on love, which binds them all together in perfect unity." God will bless us with a loving and compassionate spirit. This is our power and ability to forgive.

John Patton wrote: "Human forgiveness is not an act but a discovery that I am more like those who have hurt me than different from them; that I am capable of also hurting others very deeply. I am able to forgive when I discover that I am in no position to forgive ... at its heart is the recognition of my reception into the community of sinners —those affirmed by God as his children" (John Patton, *Is Human Forgiveness Possible*, 16).

This is a humbling statement: I am like those who hurt me. Haven't I hurt others? Sure. I am part of a community of sinners. Can I claim to be without sin? No. I need to forgive others for the simple reason that I need others to forgive me.

How do we know when we have successfully navigated the steps of hurt, hate, healing, and beginning again? One writer answered this by saying, "You know when you have forgiven when you can wish the other person well" (Norman Shawchuck and Roger Heuser, *Managing the Congregation*, 372).

With most of the offenses that come our way, we often exercise the wisdom and patience to overlook them. The act of living means bumping elbows with people, giving and receiving bruises. We can easily process these offenses without heightening the conflict.

But, for the bigger offenses that cut and maim, we need something more. We need to acknowledge the offense and work the steps to release the hurt and anger. I am thankful to God for the forgiveness we have received from him (Rom. 6:8), as well as for the means he has given us to forgive others and be forgiven by them: his love.

SHOWING PITY

> If your enemy is hungry give him food to eat; if he is thirsty, give him water to drink.
>
> Proverbs 25:21

Christian compassion can show itself in the most unlikely places and by the most unlikely people. Praise God when it does.

One of the fiercest military contests in human history took place from 1939 to 1945 in Eastern Europe and Western Russia between the Germans and Soviets. Prisoners of War numbered in the millions; battlefield dead numbered in the tens of millions.

Each side viewed the other as the arch enemy of mankind. Each was taught by their leaders to expect no quarter, no mercy, and no human kindness if captured by the other. Sometimes that was true. Horror stories abound. But, on some occasions, soldiers from both armies allowed their Christian ethics and compassion to surface and triumph over the grueling battle conditions that fueled their hatred. Gottlob Bidermann, a soldier in the Germany army, tells of one such instance.

"One morning after a probe by a Soviet Company against our defenses, we came on a Russian with an abdominal wound lying upon the railway embankment. Holding his hands over his wound as if in prayer, he was whimpering softly for water, and through his unintelligible pleas we heard him muttering "Christ" with a trembling voice. His pale face was drawn and turned toward the leaden sky, and his eyes flickered from one of us to another, seeking pity and relief from the hated enemy from whom he had been taught to expect no quarter. Hans departed for a moment before quickly returning with two Russian prisoners, who carried the badly wounded solider back to the medical aid station on a makeshift stretcher that they had fashioned from army overcoats" (Gottlob Herbert Bidermann, *In Deadly Combat: A German Soldier's Memoir of the Eastern Front*, 81-82).

"Christ."

Hearing a fellow human cry out that name in pain and misery made its impression. Bidermann and his fellow soldiers looked down at their enemy lying helplessly on the ground before them. They saw the pleading in his eyes and heard it in his voice, and they heard him whimper the name that calls us to an allegiance higher than any other.

Hans, a German soldier, left. He returned with two other Russian soldiers, and they carried the injured man to the back of the lines. To safety. To medical care. To merciful treatment. If your enemy is hungry, give him food to eat; if he is thirsty, give him water to drink. If he is injured, give him medical care.

Jesus said, "You have heard it said, 'love your neighbor and hate your enemy.' But I tell you: Love your enemies, and pray for those who persecute you, that you may be sons of your Father in heaven" (Matt. 5:43-45).

Are there any tougher commands in the Bible? Are there any commands that strike deeper against our natural inclination to avoid, withdraw from, and even do damage to the people we hate? Love your enemies. Bidermann and crew did it that day.

Jesus wants us show compassion every day. Many times a day. And then do it again the next day. Be merciful. Show pity. Offer water. Bind wounds. Heal hurts. Forgive.

If families would do that, if churches would do that, if communities would do that, if nations would do that, oh, what a world we could live in. It's a world I can't even imagine. But, it is a world that Jesus imagines, and it is a world he calls us to help create when we love our enemies.

CHAPTER EIGHT

WORDS, WORDS, WORDS

TONGUES OF SILVER

The tongue of the righteous is choice silver, but the heart of the wicked is of little value.

Proverbs 10:20

Miners, speculators, investors, and brides have always prized gold and silver. These precious metals are rare, usable, and maintain their value. They are beautiful when refined and used in art and jewelry.

Gold and silver have been cherished since ancient times. Kings and queens used them to decorate thrones and crowns. In the early days of our country, people sold everything they owned to venture out west, risking their wealth and their health to find strands of gold and silver in the earth. Today, young men and women symbolize their love for each other with shiny bands of jewelry made of gold and silver. Gold and silver is valuable and precious.

Drawing on the beauty, usefulness, and value of these commodities, Proverbs compares them to something else of great value: wisdom. Proverbs 2:4 says we should look for wisdom as a miner looks for silver and treasure. The English word "look" really doesn't convey the idea of how intense this search for silver, treasure and wisdom is supposed to be. The idea is that something is missing and you seek in earnest for it, striving with emotional intensity (Waltke, *Proverbs*, 1:222).

I remember my aunt losing the diamond out of her wedding ring. I was just a kid and was confused by the frantic search all the adults in the family were making looking for that little stone. I asked my mom, "What's the big deal? It's just a little rock, right?" Sure! I learned what intensity was that weekend. I have a friend who lost his wedding ring, and years later his wife is still angry at him for it. There is a lot of emotion tied in with those little emblems of gold, silver, and precious stone. We feel deep loss if they go missing. That, the Sage says, is what we ought to feel in our search for wisdom: earnestness, intensity, and loss if we don't find it.

With this discussion in mind, think of Proverbs 10:20 again: "The tongue of the righteous is choice silver, but the heart of the wicked is of little value."

This verse appears in the midst of an extended discussion about wise and foolish tongues. Wise speech comes from the mouth of the righteous and is a fountain of life (10:11). While a fool is busy chattering away, a wise man is busy storing up knowledge (10:14). The wise know how to hold their tongues, not speaking when it is inappropriate and not speaking too much when it is (10:19). When the wise man does speak, his words are worth listening to. The righteous speak words that are wise and fit the occasion (10:31,32), so their speech brings nourishment (10:21).

Foolish speech emanates from a heart that is not devoted to acquiring wisdom. The one who speaks foolishly stirs up hatred and violence against others and ultimately against himself (10:11). One way a foolish person stirs up hatred is in the lies he tells and the slander he spreads (10:18). The foolish mouth also stirs up anger because it simply talks too much and has no value or substance. Two times the Sage says "a chattering fool comes to ruin" (10:9, 10). The fool speaks of things that are wicked and disgusting (10:31, 32).

In the middle of this discussion is the comment about the tongue of the righteous being choice silver. The imagery of rarity, usefulness, and value are applied to the speech of the righteous person. The speech of the wise is rare because there is not enough of it. It is useful because it encourages and transforms lives. It maintains its value because it imparts life. Such speech is choice silver, having been refined to produce purity.

"The dross of evil intentions and effects" has been removed from the wise man's heart and thus his mouth (Waltke, *Proverbs*,1:471), revealing one more important reason wise speech is so critically important. It honors God's social order by promoting wholesome life for individuals and the community (Leo G. Perdue, "Proverbs," *Interpretation*, 165). The power of wholesome words to uphold God's order and impart life can be heard in the words of Jesus. "Neither do I condemn you. Go now and leave your life of sin" (John 8:11). Taken to heart, those words could perform to heal the shame of this woman and restore refreshment to her life. May our words do the same.

FITTING SPEECH

> The lips of the righteous know what is fitting, but the mouth of the wicked only what is perverse.
>
> Proverbs 10:32

Children can sense when decency has been violated. I was driving Wes and Jenny home from school when Wes asked me what a certain phrase meant. He was eight-years-old and had never heard that term before. I asked, "Where did you hear that?"

"On the playground," he answered.

"I'm glad you asked me what the phrase meant before you started using it. It's not very nice, and I'll have to explain it to you later when your five-year-old sister isn't around. She doesn't need to hear about that yet."

Jenny had been sitting in the middle of the pickup seat during this conversation. Her eyes were big with curiosity and her head swiveled back and forth between Wes and me as we talked. When she heard that she would be denied the explanation until she was a bit older, she covered her ears with her hands and said, "Go ahead and tell him, Dad, I can't hear anything."

"You can't?" I asked her.

"No, I can't," she replied. I waited until later.

Children may not know what a vulgar term means, but if they have never heard it spoken before in the home, church, or other social gatherings of family and friends, they can sense if it has the ring of impropriety about it. They sense that an order has been violated and they are curious, even uncomfortable, about what it might mean.

This order or appropriateness is what Proverbs 10:32 is about. People who are righteous or wise in matters of godliness and propriety speak words that are fitting and pleasant; people who are not wise or righteous speak words that violate sensibilities and offend. The lips of the righteous know what is fitting, but the mouth of the wicked only what is perverse.

It seems strange to speak of lips as having knowledge, doesn't it? "The lips of the righteous know what is fitting." Can lips know anything? This is an example of a common figure of speech in the Bible known as metonymy, where one object is used in place of another object it is related to. Here, lips are used in the place of a heart that is attuned to God and his will. Such a heart is filled with a sense of God, his moral teaching, and his high regard for other people. The lips of this person express the substance of a heart filled with godly wisdom and righteousness, uttering words that are fitting and pleasant.

The lips or mouth of the wicked, however, speak what is perverse. Perverse means to "turn upside down" (Roland E. Murphy, *Proverbs*, p.76). It implies that proper order has been completely disrupted and upended. Instead of an atmosphere of appropriate speech characterized by intelligent discussion, respectful tones, and encouragement for one another, perverse conversation is distasteful, even ungodly. The effect of such speech is to "confound the moral judgment of others, and to overthrow God's rule" (Waltke, *Proverbs*, 1:480).

Do Christians take the subject of appropriate speech seriously enough? Are we occasionally lured into conversation or humor muddied by base innuendo or course language? Do we engage in negative, slanderous putdowns of other people? We may regard such offenses as inconsequential, but Proverbs 10:32 challenges our casual disdain. The mouth of the wicked speaks what is perverse. Another verse in Proverbs threatens that such a tongue shall be "cut out" (Prov. 10:31).

To be perverse means to turn God's order upside down. It means to reverse the intention God had for the heart, purity and innocence, and fill it with filth and degradation. It means that when a heart that is impure speaks, wickedness flows forth. That wickedness may be gossip, slander, lies, course jokes, crude expressions, or threats of violence. All of these manifestations of perverseness give evidence of a heart in need of cleansing. Even small children with tender hearts sense this. If only Christian adults had such spiritual orientation!

Our words reveal the substance of our heart. The lips of the righteous know what is fitting because they speak from a heart influenced and shaped by the Creator.

BUILD OR DESTROY

> Through the blessing of the upright a city is exalted, but
> by the mouth of the wicked it is destroyed.
>
> Proverbs 11:11

Some personalities are so dynamic people are irresistibly drawn to them. Salesmen sell cars, politicians draw votes, and preachers win converts often on the power of their persona. Most of us may not possess such irresistible drawing power, but we all do have a level of influence that may far exceed even our own perception. Proverbs 11:11 addresses that issue.

The effect of our character, our personal power, builds or destroys communities. "Through the blessing of the upright a city is exalted." The blessing of the upright is likely the power of their pure character mediated through their speech. Verses 9 through 14 all address the effect of speech. The righteous bless with their words while the wicked destroy with theirs.

The blessing of righteous speech is to exalt a city. To exalt means "build up." A city is built up by the construction of houses for people to live in, and in ancient times, by protective walls around the city. In such an environment, people can thrive in security and safety.

The speech of the wise man does the same thing for a city. With his speech the wise man teaches firm principles of honorable living, like honesty, kindness, and hard work. More than just talking about principles, his life models them. The wise man encourages people within his charge to live up to higher standards, and he expresses appreciation for them when they do. He is also able to offer an appropriate rebuke when necessary, but always with a view toward building a life, not discouraging one. After years of exposure to the speech and life of the wise man, the city, be it a business office, church, or home, is taught and enabled to live better because of him.

"The mouth of the wicked destroys." While verses 9 through 14 address speech, most of it is about the speech of the wicked man. He derides his neighbor and betrays a confidence. Years of his influence destroys relationship and people (v. 9).

The speech of the wicked man has the following effect on people. One, he debases them, usually in front of other people. He may minimize their accomplishments in a subtle way by simply saying, "Oh wow," with a mocking grin, or more overtly, by comparing their success with others. "Well, I know people who have done even better and at a younger age." He gossips about others, reducing the esteem other people have for them (v. 9). The effect is to leave the person feeling less than what he should for his accomplishment, and creating embarrassment for him by doing it in front of others.

Secondly, the wicked man discourages others with his speech. Consistent debasement through putdowns, mockery, and belittling comments kills initiative in the victim's heart. Fear crowds out incentive to try; failure confirms the expectation of the wicked man. Children raised in such an environment may reason it is worthless to ever attempt anything worthwhile in life, or they may spend their life in vain pursuit of trying ever harder to achieve an accomplishment that will win the wicked man's approval, especially if that man is their father.

Thirdly, as a result of the debasement and discouragement, the wicked man destroys those who fall under his influence. People feel ashamed, unworthy, and incapable of doing anything to be proud of. They give up worthy aspirations, become embittered and angry, and can become wicked themselves, destroying the people they influence just as they were destroyed.

Having a forceful personality helps in selling cars, drawing votes, and winning converts. But such dynamic charisma is really not needed to affect great good. The quiet, consistent voice of a righteous man who teaches wisdom, expresses appreciation, encourages good work, and gives positive recognition for accomplishment is building a city. He is exalting the staff in his office, the members of his church, and the children and spouse in his family. The foundation of his city is firm, the walls are strong, and the inhabitants of the dwelling are free and secure to live, love, and even fail, because they know they have room to try again. Any city is blessed by such a man.

WHY THE RIGHTEOUS MAN ESCAPES TROUBLE

> An evil man is trapped by his sinful talk, but a righteous man escapes trouble.
>
> Proverbs 12:13

An evil man lives for his own pleasure and satisfaction without thought for the well-being of others. A righteous man enjoys pleasure and satisfaction, too, but he balances his own pursuits with concern for the well-being of others. His concern for others (and God) actually limits his pursuit of self-gratification.

The speech of the evil man is one clear indicator of his state of heart. Evil talk kills. The evil man uses his speech in ways that tears at the hearts of others and demeans their lives. His speech is as painful to the recipient as a punch in the belly; maybe more so, because his hurtful words lodge deeply in the heart, continuing to sting and burn years afterward.

Trouble entraps the evil man with wicked lips. He loses credibility with his lies. His harsh humor keeps former friends at bay and his mocking tone turns them into enemies. His gossip incurs the anger of others. Evil speech kills any warm feelings a person may have had for the wicked man.

The essence of the evil man displays no higher authority or love in his life than himself. He does not submit to God. He cares only for himself. The happiness of others is secondary to his own. If he hurts them with violent action or speech, it simply doesn't matter to the evil man.

Concern for others is one big thing that separates the righteous from the evil. The righteous man knows he is not inherently good; any goodness and purity in his life is from God. Since no man is saved by his own works, he has no ground for boasting. It is the grace of God at work in his life that makes the difference (Eph. 2:8-9). We do not become righteous because we overcome sin on our own or because our sins aren't as bad as someone else's. We become righteous solely because Jesus bears our sin in his life, allowing us to be declared righteous in God's sight (2 Cor. 5:21).

Something happens to us in this transformation from evil to righteousness. We become more like Jesus, and as a result, we become concerned for others. (This doesn't mean we become as good as Jesus, or can justify being 'self-righteous.' It means we take on some of his attributes, sensitivity toward others being one of them). We realize that our speech and actions can open or soothe wounds, stifle or promote goodwill, destroy or build friendships. It dawns on the righteous man that just as Jesus had concern for the happiness of others, we should, too. As we become concerned about their feelings and lives, we become more careful with our speech and actions toward them. We don't want to hurt anyone.

This change protects the righteous man. The Sage says that the righteous man escapes trouble caused by the mouth. How? Why is it that the man walking in Jesus' steps avoids hardship?

One, he doesn't lose credibility due to lies because he tells the truth. Knowing that lies function from hate and cause hurt (Prov. 26:26), the righteous man avoids them.

Two, he doesn't scare his friends off with sudden outbursts of rage. Because his speech is tempered with grace (Prov. 16:24), the righteous man always has a community around him that he cares about.

Three, he doesn't have to defend (or apologize) for slanderous speech. The righteous man will speak words that encourage people in their need, build them up, and benefit them (Eph. 4:29). That kind of speech attracts friends!

Yes, the righteous still wrestle with their old nature and will slip into selfish pursuits and damaging speech. They will sin with their mouths. But what separates the righteous from the evil is that the wicked will not care that they hurt others. The righteous man will care, and because of that he will feel guilt and pain for the harm he caused others, and he will repent before God. He will also apologize to the one he offended. This humble response to his own sin keeps the righteous man on the godly path, and frees him from the trap of trouble.

PLEASANT WORDS

> Pleasant words are a honeycomb, sweet to the soul and healing to the bones.
>
> Proverbs 16:24

There are many warnings in the Bible about our use of words. Paul wrote, "Let your conversation be always full of grace, seasoned with salt, so that you may know how to answer everyone" (Col. 4:6). What does salt do to food? It flavors and enhances it. Our words should do the same thing for our speech and relationships. Words aptly spoken, with kindness and grace, enrich the quality of good speech and deepen the bonds of kinship with others.

We have a saying for salt that I'm not sure they had in ancient times: "Take what he says with a grain of salt." That means filter it. Don't just take his words at face value, and don't take them to heart. His words are often untrue and hurtful, so ignore them. What Paul seems to be saying is that the refining process needs to be on our tongue rather than in the other person's ear. We need to taste the words first. This admonition is in the Bible because tasting and filtering our words before we speak them is something we often don't do.

This thought is brought home in Matthew 12:36-37: "I tell you that men will have to give account on the day of judgment for every careless word they have spoken. For by your words you will be acquitted and by your words you will be condemned." Careless words can take you away from God. Can you think of some jokes you wish you hadn't told? Some stories you wish you had not repeated? Some accusations better left unsaid? I shudder when I think of meeting my own words at judgment. The good news is, careless, cutting speech spoken to harm another does not have to be the final, defining words that hang over us in judgment. At judgment, we can also meet words that grant life, words such as, "I know you are one of mine. You are forgiven." These are words that acquit.

This thought gives added value to Proverbs 16:24 and the healing quality of pleasant words. The sweet, soothing attributes of honey to a sore throat give it a medicinal value. Proverbs says pleasant words have that same soothing and healing nature to a soul that has been wounded.

Before David was a great man of Israel, he was a young man who was alone and fearful. His life was upended when his boss, the king, said, "I'm going to kill you." The king's words were not vain; he tried more than once to run David through with a spear.

David had to flee. Before his departure, he met with his friend, Jonathan. Their friendship was deep and abiding. Jonathan had shared his royal clothes and military equipment with David, but they shared more than this, they shared their hearts.

At their final meeting, Jonathan said to David, "Go in peace, for we have sworn friendship with each other in the name of the Lord, saying, 'The Lord is witness between you and me, and between your descendants and my descendants together'" (1 Sam. 20:43).

David was a young man and he was a trusted servant of the king. He was rising in the ranks of the kingdom. Now suddenly, he is a fugitive on the run. He has a price on his head. Life as he knows it is over. But one man extends his hand and says, "David, I'm still your friend."

Proverbs 18:21 says, "The tongue has the power of life and death ..." When Saul said, "I'll pin David to the wall" (1 Sam. 18:11), his tongue was expressing the murderous rage of his heart. With the power embedded in him as the king, Saul's words literally carried the weight of life or death. If "reckless words pierce like a sword" (Prov. 12:18), so do words that are designed to cut and tear. Many are the victims of an unruly and perverse tongue.

Thankfully, many are the recipients of the healing work of the tongue as well. Pleasant words are a honeycomb, sweet to the soul and healing to the bones. Jonathan's words of support must have seemed liked honey to David's hurting soul: "I am your friend." David was despised and rejected by the very man who called him to service. That is a devastating blow to a man's ego. Then the king's son extends his hand and says, "We're still friends, and will be for life."

Honey to the soul. Do you know how an affirming moment like that feels? What it does for one's heart? A student who sits alone at lunch every day knows that feeling when someone says, "Hey, why don't you come over here and eat with us?" An AIDS patient knows what that is like when someone says, "Hi" and extends their hand in friendship. The woman in John 8 knew how David felt when Jesus said to her, "I don't condemn you either, but go, and leave your life of sin." A husband and wife know the healing power of words when their spouse hugs them and says, "I forgive you."

The pain of harsh words, rejection by friends, and condescending looks cuts deeply. The Bible describes the pain as going into our souls and our bones. We can carry that pain with us for years, and it can color and cloud every other relationship we are ever in. Openness and conviviality can give way to indifference and fear. We can shut other people out of our lives.

The pleasantness of words goes just as deeply as the pain. "A word aptly spoken is sweet to the soul and healing to the bones" (Prov. 25:11). A word of understanding, care, tenderness, and acceptance can work through the hurt and pain, filling a heart with hope and healing.

I'll bet David never forgot that moment when his friend offered pleasant words of affirmation. Even with all the uprooting and change his life would experience, that moment was forever implanted in his psyche. In fact, years later, when Jonathan met his death on a battlefield, David cried, "I grieve for you, Jonathan my brother; you were very dear to me" (2 Sam. 1:26).

We may never know the effect our words will have on someone's heart and soul. But knowing the power those words have to work for good or evil, let's be careful. Appropriate words are a sign of godly wisdom and a righteous heart. Let's pray for God's Spirit to work in us to give us the discernment to know when to speak, what to speak, and how to speak. And as Paul prays for the Colossians, "Let your conversation be always full of grace, seasoned with salt so that you may know how to answer everyone" (Col. 4:6).

CHOICE MORSELS

> The words of a gossip are like choice morsels; they go
> down to a man's inmost parts.
>
> Proverbs 18:8

Good food has sensual appeal. It looks and smells inviting, tantalizing us with its delectable qualities even before it touches our lips. Good food explodes with flavor and delights our inmost parts, nourishing our entire body with beneficial nutrients.

Sometimes the food we eat has sensual appeal without the beneficial nutrients. It may look and smell inviting and burst with flavor, though its taste comes not from God's natural ingredients but unnatural, artificial flavoring. It may please the palate and the inmost parts even though it lacks any healthy qualities that would nurture the body. Such food may even damage the body, messing with insulin levels, causing obesity, and clogging arteries.

Yet we love that unhealthy food, don't we? During the movie do we reach for something natural and healthy to curb our hunger, or something processed and packaged? It is amazing how chemicals can combine to make a snack look, taste, and smell so inviting that we are compelled to indulge, even though we know it is detrimental to our system.

Gossip is like processed food. It's a negative report delivered "to inappropriate people at an inappropriate time" and is "based on uncertain evidence" (Longman, *Proverbs*, 356). Even if the information turns out to be accurate, it is still gossip if its intention is to injure someone. Gossip, like junk food, is so inviting that we are compelled to indulge, even though we know it is detrimental to our system.

The Sage wouldn't refer to gossip as a choice morsel that feeds our inmost parts unless he knew from experience that most of us, at some time, relish tidbits of information about other people that defame and slander. Why? What is the appeal of gossip that keeps us feeding at its trough and relishing it like a choice delicacy?

One, gossip is often delivered in a tantalizing manner. Like a richly decorated table at a fine restaurant, gossip comes to us packaged in richly decorated verbal decor. "If you've heard this already let me know." "I don't want to gossip but ..." "Has anyone told you the latest about ...?" The hushed tones, furtive glances, and wry smiles accompanying the gossip are the fancy table setting adorning the poisoned meal to follow. The gossiper is "artistically skilled," but unfortunately his skill delivers destruction (Bland, *Proverbs*, 241). Though it tastes good, going down like a choice morsel, gossip is junk food that clogs the arteries of compassion, truth, and integrity. It kills both the giver and receiver.

Two, gossip puts us in the seat of power and prominence, imbuing us with a sense of self-importance. When we gossip, we sit in judgment on someone else. We pass sentence on their work performance, personal and family life, and their character. In truth, the only Being capable of performing such an evaluation is God. So, when we gossip, we presume upon God's position as Judge, deluding ourselves into the dangerous position of playing God.

Finally, gossip allows us to feel connected. If even for a brief moment, our hearts are joined with our fellow rumormongers when we give and receive those tidbits of information that leave everyone smiling, sneering, and yearning to spread the choice morsels to others. In their attack against other people, gossipers are trying to form a community of their own where they will feel accepted and loved. That is sad. Acting with greater character would allow them to enjoy a healthier community than they will ever find with their current compatriots.

Ironically, gossipers reveal more about themselves than they do the people they are maligning. They reveal a lack of Bible knowledge, self-esteem, and integrity. The choice morsels have fed their inmost parts, perverting their values and moral fiber. Pray for them. And pray for us, that we don't indulge their fare, and that we have enough sensitivity to repent when we do.

RESTRAINING THE TONGUE

> He who guards his mouth and his tongue keeps himself
> from calamity.
>
> Proverbs 21:23

When Richard heard that Ron lost his temper at a church meeting and yelled obscenities, threw a Bible across the room, and stormed out of the building, restraining his tongue was impossible. This report went into his "inmost parts" (Prov. 18:8), warming and titillating him all the way down.

Ron wasn't Richard's favorite person anyway, so hearing a negative report simply confirmed the negative feelings he already felt toward the man. Also, news like this was too juicy to keep to himself; it begged to be shared. Richard wasted no time doing just that.

By the time Richard's version of the church meeting was countered by a more accurate assessment of what happened, Ron's reputation had been seriously tarnished and many people were asking for his resignation from several church positions. Too late Richard learned that he was third in line to receive this story, and it had been significantly enlarged and embellished with each telling. Ron had lost his temper briefly, he had spoken in angry tones, but he was not guilty of the violent words and actions of which he was accused.

Gossip had done its dirty deed. It tarnished a man's name, hindered his further work in the congregation, and seriously disrupted God's community. It is no wonder that gossip separates close friends (Prov. 16:28) and is prominently featured in a couple of the "hall of shame" lists in the Bible (Rom. 1:29; 2 Cor. 12:20). Gossip kills good feelings, friendships, healthy working relationships, and community solidarity.

Gossip is only one example of failure to restrain the tongue. Anger is another. "A fool gives full vent to his anger, but a wise man keeps himself under control" (Prov. 29:11). Not all anger is wrong. Jesus himself experienced anger and expressed himself in bold and decisive action (John 2:12f.). Paul cautions against acting inappropriately in our anger but doesn't seem to deny the legitimacy of anger at certain times (Eph. 4:26). The problem with heated emotion is how we use it to hurt other people. Like a cough, anger will come out, and unless we release the pressure appropriately we will damage lives around us, including the people we love. "A hot tempered man commits many sins" (Prov. 29:22). It wasn't a spirit of calm reflection that led ten boys to sell their brother into slavery (Gen. 37). It was unbridled anger that festered into vengeful rage. Restraining the tongue and vengeful spirit gives us time to diffuse our anger through contemplation of its harmful effects, talking to someone else, and prayer.

Finally, simply speaking without thinking and tempering one's words is failure to restrain the tongue. "Do you see a man who speaks in haste? There is more hope for a fool than for him" (Prov. 29:20). Too many times I have spoken in haste, only to regret seconds later the barrage I'd released.

Many people who say hurtful things do not mean for their words to be so damaging. They simply don't exercise the care and discipline of considering another's feelings and guarding their speech. They speak before they think.

This problem causes heavy damage in marriage. A husband or wife experiencing frustration in their relationship can lose patience with each other. When they meet with another disappointing episode, they are not inclined to restrain their tongue and allow their emotions to cool. Instead, they speak in haste, exploding with the first words of frustration and anger that come over them. Speaking in anger or in haste creates enough problems; combining the two creates sure devastation.

Thomas Carlyle said, "Consider it the greatest of all virtues to restrain the tongue." Perhaps you've experienced tense situations when you wanted to say something but restrained, waiting for a cooler moment to think. Later you wished you'd spoken out and made your thoughts known. You can still express those thoughts, but now in a calm, orderly manner. The emotional impact might be missing, but so will the possibility of shame and regret for having spoken harmful words in anger and haste. He who guards his mouth and his tongue keeps himself from calamity and never has to feel the burn of remorse.

AN APT WORD

> A word aptly spoken is like apples of gold in settings of silver.
>
> Proverbs 25:11

Knowing what to speak, to whom to speak, and when to speak is a function of godly wisdom. "It is only fools who speak all the time, without regard for the circumstance ... The wisdom formula is to speak the right word to the right person at the right time" (Longman, 453).

A well-timed word has several positive attributes to it. One, it reaffirms our value. A teenager cut from the basketball team, a man terminated from his job, and a woman reeling from an unsought-for divorce all suffer from devastating hits to their lives and psyches, pain felt deeply within their being. A corollary to such blows is that we question our own worth and value. If we have just been rejected by a team, business, or relationship from which we drew a significant sense of our own identity, we may wonder if we will ever find another place or person to belong to. A well-timed word at this juncture can rescue us from swimming in the sea of self-doubt and reaffirm that we are people of worth.

Two, an apt word refocuses our vision. Lingering in the shadow of our damaged self-worth is blurred vision. The future looks foggy at best, and any vision we may have left is bleak, even ominous and threatening. It is natural that humiliating defeats and emotionally disturbing setbacks would cause reticence to face the future. What lies ahead? If I have failed now, what prospects do I have for better results in the future? If I have been rejected, can genuine love ever find me again? A timely word to such a person is one that considers their circumstances, acknowledges the pain and uncertainty choking their heart, and offers hope that the future can be faced.

Three, an appropriate word is one that rekindles hope. The future is very uninviting when it seems to offer only prospects of continued gloom and doom. Living with the fear of never belonging again, lacking financial resources, or having no one to bond intimately with is gloomy. But that well-timed word, if embedded and nurtured in the heart of the sufferer, can eventually sprout and grow, offering vision, and hope of a brighter future that we can participate in.

Finally, a well-timed word can even deliver necessary rebuke. To rebuke someone is to expose them to the truth of their situation, their attitude or behavior, and the appropriate response they need to make. Rebuke is usually appropriate for someone who persists in inappropriate or dangerous behavior. Rebuke may not apply initially to someone struggling with situations of rejection and hurt as described above, but, there may come a time when even they need a gentle nudge to open their eyes. "Okay, you lost your job, I'm very sorry. But you are not likely to find another job by watching TV all day, seven days a week. It's time to pull yourself together and get back out there." It may seem out of place discussing rebuke after describing an apt reply as one that reaffirms value, refocuses vision, and rekindles hope. But, an apt reply isn't limited to situations of encouraging the broken-hearted; it can also apply to those pursuing paths that can render them hard-hearted.

The finesse of Jesus' response to the woman entrapped in sin demonstrates the power of the apt reply. Even if she didn't know the law, the woman knew the Pharisees advocated stoning her. That is quite a blow to one's self-composure and image! Jesus said, "Neither do I condemn you." But he didn't withhold rebuke. "Leave your life of sin," he said next. He acknowledged her sin and told her to abandon it, choosing instead to live morally and spiritually. With this gentle rebuke and freedom from condemnation, the woman's value was affirmed, and she was free to envision a future of hope and second chances (John 8:1-11).

An apt word delivered to a hurting soul is "a masterpiece of human art" (Bland, *Proverbs*, 225), comparable to richly designed apples of gold in settings of silver. The beauty of the gold and silver setting and the apt word both enrich our lives and testify to the wisdom and skill of the master artisans who crafted them.

STRIFE

> Without wood a fire goes out; without gossip a quarrel
> dies down. As charcoal to embers and as wood to fire, so
> is a quarrelsome man for kindling strife.
>
> Proverbs 26:20-21

A lightning strike, a dropped cigarette, or a campfire not properly extinguished can smolder for days, finally igniting a few dry leaves culminating in a forest fire that can burn for weeks, even months. Trees and homes miles away from the spot where the fire began can be torched in minutes from the inferno unleashed by that original smoldering ember. Under the right conditions, forest fires can become impossible for even multiple teams of fire fighters to put out. It may take the arrival of fall snows to finally extinguish the blaze. Or, as the Sage says, a fire may not play out until it is deprived of a substance to burn. There is a three-step progression in the scenario just presented: a smoldering ember, dry kindling, and finally, a raging fire.

A similar three-step progression is present in these two verses in Proverbs. First, there is the smoldering ember, a quarrel between two people. Then there is the dry kindling to feed that ember and give it greater life, gossip. Gossip is the spreading of tales by the participants in the quarrel. With enough time and gossip, the third step is realized, strife. The quarrelsome man who can't or won't keep his discontent or disagreement contained, but must spread it through the kindling of gossip, fuels the fire until it becomes a bitter conflict involving numerous parties. Strife, or discord, is one of the acts of the sinful nature (Gal. 5:20), and it can burn out of control, scorching and burning people miles away from the original smoldering ember.

A quarrel is simply a verbal battle between two people. There is usually some degree of heat and flame of emotions in the verbal feud, but in time quarrels usually die down.

Like a fire, though, quarrels can be fed highly combustible material. For a fire it is dry wood; for a quarrel it is gossip. Gossip in this verse also means "whisper" in Hebrew. The idea is that one is going around on the sly whispering damaging things against someone else's character and position. Should one or more of the participants in the quarrel take their grievances to others, not for wise counsel on how to handle the situation but rather to whisper against and slander the other party, then more people are dragged into the fray. Soon five, six, even ten, or more people may be agitated and riled up against each other, and they may not even know why!

I have seen situations of two people frothing in anger towards each other over what other parties in the quarrel had told them. These guys were not original participants and didn't even know all the details of the initial argument. They were just dragged in and began burning like dry timber and they didn't know why. Situations like this can erupt at work and church, burning with a fury that can last for weeks. It may not die out until everyone involved is literally exhausted and singed from the heat of the verbal and emotional blaze.

After once such inferno, I asked a participant in that holocaust, "What happened? What was going on to create such a blaze where people were fighting and seemed to hate each other?" She said, "I don't know. Everyone was just so angry and excited and saying things that were so mean. I don't know how it started and why it went on for so long. But it was very ugly and unnecessary."

It started as a disagreement between two people that became a quarrel. The quarrel was not allowed to die down but was fed with the kindling of gossip and slander, causing it to burn hotter and wider. Soon, a dozen people were sucked into the blaze of bitter conflict, angry, hot, and ready to do battle on a larger scale. And no one really knew why.

Quarrels, gossip, and strife are the external manifestations of a deeper issue in the heart of the one engaged in these unholy activities. The inner issue is an evil and malicious spirit. The evil spirit of one who creates discord and contention among other people is discussed in the next several verses, where the Sage says, "A malicious man disguises himself with his lips, but in his heart he harbors deceit" (Prov. 26:24). Verse 26 says his wickedness will eventually become known.

Families, churches, businesses, and community programs can be devastated in the incineration caused by the slanderer. To protect yourself and those around you, simply do not engage this man or woman. Only by joint refusal to participate in the ungodly triad of quarrels, gossip, and strife can we starve the fire of fuel and save our relationships.

CRAFTING OUR WORLDS

> The lips of the righteous know what is fitting, but the mouth of the wicked only what is perverse.
>
> Proverbs 10:32

The righteous know what is fitting because they know three important things: the heart of God, the heart of others, and their own hearts.

"The lips of the righteous know what is fitting" refers to speech. Fitting speech refers to words that are spoken at the right time to the right people in the right circumstances. People who handle words this appropriately are artists and craftsmen.

My girls were excited when I arrived at home with a bunk bed kit for their room. But excitement turned to disappointment when several pre-cut pieces didn't fit and pre-drilled holes for the screws didn't line up. Someone in the factory was not careful enough with the measurements, cutting, and drilling.

It is too easy for our speech to be as haphazard and ill-fitting as the pieces of the bunk bed. For the wicked, speech is perverse, meaning it violates moral and societal standards. Perverse means to "turn upside down." It is immoral, offensive, and inappropriate. Children exposed to this kind of speech often grow up without the internal apparatus for tuning in to spiritual thoughts or behavior.

Inappropriate speech doesn't just emanate from those with impure and wicked hearts, nor is it limited to that which is immoral or offensive. Inappropriate speech is that which fails to take into account people's feelings and situations.

One year after losing their oldest son, friends of ours were asked by a lady at church, "Are you still grieving for him? It's been a year." She had no idea how she cut the heart of our friends. It wasn't wickedness that prompted her cruel comment; it was simply an unsympathetic and undiscerning heart. Because she didn't know the heart of God, the heart of her friends, or even her own heart, she spoke words that tore the spirit.

The heart of God is compassionate, gracious, slow to anger, loving and faithful (Ex. 34:6). To know his heart is to walk in his kindness, showing compassion to the hurt and suffering. Someone attuned to the heart of God would never so callously dismiss the constant ache felt by grieving parents. God himself knows the pain of losing a child.

Secondly, to know the heart of another person is to place ourselves in the drama of their lives and feel, as best we can imagine, the joys and hurts they experience. Though our children may be alive and healthy, can we imagine what it would be like to visit our own child in the cancer ward? Can we stretch to think what it must be like to make the funeral arrangements for our son or daughter? Such thoughts are not pleasant, but neither are they morbid if the focus of such thoughts is to enter into another's suffering and experience life with them.

Finally, to be able to speak words that are fitting, we must know our own hearts. "The heart is deceitful above all things and beyond cure. Who can understand it?" (Jer. 17:9). We all have an amazing capacity for thoughts, speech, and behavior that is inconsiderate, selfish, and even evil. We can become so absorbed in our own lives that we become blind or insensitive to the circumstances of others. For those of us who have never experienced loss, grieving for a year may seem like sufficient time to calm the ache of a heart. But have we really put ourselves in the place of those parents who still see the empty chair at dinner time?

It takes a craftsman who knows wood to fashion furniture so that the pieces fit and are aesthetically pleasing. Likewise, it takes a craftsman who knows hearts to fashion words so that they fit the setting, offering peace, comfort, or even rebuke, as the situation may demand. To become a craftsman of words, study hearts, beginning with the heart that yearns to make us righteous so our speech can be fitting: God's.

CHAPTER NINE

RELATIONSHIPS

LISTENING IS MINISTRY

He who answers before listening – that is his folly and his shame.

Proverbs 18:13

"Listening carefully and responding accurately to the story of another is a true ministry. To be understood and accepted by another person is a treasured dimension of human living. It is also the first movement of any kind of care" (Herbert Anderson & Edward Foley, *Mighty Stories, Dangerous Rituals*, 45).

Ridiculing someone's ideas or mocking their serious questions are effective ways of making them feel belittled and inferior (they may also be sinful, just for the record). Though these verbal offenses cause great harm they are committed frequently and enjoy fairly widespread acceptance, which is too bad.

There is a less aggressive but equally effective way to make a person feel emotionally debased and hurt: just ignore them.

Maybe you've had the experience of trying to speak to someone and they totally ignore you. They know you are speaking to them, but they don't even acknowledge your presence or speech. Equally bad is when they do address you, but it is not in response to what you said or asked. Rather, it is for them to express what they want to say to you. They are controlling the agenda by ignoring you and redirecting the conversation.

Pointing out these inconsiderate ways of treating people will, I hope, make us wise and sensitive to the problem, and will encourage us to be aware of any tendencies we may have to practice them. I certainly hope no one reading this will respond with, "Oh, so that is another way I can annoy someone. Ignore them."

I often give too little thought to the power of listening. The first time I realized how deeply some people need to be heard was when I was seventeen, and a woman I met at a summer job told me about the death of her teenage son the summer before. She told me about the accident, the sense of loss, the annoyance of legal and insurance issues, the constant darkness of his absence, and the cancerous pain that ate at her soul every day. She cried. I listened. I was overwhelmed. My heart ached for her, but I had no way to comfort the incredible hurt other than to listen to the flood of words that poured out of a soul desperate to be heard. After an hour the clock chimed it was time to resume work. My summer job was soon over and we never talked again.

I've thought about that experience many times and the lessons it teaches about the power of listening. No one could bring the woman's son back, dull the pain, or ease the loneliness. But anyone could listen. A group of listeners might have saved her marriage. When her husband, suffering horribly with his own grief, could no longer bear his wife's burden with his own, he left. A group of five to ten caring friends and fellow church members, meeting regularly with both the husband and wife, taking turns listening and shouldering the pain with them, may have saved their marriage.

Listening is ministry, whether it is over a kitchen table, in a hospital room, after a funeral, or over a cup of coffee. "Listening carefully and responding accurately to the story of another is a true ministry. To be understood and accepted by another person is a treasured dimension of human living. It is also the first movement of any kind of care."

Listening is a way to honor a person's dignity, reassure them of their value, relieve them of intense inner burdens, and sometimes save their families and lives.

What do you think Jesus was doing with the sinners and social outcasts of his day? We assume he was preaching.

I think he was listening.

ABERRATIONS OF FRIENDSHIP

> A man of many companions may come to ruin, but there
> is a friend who sticks closer than a brother.
>
> Proverbs 18:24

A genuine friendship is a relationship of mutual concern and is built upon the foundations of trust, loyalty, honesty, and tough love. Such friendships can take years of intense labor and effort to form and maintain. Repentance, forgiveness, compassion, and overlooking character flaws and slips all go into the formation of genuine friendships.

Some people lack knowledge of how such friendships take shape and are sustained, or they don't have the energy to devote the effort it takes for them. Still others do not have the emotional strength to participate in such open and honest relationships. They undermine such potential friendships with gossip (Prov. 11:9; 16:28; 17:4; 17:9), harsh words (Prov. 15:1), angry words (Prov. 29:22; 30:33), evil desires (Prov. 6:14; 17:19), and numerous other unwholesome or sinful attitudes. They may desire a healthy relationship enjoyed by others and may even be envious of those who do enjoy one, but they cannot or will not expend the effort to have such friendships themselves. They may know something is awry in themselves that prevents such bonding with others, and they hurt over that. But rather than exercising introspection and working to change possible character flaws, they make various superficial attempts to connect with other people.

One such attempt at friendship is short-circuiting. Real intimacy between two or more people often takes years of mature interaction. In an attempt to bypass this long and necessary process, the short-circuiter will substitute a real connection for an immediate, but shallow, one. But that superficial connection becomes the bond that cements them together.

They then project themselves into the other person's life, presume upon their schedule, make themselves a frequent guest at the other person's home (Prov. 25:17), and speak about this person to others as "my best friend." Whether they mean it or not, the short-circuiter becomes a manipulator of your life. You are being manipulated to meet their emotional needs.

This process is especially easy to pick out at church. We enjoy a lot of open, honest, and loving connections with our church family. How does that make the person feel who doesn't enjoy them? Alone. Left out. Incomplete. Their options are to work hard to have them, leave the community, or short-circuit. The benefit of short-circuiting is it at least looks like they have close friends.

Short-circuiters are not necessarily bad people. They may just be unaware of the dynamics of friendship or may lack the esteem to extend themselves to others. But whether through serious character flaws or just ignorance, the short-circuiter can become a serious drain on your emotional reserves. Also, if you give them a lot of attention and then draw back from them later because of exhaustion, they can turn on you. They will likely become best friends with someone else very soon.

A second superficial attempt at relationship is friendship by opposition. This means we become friends not because of shared mutual interests or similar ethical or moral foundations, but because we share a common enemy. This attempt at friendship is always superficial because the common element we share is a disdain for someone else. That's it. There is nothing noble or honorable about the attitudes that draw us together. Is anger and animosity a healthy element to draw and bind us into friendship?

The irony of friendship by opposition is that former enemies become friends on the basis of their mutual dislike for a third party. This can happen to individuals or even nations, as with our alliance with Stalin and the Soviet Union during World War Two. We were drawn to the Soviets because of a shared enemy: Germany. This was a national friendship by opposition. But, did Stalin prove to be a particularly good friend? Prior to World War II and for some years after, Stalin ordered the wholesale persecution of Christians, quipping that "To make an omelet you have to crack a few eggs" (Martin Amis, *Koba the Dread: Laughter and the Twenty Million*). Literally tens of millions of Russian and Eastern European believers perished at the hands of the anti-Christian government. Communism prevailed and spread throughout Europe, Asia, the Orient, Africa, and South America because friendship by opposition allowed Soviet communism to prevail and prosper.

On an individual basis, friendship by opposition can be seen to wreak havoc in families, businesses and churches. When people who were formerly at odds suddenly start lingering after worship services and talking about another member, or start drinking coffee together because of their anger at the manager, or start complimenting each other in meetings, the leadership needs to pay attention. These people are working an agenda. Their sudden bond is not the result of character transformation; it is the meeting of negative attitudes. They sniff out other angry, discontented people in the body or organization and form their friendships on this basis. Their friendship and work will not be redemptive in nature. The home, church, or workplace will not enjoy a friendlier atmosphere because of their association with one another. Anger breeds anger, and their anger will eventually spew toward the one they share a common disdain for, often burning others in the process.

Genuine friendship is based on character and hard work over the long haul. There is no short-circuiting of the process. There is no friendship by opposition that can be healthy because it is not based on character or hard work. Both attempts at friendship will fail.

Refuse to participate in these devious ploys. They drag you into unholy alliances and denigrate sincere friendship. Maintain your character. Be kind to those who practice scheming ways, but do not participate with them. When possible, practice godly rebuke against those who practice insincere and manipulative forms of relating (Prov. 27:5). You may be ostracized and slandered by the schemers, but you will have your integrity intact.

SEEKING GOODWILL

> The desire of the righteous ends only in good, but the
> hope of the wicked only in wrath.
>
>   Proverbs 11:23

"One man gives freely, yet gains even more; another withholds unduly, but comes to poverty.

A generous man will prosper; he who refreshes others will himself be refreshed. People curse the man who hoards grain, but blessing crowns him who is willing to sell. He who seeks good finds goodwill, but evil comes to him who searches for it" (Proverbs 11:24-27).

In proverbial wisdom, the wise or righteous man lives to the glory of God and for the betterment of others. He realizes he is part of a community of people, in the home, church, workplace, and neighborhood, and he uses his influence and behavior to enhance their lives.

The foolish or unrighteous man lives for his own glory and for the betterment of himself. He may realize he is part of a larger community of people, but his thoughts are not about how he can bless their lives, but of how others can bless him. He uses his influence and behavior for self-gain and aggrandizement.

Bruce Waltke summarizes the distinction between the wise and foolish (or righteous and unrighteous) man in this way: The wise man disadvantages himself for the good of the community while the foolish man disadvantages the community for the good of himself. The wise man will disadvantage himself by sharing his money, food and time to bless the lives of others. The fool expects others to disadvantage themselves by spending their money, food, and time on him.

Since this idea is an underlying theme of Proverbs, it is also likely the idea behind verse 27 and several preceding verses. Verse 24 says that a man who gives freely (perhaps of money, food, and time) receives even more, but the one who is miserly will eventually lose all he has. The generous man in verse 25 shares what he has with others and enhances their lives. In turn, some of that enhancement comes back to him and he is refreshed.

This point can be seen in the Jimmy Stewart movie *It's A Wonderful Life*. Jimmy's character, George Bailey, made a career of helping his neighbors buy houses and start businesses with affordable loans. He gave up his personal dreams of travel to stay in Bedford and defend the people against the wiles of the treacherous financier Mr. Potter. Later, due to an employee's mishandling of his money, George's career and livelihood is threatened and George contemplates suicide. When it looks like he and his family are about to go under, appreciative neighbors show up at his house and place money on his table, enough to cover his financial need and allow him and his family to continue their lives in the community. George's gift of care and service to his neighbors came back to bless him abundantly.

The opposite of the good and generous man is the one who gathers for himself and hoards what he attains, refusing to share. Verse 26 describes a business man who buys grain but holds it until prices climb, giving little thought to the people of the village who need food. This man is thinking only of profits and not of his community's needs. He is disadvantaging the community for the advantage of himself. While this may seem like a reasonable business practice in a profit-driven economy, it is not considered wise or righteous in God's spiritual economy. The man who can conduct business while still maintaining concern for his fellow man will be crowned with blessings (v. 26b).

The essence of verses 24-26 are restated as a principle in verse 27: "He who seeks good finds goodwill, but evil comes to him who searches for it." This should not be understood as a fixed rule or people will be kind and generous not out of sincere motive but to manipulate others for self-interest. You don't give food to the hungry or clothing to the cold so you can demand favor from God. Rather, it is a principle that the kind of relational energy you unleash into the lives of others is what will find its way back to you. Jesus' statement that what you seek you will find (Matt. 7:7; also 6:33) "takes on new meaning; what you seek for others, you will find for yourself." (Waltke, *Proverbs*, 1:509).

CAUTIOUS IN FRIENDSHIP

> A righteous man is cautious in friendship, but the way of
> the wicked leads them astray.
>
> Proverbs 12:26

To be cautious is to be careful. It is to approach something with all senses alert for possible danger. A hiker is cautious in deep woods, his eyes and ears tuned for the presence of a bear or mountain lion. A sailor is cautious on rough seas, navigating the choppy water with great care. A wise man or woman is cautious when making friends, concerned that their genuine affections and good intentions are shared with one of worthy character.

A literal translation of the first part of this verse could read, "'the righteous one will seek out his friend," meaning "one who is righteous takes care in identifying the kinds of friends with whom he or she associates" (Bland, *Proverbs*, 129). Developing a genuine, abiding friendship is not something that can be left to chance or luck. The Hebrew word used for seeking is also used in the Old Testament of Israel spying out the land. It denotes "a careful, diligent, and penetrating examination in order to find what is concealed" (Waltke, *Proverbs*, 1:542-41).

The greatest honor we pay another person is to trust them with our hearts, our secrets, and even our lives. Great care must be exercised to ensure that the one in whom we deposit our treasure is noble and trustworthy, and will treat the exposed contents of our hearts with respect and dignity. Our lives can be damaged, even ruined, if the object of our trust proves unreliable.

A young man's heart burned for a beautiful woman. But because she was a close relative and his desire was inappropriate, his heart and mind were tortured. He dwelled on his desire, increasing his frustration and rendering himself ill.

"What's wrong with you?" a friend asked. "You look pitiful."

"I am pitiful," the young man said. "I'm in love with a beautiful girl but I can't have her. We're too closely related."

"Ah, what are you worried about," the friend replied. "There are ways to get whatever you want. You go to bed and pretend to be ill. Her dad trusts you. Tell him you want his daughter to come fix you something to eat. When she does, well, I think you know what to do then."

The young man pondered the words of his companion. This was indeed a friend, a man with whom he shared his heart, his secrets, even his very life. Hadn't he told the friend about his forbidden desire? He bared his very soul. He trusted his friend and the direction that companionship would take him.

"Sir, I'm quite ill. Would you send your daughter over to fix me something to eat?" The father trusted the young man. The father sent his daughter. And if you have read 2 Samuel 13 you know the rest of the story. The young man, Amnon, followed the advice of his friend. He attacked the object of his desire, the beautiful young woman, Tamar. She was left a broken woman, sentenced to a life of desolation in her brother Absalom's house. Hatred festered in the family until Absalom murdered Amnon. A rift erupted between Absalom and his father David, culminating in Absalom's violent attempt to overthrow David and assume the kingship. Eventually, Absalom died in a brutal, humiliating manner.

A righteous man is cautious in friendship, but the way of the wicked leads them astray. Amnon wasn't cautious. So, instead of experiencing a friendship where each party in the union taught, encouraged, and spurred the growth of the other, Amnon was led astray into horrible behavior with devastating consequences.

We are cautious in friendship because we are influenced by our companions. Righteous friends will lead us on a path of noble and honorable living. Friends who mock at morals and flaunt ethical codes will drag us into destruction with them.

We are cautious in friendship because we become like our friends. Amnon never acted on his lust until led to do so by his friend, Jonadab. It is still Amnon's fault; he made the decision to trust Jonadab, listen to his counsel, and act upon it. But how different the course of his life might have been if he had a companion who said, "Amnon, are you crazy? That is so wrong! You stop this right now!"

Finally, we are cautious in friendship because friends can hurt us. In the case of Jonadab and Amnon, their influence can even kill us.

Among the cries of hurt, remorse, and grief I hear this recurring phrase: "Why did I listen to him/her? Why didn't I just say, 'Go away and leave me alone!?'" From shoplifting to beating up a loner, to alcohol and drug abuse, to sneaking out of the house at night, and to moral indiscretions, we are led like an ox to the slaughter when we listen to the wrong voice.

It was true in Solomon's day; it is true in our own: A righteous man is cautious in friendship, but the way of the wicked leads them astray.

A CHEERFUL LOOK

A cheerful look brings joy to the heart, and good news gives health to the bones.

Proverbs 15:30

Henry David Thoreau wrote, "The mass of men lead lives of quiet desperation. What is called resignation is confirmed desperation...." (Walden). Thoreau applied this saying to men whose work is oppressive and they fail to find satisfaction and enjoyment. But, it could equally apply to those who suffer in silence from any number of blows life can deliver. Think of a family that struggles financially all their lives but never gets their head above water. They miss vacations, new vehicles, and a retirement program they hear so many others talk about.

Think also of a family that struggles with perpetual health issues. They can't eat this; they can't eat that. As neighborhood children gather to play baseball and football, their son or daughter watches from the safety of the living room window, but inside they hurt with a burning desire to be out there among friends, having fun.

A middle-aged man faces his failure every day. Co-workers receive significant promotions and raises while he still languishes in obscurity. None of his hard work and devotion has caught the attention of company executives. He'll end his career largely where it began, low on the rung of corporate position and pay scale.

Every teenage boy and girl knows the feeling of quiet desperation. Every teenager at some point feels alone, isolated, judged, and unworthy. It may be acne, a body that doesn't measure up to the image of feminine beauty or masculine toughness, or general insecurity, but every teenager has felt those devastating emotions. More than few adults have, as well.

A mother of a special needs child wrote this a couple of weeks before Christmas: "We did skip Christmas last year. We had the Christmas morning thing with Stephen and my parents came by on Christmas Eve to bring his presents, but we skipped our family get together. That's right. No Mia's famous cheese ball, no cakes, pies, or fudge. No eggnog, no hot apple cider. Baaah! It was almost as if Ebenezer Scrooge himself lived here (before his transformation). When did I start disliking the holidays so? What used to be my favorite time of year is now something I dread like a root canal. No, that isn't true. I'd rather have a root canal. I think as Stephen has gotten bigger and the care giving has gotten more difficult, I've gotten older and more arthritic. Therefore, the part of me that once enjoyed doing those things was shoved aside as real life, as we know it, forced its way in. I want to enjoy the holidays; I just don't have the strength to get there. Exhaustion is a wicked, wicked little monster."

The feelings of weariness, failure, aloneness, and futility assail most everyone at some point. When those emotions linger, they become stifling and oppressive. Elsewhere the Sage writes, "All the days of the oppressed are wretched" (Prov. 15:15a).

Writing and reading this seems heavy, even oppressive. But, it is the stuff of life, and Proverbs is not afraid of tackling some of the stickiest burdens we face. Proverbs acknowledges that sometimes the painful issues of life attack without mercy and leave our hearts and bones aching.

Proverbs 15:30 addresses the inner being of a person. The heart is the center of emotions and thoughts. It is the inner concept we have of ourselves. We may feel like we are a failure, an outcast, a worthless being. These kinds of negative impressions of ourselves can come from the way others treat us or from our own misbehavior. When David summed up his feelings about his sin with Bathsheba he wrote, "Create in me a pure heart,

O God, and renew a steadfast spirit within me" (Psa. 51:10). David wanted purity of heart to replace the sinful images he had of Bathsheba. But I think he also wanted to feel freedom from condemnation. We repent after we sin and know in our heads that God has forgiven us. But sometimes we carry that shame and reproach of that sin, and we can't feel the freedom of forgiveness. I think that is what is troubling David.

David writes further, "Let me hear joy and gladness, let the bones you have crushed rejoice" (v. 8). God didn't literally crush David's bones. But David is feeling such intense inner pain, it is as if his bones are fractured. You can't do much with fractured bones. You may not be able to stand, walk, or lift anything. Life shuts down. A fractured spirit does the same thing to us. The weight of failure, shame, and loneliness can shut us down like a fractured leg. "Heal me," David pleads. Let the feeling of fractured bones deep in my heart heal so I can enjoy life again."

What can we do for someone who is suffering from any of these debilitating emotions? Proverbs 15:30 mentions two things we can do for the weary spirit.

One, we can give them a cheerful look. A cheerful look may be as simple as a smile or a kind greeting. But the effect of the cheerful look is immeasurable. The cheerful look is "probably the eyes of persons whose good demeanor encourages those with whom they come in to contact" (Longman, *Proverbs*, 323). A sincere cheerful look communicates forgiveness, value, and dignity. That gives fresh hope and life to an aching heart that thinks it is unworthy.

Two, we can speak good news. "Good news gives health to the bones." Sometimes it is hard to know how to speak good news. What do you say to someone who has lost a job, their health, or a loved one? Great care must be given. Ultimately, good news is associated with what we know about Jesus: he loves us, he values us, and he wants to forgive us, no matter what we have done.

The Luke 7 woman could tell us about a cheerful look and good news from Jesus. In her quiet desperation, she barged into a luncheon of Jesus and some important Pharisees. She was a sinful woman, and everyone there knew that. When she touched Jesus' feet, one of the Pharisees thought to himself, "How could Jesus let her touch him? She is a sinner!" Implied in his evaluation of this woman was derision and disgust. No doubt the woman felt the eyes of the Pharisees boring into her with the unspoken message: "You are sickening."

But Jesus let her touch his feet. Then, looking at the woman, he spoke to Simon the Pharisee and said, "Her many sins have been forgiven—for she has loved much." Remember, he spoke to the Pharisee, but looked at the woman as he spoke. And what do you think his stare was like? I'll bet it was cheerful. Jesus gave a cheerful look and good news to this desperate woman. Then he told her, "Your faith has saved you; go in peace." She could go in peace because Jesus brought joy to her heart and health to her bones.

A cheerful look brings joy to the heart, and good news gives health to the bones. We know the one who delivers joy and is the good news—Jesus. We have experienced his healing.

There is a mass of people leading lives of quiet desperation. We can't change their circumstances. They still have to work jobs that may not be fulfilling, work through feelings of failure, loneliness and worthlessness, and struggle with health issues. But we can help change their lives. We can deliver joy and health with the power of our look and the story we tell of Jesus.

PROBLEMS IN COMMUNITY

> He who listens to a life-giving rebuke will be at home among the wise.
>
> Proverbs 15:31

It isn't by accident that God creates community. There is something about the nature and dynamic of people coming together and rubbing shoulders that accomplishes things God wants.

Think about two important communities God puts us in: family and the body of Christ. As a baby, every need is met by the loving care of mothers, fathers, older siblings, and other family members. For the first several years, nearly every aspect of our lives is closely observed and monitored. From eating baby food to saying our first words to taking our first steps, caring adults are hovering over us, helping us along, picking us up, encouraging us, showering us with love, and taking photographs to record key events.

As we grow older, the monitoring stops but the care certainly doesn't. Parents can't be with their children for every step they take, but their hearts and prayers go with them. That's true when they are four, fourteen, or twenty-four. The connection we forge with family members from our debut into the family remains with us for life.

A similar dynamic occurs in the body of Christ when we are born into it. We are now clean and whole; sins are forgiven, stain is removed, and hope reigns. We feel alive. We are greeted by older members with handshakes, hugs, and a lot of encouragement. We take baby steps in our new life, fall down a lot, and get helped up by the encouragement and teaching of our brothers and sisters in Christ.

I remember a young woman struggling to leave alcoholism. She was still young in her sobriety when she climbed the steps to her apartment. At the door of an apartment next to hers was a bottle of wine someone had dropped off. She looked at it and immediately her mind was transported back to her drinking days (which were only a few weeks ago). She sat at the top of the steps frozen in fear. She was afraid to go back into her apartment where she used to do much of her drinking for fear that the feelings would overpower her, she'd get that bottle of wine, and she would drink again.

She was taking baby steps, and she could have fallen very hard. But she didn't. Friends at AA (another powerful community) and some Christians encouraged her through this near-crisis. Even if she had fallen, those same friends would have been there to help her back on her feet. That is what God's communities do for their members, whether it is the biological family or spiritual family of Christ. Community is essential for life.

I'm impressed that God chose to have his son born into a human family and to be nurtured in faith in the spiritual body of Israel. When he began his ministry, Jesus called twelve men to himself that they might be with him (Mark 3:14) and become like him (Acts 4:13). He built a community, one that lasts even today.

Unfortunately, there are sad and hurtful things that happen in families and in the body of Christ that can disillusion us to the value of community. Slights, insults, violent behavior, deceitfulness, immorality, greed, unrestrained anger, and a host of other manifestations of darkness and flesh can crowd out light and life. We can despair of family and church and separate ourselves from them, seeking peace and wholeness in isolation. But, invariably, we will seek out other communities, other connections with people, sometimes even unhealthy connections.

I'm sorry for the pain some people experience in their families and churches. It shouldn't happen, but it does. We get hurt and we hurt others. But I hope that in that pain and disillusionment we can remember where we experienced our biological and spiritual births: in community.

Our communities are imperfect, but even with their faults they can fulfill important functions. "Even with the imperfections of all human community, Jesus sought it out and believed in its power to support and change lives" (Reggie McNeal, *A Work of Heart*, 63). We can believe in it, too.

CHARGING GRIZZLIES

> Better to meet a bear robbed of her cubs than a fool in
> his folly.
>
> Proverbs 17:12.

I've never met a bear robbed of her cubs, and I don't want to! Newspapers in Wyoming and Montana frequently carry stories of hunters or hikers who happen upon a bear cub. Suddenly, charging from the brush comes an 300 pound sow grizzly bearing down ferociously upon the unsuspecting intruder. Time to look for a nearby tree! Too late! The momma grizzly now has the hunter or hiker in her teeth, her ten-penny claws ripping into his arms and legs. After a few seconds, she gives her head a jerk, releases her victim, and sends him flying.

I've read a lot of stories like this one, and I've spoken to guys who've been through this experience. I have a friend with scars on his scalp from his encounter with a grizzly. But, Proverbs says, "You haven't seen anything! You think a quarter-ton of savage grizzly is fearsome? Just wait until you bump into a fool. Even a grizzly would steer clear of a fool."

To appreciate Proverb's comparison of an angry bear to a fool, we need to know something of what the Bible means by a fool.

One, a fool denies God. "The fool says in his heart, there is no God" (Ps. 14:1). Because he lacks faith in a higher power, the fool has no source higher than himself to determine right and wrong. His tendency will be to make decisions that he judges to be good for himself, without adequate consideration for how his decisions will affect others, even his own family. So, Proverbs says, "To have a fool for a son brings grief; there is no joy for the father of a fool." (17:21).

Secondly, a fool does not think or learn. "A rebuke impresses a man of discernment more than a hundred lashes a fool" (Prov. 17:10). This verse implies that even a beating won't knock sense into a foolish person. Ecclesiastes 10:3 is anything but subtle on this: "Even as he walks along the road, the fool lacks sense and shows everyone how stupid he is."

Three, a fool lives without consideration of others. This can make him dangerous. Proverbs 26:9 says "Like a thorn bush in a drunkard's hand is a proverb in the mouth of a fool." A drunk with a thorn bush is going to hurt people. So will a fool, Proverbs says. Even when he may not want to, he cannot help it.

Finally, a fool thinks he is always right and won't listen to the advice or counsel of others. "The way of a fool seems right to him, but a wise man listens to advice" (Prov. 12:15). This is why there is so little help for a fool.

So, how is a fool more dangerous than a ferocious momma bear protecting her cubs? There is a certain order and predictability to her behavior: she wants to protect her cubs. She may only feign an attack in an attempt to scare you away. Or she may actually sink her teeth into your ham bone. You won't know for sure until she actually makes her move. But she is acting on a reasonable presupposition: she fears for the safety of her cubs and wants to protect them. Any attack on you is a defense of her loved ones.

A fool knows no such order and offers no such predictability. Denying God, acting without thinking, and treating others with contempt, he hurts without discrimination. Anyone and everyone, both friend and foe, is potentially a victim. One writer says, "Experiencing the folly of a fool is worse than being the victim of road rage" (Bland, *Proverbs*, 164.)

I don't want to meet any angry momma bears, but my chances of emerging intact are better with her than with a fool. So, exercise caution and steer clear of enraged bears and fools. And let's not be that person, either.

FORGIVENESS HAS A FACE

A man's wisdom gives him patience; it is to his glory to overlook an offense.

Proverbs 19:11

"He did it again, but it will be his last time."

"What are you talking about?" his friend asked Ryan.

"A co-worker up for the same promotion as me undermined my proposal and plans for a project we are working on. His insult left me in a bad light with the boss. If the boss sides with him, I lose the promotion."

"What do you plan to do?"

"At our next staff meeting, I am going to turn this whole thing back on him. I've been working on my presentation, and it includes a very subtle but fatal attack on him. He'll never know what hit him, and I'll ruin his standing in the company."

"Are you sure that is what you want to do?" asked his friend. "You might hurt him and successfully scuttle his career, which will leave you with the promotion. But what does that say about you and your character?"

"What it says about me is I'm standing up for myself and finally putting this guy in his place," Ryan replied.

"Let me encourage you to think about three things," the friend challenged. "One, are you being too sensitive? Your wrath at how you were treated may be justified, but are you taking it too deeply and personally? To me, your anger seems to be out of proportion to the insult you experienced. That could indicate a heart that is too sensitive. You may look for reasons to be hurt, and then for reasons to propound the injuries of the offense. We need hearts that are sensitive to the hurts and needs of others, but we do ourselves an injustice when we apply all that sensitivity to our own situations. It isn't healthy to leave open wounds."

"Secondly, what is your history of feeling insulted, disrespected, and injured? Have you resolved your anger at the perceived injustices perpetrated against you five, ten, and twenty years ago? If not, then you are carrying the emotions of those experiences with you even now. So, your response to your current situation is not isolated to this incident alone, but carries the freight and momentum of many episodes over many years. That is not healthy. And, if you confront your co-worker now, you will unload your past grievances with this new one against him. It is not fair to make him bear your animosities held against other people."

"Thirdly, how are you at letting go? Are you able to lay offenses down and forgive the perpetrator? If not, and you continually relive them, you keep negative emotions brewing. You must learn to forgive.

"Genuine forgiveness has a face on it. Without real people and pain to forgive, forgiveness is just an idea. Real forgiveness wears the faces of the people who have hurt you. How are you at letting go, Ryan?"

Remember this commandment from the apostle Peter: "Do not repay evil with evil or insult with insult, but with blessing, because to this you were called so that you may inherit a blessing" (1 Pet. 3:9). How can we respond so kindly to mistreatment? Remember Jesus. "When they hurled their insults at him, he did not retaliate; when he suffered, he made no threats. Instead, he entrusted himself to him who judges justly" (1 Pet. 2:23). Because Jesus bore insult and personal abuse, we can too. We don't have to seek revenge, get even, or go tit-for-tat. We can overcome hyper-sensitivity, accumulated grievances, and difficulty in forgiving. With Christ's example and empowerment, we can respond in patience and overlook an offense.

WOUNDS FROM A FRIEND

> Wounds from a friend can be trusted, but an enemy multiplies kisses.
>
> Proverbs 27:6

For a year, a Wendy's franchise allowed Cheryl and me to eat their food for free. We would go through the take-out and eat in the restaurant. We were actually being employed to evaluate the quality of the service and food. We had to critically evaluate the promptness of the service, cleanliness, friendliness of the employees, and quality of the food. It was great! But Wendy's wouldn't let me do it for another year. It seems I didn't find enough things wrong to criticize.

Most people don't want to hear, "You were wrong," or "Your performance was lacking," or "Here is how you could do better." Most of us want to hear, "You are the best." How interesting that Wendy's was paying us (the price of the food) to find fault with them (and I was at fault for not finding enough fault!).

There is value in criticism. Granted, the constant critic likely has problems himself, often more severe than the person he is criticizing. But, that does not discount the potential value of at least some of what the critic says. Proverbs 27:6 acknowledges this fact. "Wounds from a friend can be trusted."

Wounds are painful, thus generally unwelcome. We associate wounds with war zones where enemy soldiers shoot at and try to cause harm to each other. Blood, tears, pain and even death accompany battlefield wounds. Such discomfort often accompanies the wounds that occur between people in the home, workplace, and church. These places that should be centers of peace and cooperative effort often resemble a battlefield between enemies rather than places of peace and mutual support.

Wounds can be caused by criticism, rebuke, gossip, putdowns, mockery, even condescending glances that communicate, "You are a nobody."

Such mistreatment hurts deeply in the core of our being. It can make us feel incompetent, insecure, unloved, and like we don't belong in the group. That is painful.

Usually, the wounds caused by unfair criticism, gossip, putdowns, mocking humor, and condescension are meant to hurt us. They are not usually administered by friends, but by those who don't like us or feel threatened by us. They want us to feel every negative emotion that their wounds generate in our hearts.

But the truth of Proverbs 27:6 still stands: Wounds from a friend can be trusted. There is a difference between the office grizzly who seeks to devour all competition or the neighborhood wolf who slinks and stalks until he can deliver a sudden and unexpected attack, and the caring though painful words of a friend. A friend's words may seem to hurt as much as that of the grizzly or wolf, but there is a difference. The friend's wounds are intended to help and heal, not hurt and destroy.

The previous verse says, "Better is open rebuke than hidden love" (27:5). Hidden love is not really love. It is reluctance to confront or tell the truth for fear that you will lose a friend or loved one. Hidden love is remaining silent when someone you care about is careening toward danger or destruction. Hidden love really isn't love. Better than hidden love is a real love that is willing to risk rejection and risk the friendship in the interest of helping the person you care about. Open rebuke is a parent disciplining the child; a spouse confronting the partner about behavior that is threatening the health of the marriage or family; a Christian confronting a brother or sister about behavior that is spiritually immature or unsound.

Jared's preacher pulled him aside after a Sunday service. "Jared," the preacher said, "You are a fine young man with a wonderful family. But there are some things you need to give attention to. Your wife often takes your children to Sunday school, and you are not with them. You are communicating to your sons that Bible study is for women and children, not men. On the occasion you are in class, and we are having a serious discussion about responsibility and family roles, you make jokes. This is not a joking matter. Rather, I feel it is a way for you to evade looking at your role in the home. It is okay to make some jokes, but not at the expense of being serious about things that are very important. Jared, I just think it is time for you to step up and be the man God is calling for you to be."

Jared listened to what his preacher told him. Because of his respect for the older man, he held his tongue and didn't rush to defend himself. But, he didn't like what his preacher told him. He went home and stewed over it. He didn't sleep much that night, and his productivity at work the next day was nil. When his wife inquired about what was bothering him, Jared finally opened up and poured out his contempt for what the preacher said. When he finished his wife calmly asked, "But what if he is right? I do wish you would take a more active role in the home and in the spiritual training of our kids. Even if he overstated the case, don't you think there is some truth in what the preacher said?"

It took time, but Jared finally calmed down enough to soberly reflect upon the rebuke his preacher gave him. As the wounds began to heal, the truth that caused them began to work in Jared's life. He still isn't teaching a Bible class yet, but he is in attendance more, setting a positive example for his kids. He can't help telling the occasional joke, even some poorly timed ones, but even if he isn't comfortable engaging in serious discussion in class yet, he will listen, and he tries taking truth to heart.

Jared experienced wounds, wounds from a friend who cared deeply about him and his family. But he realizes now those wounds from a trusted friend can be trusted to work good in his life, not harm or injury.

Proverbs 20:30 offers further insight into the curative effect of well-timed wounds. "Blows and wounds cleanse away evil, and beatings purge the inmost being." This verse sounds like some of the parenting verses in Proverbs that talk about spanking children. Proverbs 22:15 is one example: "Folly is bound up in the heart of a child, but the rod of discipline will drive it far from him." We know this works on children. Discipline can discourage folly in a child's heart and replace it with serious and mature behavior. But do blows, even if not literally but figuratively, work on adults? They can, if we are humble enough to accept them. "Listen to advice and accept instruction, and in the end you will be wise" (Prov. 19:20).

Advice and instruction don't always come to us in pleasant and palatable ways. Sometimes it is bitter and painful. But if it is true, and if it can improve the quality and spirituality of our lives and family, it is necessary medicine.

There are three things we can do to prepare our hearts to accept rebuke and process the helpful wounds that caring people bring into our lives.

1. Prune our pride. Pride rushes to erect defenses to protect us from the criticism, even the just criticism, of others. Pride seeks to keep our inflated view of ourselves intact. Suppress that urge.

2. Consider the critic. Are the wounds coming from the office gossip or from a person who we know loves us? Knowing the criticism emanates from a caring source can help make it more bearable.

3. Face the future. Does the rebuke have the potential to make us better people in the future? Then let the prospect of becoming a better person soften the blow of the wound.

Two people wielding a knife can have dramatically opposite intentions. With the knife one person can take a life and another can remove damaged or diseased tissue and save a life. If we can resist the impetuous urge to throw up immediate defenses, and consider the intent of the person wielding the weapon, we can endure the wounds designed to make our lives better.

RUDE NEIGHBOR

> If a man loudly blesses his neighbor early in the morning,
> it will be taken as a curse.
>
> Proverbs 27:14.

The Hebrew word for neighbor also means friend. It is used in other verses in the Bible. Leviticus 19:13 says, "Do not defraud you neighbor or rob him." Leviticus 19:18 says, "Love your neighbor as yourself." Both of

these occurrences of neighbor are used in a broad sense, indicating anyone an Israelite would have contact with. But neighbor was also used in
reference to people living in close proximity to each other. Exodus 22:10
discusses the legal issues involved in the injury or theft of farm animals
entrusted to the care of a neighbor. It is reasonable to assume that the
care of these animals would be given to someone living close by. Proverbs
3:28 describes a situation of neighbors borrowing and sharing personal
possessions, something likely to occur among people living in close proximity and are on friendly terms with each other.

To be a friend or neighbor entails certain responsibilities. Our relationships with neighbors should never be damaging or harmful. Proverbs
3:29 admonishes, "Do not plot harm against your neighbor who lives
trustfully near you." Those who do harm their neighbor are considered
godless (Prov. 11:9) and perverse (Prov. 16:28-29). Instead of bringing
harm to his neighbor, the godly man should be caring and thoughtful
of all around him. "A friend (or neighbor) loves at all times" (Proverbs
17:17).

Friend or neighbor has been a key term in this section of Proverbs.
In 27:9, genuine friendship is compared to the sweetness of perfume and
incense. Verse 10 admonishes the honoring of friendships, even those of
one's father, and the blessedness of having a friend or neighbor nearby
when tragedy strikes. Both of these verses emphasize the sweetness and
blessedness of sincere friendships where everyone is thoughtful of each
other. Such relationships are mutually beneficial to all the parties.

But 27:14 introduces a new dynamic: insincerity in relationships. In
this verse a man blesses his neighbor or friend, but the neighbor does not
regard it as a blessing. Instead, he feels the weight of a curse.

Two features of the blessing indicate it is insincere and masks underlying attitudes and intents that are malevolent. One, the blessing is loud.
The Hebrew word means "loudness in sound, being old in years, great in
importance" (Smick, *Theological Wordbook of the OT*, 1:151). In 1 Kings
8:55, "loud" is used in reference to Solomon standing before the entire
congregation and speaking loudly enough for all to hear him. As the king,
Solomon was great in importance and speaking before a large crowd

would necessitate his speaking boldly and with great volume. The use of this word in reference to greeting a neighbor would indicate this was not a typical expression of "good morning," but was unusually boisterous for a greeting between neighbors and likely had a pompous flair.

Another feature of the blessing is that it was early in the morning when the neighbor was possibly still at rest or preparing for the day. The greeter "aims to make the impression that he has a deep veneration for his neighbor ... (but) his unnatural voice and timing betray him as a hypocrite" (Waltke, *Proverbs*, 382). The greeter has less concern for the welfare of his neighbor than he does for his own convenience. He is actually abusive, inconsiderate, and rude, so his insincere greeting is taken as a curse.

Proverbs 27:14 exposes the insincerity we may mask with shallow politeness. Overt rudeness is hurtful and unappreciated, but it at least has a degree of sincerity to it. The loud blessing in the morning is rudeness masked in hypocrisy and is to be avoided by one walking in proverbial wisdom.

FRICTION

> As iron sharpens iron, so one man sharpens another.
>
> Proverbs 27:17

Iron sharpens iron through friction. Friction is the result of pressure. Two things rubbing together cause the pressure, resulting in heat. As a result of the friction, the iron, as in a knife, becomes sharper.

The same thing happens to people. As we rub against each other in family or church, we create friction. We can make each other "hot" with our displeasure toward each other. The desired result of this proverb is that we become better people.

We often read Proverbs 27:17 and think we sharpen and make each other better people by positive influence, friendliness, and encouragement. And that is true. Positive relationships and encouraging personalities can motivate our personal improvement. But, the emphasis in this verse does not seem to be on the pleasantness of relationships, but on the stress and strain of them.

Friction in a relationship means there is a problem. There is heat between people caused by disagreement or even bad behavior. Someone in the relationship may be rude, judgmental, or mocking. Such a relationship is anything but pleasant. This seems to be the relationship that Proverbs 27:17 has in mind when it says that iron sharpens iron.

What do we commonly do when there is negative pressure with other people? One, we try to avoid the friction. We get away from the other person or situation. Sometimes that may be necessary. The Bible warns us to steer clear of dangerous situations and personalities (such as an angry person, Proverbs 22:24-25).

Two, we crumble. If we are too soft, or too sensitive, we may cave in from the friction of the abrasive personality. We may get our feelings hurt and shut down emotionally.

Three, we get defensive. We may get mad and even hostile, leading us to focus on the faults of the other person and criticize them.

These are not the only choices we have toward someone when our relationship with them is strained. We don't have to avoid the heat, crumble under it, or get defensive. All three of these approaches blind us to what we can learn from the situation, including any character flaws that may be operative in our own lives. For example, if we experience anger at another, does that necessarily mean they have wronged us? Couldn't it reveal that we have wronged them, and anger blinds us to our own contribution to the problem?

Friction means we are rubbing up against another person's personality or habits and it isn't working very well. Instead of assuming the heat is bad, look for something good. It may mean our own rough edges are being rubbed off by the abrasive nature of the relationship, forcing us to change to live successfully in community.

Don't run from the friction. Stay in there with the other person. Look at your life. Ask what is going on; why you feel annoyed; why you want to run; why you feel like you are crumbling; why you want to react against the other person. Your answers may tell you something about the other individual. More importantly, your answers may tell you something about yourself.

Remember, when there is friction between two people, God maybe be trying to make something good happen. Work with him on that. You may be the iron God is trying to sharpen.

IRON SHARPENS IRON

> As iron sharpens iron, so one man sharpens another.
>
> Proverbs 27:17

Two "irons" are mentioned in this verse. One iron is the knife or sword and the second iron is the sharpening iron that hones them. The pressure of iron rubbing against iron is an abrasive action that creates friction. Through this friction the hardness of the one material wears and shapes the other. The knife or sword is worn and sharpened by the harder iron, making it more useful and effective as a tool. In the same way, friends, over time, have the effect of changing and shaping each other, hopefully for good.

The hardness of the iron images the hardness of a caring friend's persistence. As a result of his untiring devotion to a relationship, the "hard" man (that is, the man with a firmly shaped and honed character) is able to sharpen his friend. This sharpening may occur through offering encouragement and instruction in wisdom, but can also come through offering rebuke.

"He who tends a fig tree will eat its fruit, and he who looks after his master will be honored" (Prov. 27:18).

The wise take care of and honor those who employ them. "Fruit" is a metaphor for the consequences of one's behavior. Those who take care of the fruit tree will enjoy the results of their activity; they will get to enjoy the fruit. Similarly, those who tend to the needs or expectations of their master will enjoy the fruit of honor.

Bruce Waltke identifies numerous truths in the metaphors of the fig tree and the diligent servant. One, the fig tree was one of the most highly prized trees in Israel and was given great care. This is the mindset a faithful servant should have toward his master. Two, to protect meant to be "careful, precise and vigilant." Three, protecting and guarding is not an occasional disposition of the farmer or servant, but one of constant devotion. Four, just as it takes years of gentle planting and care of fig trees to enjoy its succulent fruit, it may take years of devoted service to earn the honor of a master. Five, as the fruit of the fig is sweet and refreshing, so is the honor received from a master. Six, the rewards are enduring. A healthy fig tree will continue to bear fruit for years, and a pleased master will bestow his favor upon a trustworthy servant for the duration of their relationship. (Waltke, *Proverbs*, 2:385)

Each of these truths mentioned above have bearing upon the interpretation and understanding of the rude neighbor and the argumentative spouse mentioned two verses earlier. These latter verses deal with the theme of friction in relationships, patience, endurance, change, and ultimate reward. Verses 17-19 describe how the offended neighbor and the verbally abused husband are to respond to the affronts paid to them.

Just as the farmer is to tend the fig tree with diligence and the servant heed the will of his master, so is the offended neighbor and spouse to give devoted attention to the needs of the friend and wife. They may have to provide care and attention for years before they get to enjoy the delicious fruit of the relationships (mutual respect for the neighbors; peace and intimacy for the spouses), but such a positive outcome can only happen if they exercise diligent care, service, and even rebuke.

Interaction with others can be peaceful or chaotic. While it could be hoped that every encounter would be friendly and pleasant, they are not. Frequently in involvement with the lives of others, rudeness, disdain, and even open hostility are experienced. But, while such encounters are not pleasant, from the perspective of proverbial wisdom and character building, they are not without value, either. It may be that from some of the more distasteful and painful experiences with other people, including one's neighbor or spouse, character growth and development takes place (Bland, "Iron Sharpens Iron" in *Leaven*, 8:2, 2000).

ABSOLUTE SURRENDER

In all your ways acknowledge (or, submit to) him, and he
will make your ways straight.

Proverbs 3:6

Unconditional surrender refers to the complete capitulation of
the enemy. Unconditional surrender means we are not going to negotiate terms of surrender with them. There won't be any discussion about
whether or not we will let them keep a certain portion of their military
or weapons. They won't get to negotiate about if they have to make repa-
ration payments after the war to pay for the expenses of their conquering
enemy. They don't get to discuss border issues. If one of the conquering
nations wants to take land, property, houses, even factories and businesses from the losers, they just take them. They don't even get to negotiate
the treatment of their people. A nation that offers unconditional surrender means that even their own citizens can be taken into a foreign country
for slave labor. There are no negotiations, no pleas, no agreements. The
winner dictates every term of the surrender and the loser has no recourse
but to obey. Terms of surrender under such conditions can last for generations.

World War II is a recent example of an unconditional surrender being offered to Germany. The Germans would have terms dictated to them
and they would obey, completely. In the end Germany gave up land to
foreign countries, citizens to foreign labor, and billions of dollars in repa-
ration payments. Unconditional surrender is tough.

But there is a place for unconditional surrender, especially in our own
lives. Unconditional surrender is something we must practice personally.
Remember that unconditional surrender means we have no rights, freedom, or privileges. It means we are at the mercy of others. It is a miserable
state! But sometimes, unconditional surrender is the only hope we have.

In her book *When His Secret Sin Breaks Your Heart*, Kathy Gallagher
addressed a letter to a wife whose husband had committed some terrible
sins against her. The woman first wrote to Kathy and said, "He doesn't
love me or the babies at all; he's just consumed with himself." Kathy tells

the wife that her husband is totally self-absorbed.

His total self-absorption could crumble. The terrible sin he is prac-ticing will one day weary him out. He may then come crawling back to his family pleading to be let back into the home. He will have to confess his sin and bring it into the open to be dealt with. Kathy says, "It takes sin like this in some lives to bring them to the place of total and absolute surrender" (p.127).

Kathy uses the term, "absolute surrender," a parallel term for uncon-ditional surrender. It means the husband, if he ever wants to come home and be restored to his family, is going to have to swallow his pride, his dignity, and his honor. They are actually all destroyed anyway by his be-havior. But now he even has to give up any pretense of them. He can't pretend to be in control or in charge. He can offer no self-defense. He has no control over his life or situation. All he can do is throw himself at the mercy of God and his family and beg for mercy and forgiveness. He must pray that over time God will restore his character and hope his wife and children will love him, trust that he has changed, and welcome him home. He cannot make any demands or set any of the rules. When you sin big, you lose big. But in your loss is your only real hope for something better to come from it— restoration to God and your family. When God destroys your pride and love of sin, he allows something else to grow in its place: humility, love, life, salvation, and restoration. So, go ahead, give it a try, unconditionally surrender to the will of God and his power in your life.

ACTING OUT

The words of a person's mouth are deep waters ...

Proverbs 18:4a

A teenage friend of ours was being uncharacteristically rude on a youth trip. One sponsor suggested taking her home. "She has no right talking the way she is."

Since this was not her normal behavior, we knew there was some-thing operating beneath the surface level. Something was eating at her heart and soul.

Young people (perhaps all of us) act out for several reasons. One is that acting out is fun. There is a certain thrill that comes with crossing forbidden lines.

A second reason is that young people are sinners. Why do any of us sin? Before we give ourselves to Christ we have an unregenerate nature that exerts its will and pushes us into rebellious behavior.

Thirdly, kids act out because they want attention. It is horribly chilling to feel we are all alone. Kids see others in what appears to be genuine relationships, and they yearn to be in one themselves. If they have any estrangement with their family, they are doubly lonely. So, they may act out just to get recognized. In *Blind Spots* author Bill McCartney notes this tendency in kids who act out, and says they "are often comforted just from the fact that their parents care enough to get angry and come back at them" (p.74). Taking the time to engage with your child through sports, music, or whatever interests them can prevent much heartache later on.

Finally, kids can act out because they are carrying a terribly heavy burden. In the case of our young friend, we learned shortly afterwards that she had an abortion just before the youth trip. When the baby's father found out she was pregnant, he yelled at her and said, "Get rid of it! Get rid of it!" Her parents thought she was too young to have a baby, so they supported the abortion as well. Everyone seemed to want the abortion except this sweet girl. Now, weeks after the abortion, her heart was bursting with sadness, shame, and guilt. That is why she was so verbally offensive in the vehicle. She was crying out, "There is something horrible in my life that I need help with, but I can't tell you! I'm too ashamed! Instead, I'll act like the terrible person I think I am and I hope you can pick up on it. Please don't be put off by my mean speech. Read beneath the lines and help me, please!"

It is hard for a teenager that is lonely or carrying a secret sin to make themselves vulnerable to anyone. Being vulnerable in a relationship (as with the teenage girl above) may be the reason they are hurting now, so why risk any further hurt or rejection from an adult? Acting out with offensive behavior or speech seems a better option, since it now places the burden to act on the adult.

The Bible warns that our speech should be wholesome and our be-havior thoughtful of others (Eph. 4:29-32). Improper talk and behavior must be addressed. But, remember that lurking underneath the offending words and actions may be something more than a mischievous or sinful heart. There may also be a heart that is lonely and broken, one crying out for healthy attention from a concerned adult.

If someone has singled you out for some uncharacteristically sharp words, resist responding too quickly. Pause and look beneath the surface. There may be a heart crying out to you for help.

CHAPTER TEN

MATTERS OF THE HEART

DO YOU HAVE THE WISDOM OF SOLOMON?

These are more Proverbs of Solomon ...

Proverbs 25:1

Some historians consider Thomas Jefferson to be the smartest man to hold public office in America. Jefferson was a voracious reader on government and economics, so he was able to compare the various systems of government in history and help devise the American system. When he was in France and the American leaders were working on our constitution, Jefferson sent books to James Madison to educate him on republican forms of government.

Jefferson never wrote a book, but he did pen thousands of letters on a dozens of subjects. Many of his letters have been collected and published. Jefferson wrote about theology, architecture, orthography, exploration, grammar, prosody, animal husbandry and breeding, medicine, surgery, arts, manufacturing, philosophy, history, educational theory and practice, economics, monetary science, anatomy, zoology, botany, inventions, patents, mathematics, pendulums, geology, anthropology, antiquarian society, sculpture, painting, naval warfare, military science, languages, aeronautics, physics, meteorology, astronomy, paleontology, natural history, civil engineering, agriculture, rural development, and human advancement. Thomas Jefferson could have taught college level courses on many of these topics (Martin Larson, *Jefferson: Magnificent Populist*). But as brilliant as he was, another man eclipses him: Solomon.

Solomon prayed for wisdom and received instruction in wisdom from his father (if we can take Proverbs 4 literally). First Kings 4:29-34 says Solomon wrote 3,000 proverbs and 1,005 songs. He studied botany, zoology, and other subjects. People of many nations came to listen to Solomon speak. His wisdom was known world-wide.

Reading about these two guys makes me think, "I'll never have the intellectual grasp of the subjects these men have." And that may be okay. I don't know if it matters how much we know as much as what we know. Two things about what Solomon knew and his application of that knowledge stands out.

One, Solomon's learning didn't penetrate the depths of his heart. He had this tremendous knowledge in his head, but for some reason key elements of it didn't make it to his heart. Solomon did not direct his worship to God alone (1 Kings 11:7-13). Because he worshiped foreign Gods, his kingdom eventually split.

Two, Solomon didn't pass all of his knowledge on to his kids. His son Rehoboam became the next king of Israel. 1 Kings 12 relates the story about the northern part of the kingdom wanting Rehoboam to make work and living conditions easier. Rehoboam asked the aged men of Israel for advice, and they told him to lighten the load on his subjects. Then he talked to the younger men, his own peer group, and they told him to make the load heavier. They said to threaten to beat the people more severely than Solomon did. Rehoboam took the advice of the younger men and the kingdom split. Rehoboam was left with only two of the twelve tribes. When you read the proverbs, which Rehoboam's father helped write, you see over and over how younger men are to listen to the advice of older men. Rehoboam didn't do that. He listened to the advice of the younger and lost.

With all of Solomon's wisdom, two things stand out: he didn't follow his own advice, and he didn't thoroughly instruct his children. That's why I think what we know probably matters more than how much we know. Here is what Paul said, "I resolved to know nothing while I was with you except Jesus Christ and him crucified" (1 Cor. 2:2).

One thing that ultimately matters is that we know Jesus Christ. In Christ we have the forgiveness of sins (Acts 2:38), salvation (Acts 4:12), and eternal life (John 3:16).

Do you know the genus of all the animal kingdom? The latest stock figures? Statistics of the professional football and baseball players? Well, it really doesn't matter. But, do you know Jesus Christ?

Secondly, what we do matters as much as or more than what we know. Many people know about Christ, but have they confessed his name? Repented? Been baptized? It is one thing to have the information; it is another thing to act upon it.

Solomon knew to worship only the one God of heaven, but he didn't; he worshiped other gods. Solomon knew to pass on the instruction about wise living to his son. Apparently he didn't. What we know matters, and what we do with that knowledge matters more.

LAND MINES

> The path of the righteous is like the first gleam of dawn,
> shining ever brighter till the full light of day. But the way
> of the wicked is like deep darkness; they do not know
> what makes them stumble.
>
> Proverbs 4:18, 19

Into the black of night shines the first gleam of dawn, dispelling the darkness and giving sight to our eyes. This experience of first light and the ability to see is a metaphor for the spiritual light that shines into our hearts when we follow the way of godly wisdom and walk in the path of righteousness. The righteous can see the dangers of foolish living because God's light, mediated through the wise words of the Sage and other godly teachers, enlightens their heart. In the wisdom of Proverbs, such behavior as anger, resentment, adultery, excessive spending, gossip, miserliness, inconsiderate humor, lying, violence, theft, laziness, incessant talking, and unreflective speech are foolish and sinful. The wise pursue the path away from these things, continually seeking the light of God.

The wicked do not live in the light but in the darkness, so they cannot see the dangers that follow sinful and foolish living. They stumble along, as in the black of night, losing friendships, getting into trouble, losing their money, constantly arguing and fighting, shattering families, and they "do not know what makes them stumble," even though it is their own behavior. Two common responses of foolish people to the harm that comes into their lives are: "It is someone else's fault" and "Why am I always so unlucky?"

Even those who pursue the light and try living wisely encounter situations that make them stumble, and they do not know why. They try to maintain healthy attitudes of love and gratitude, and they try to live righteously, but they occasionally find themselves inexplicably acting out of character. They may explode in anger, flirt, be immoral, or tear down another's reputation. How can ten or fifteen years of righteous living be disrupted by such unusual behavior in a good person's life?

A preacher meeting with a young ministry couple told them, "If you have any unresolved issues in your lives, address them now, early in your marriage and ministry. If you have any neglect, abuse, deep-seated anger, or aberrant behavior, get it out and address it now. Seek counseling if you need help identifying and addressing some of the problems. A few years from now the pressures of marriage, family, and ministry will squeeze you like a sponge, and if you don't have your inner issues resolved, they will erupt out of your life with ugly and destructive force."

Leslie Chapman says we all have land mines in our lives. A land mine is an explosive device used by the military during a war. It is buried just under the surface of the ground, typically on a path frequented by the opposition. An enemy soldier walking along will unknowingly step on the land mine and trigger the mechanism, causing an explosion that will surely maim, and possibly kill, the one who stepped on it and others standing nearby.

Usually after a war, land mines are removed. But, they can't all always be accounted for and some remain in place. For years after the war is over, civilians can be injured and killed when they unsuspectingly step on one.

Land mines in our lives are like that, too. Even after righteous living for many years, an event or conversation can trigger a land mine that has been buried in our lives for years, even decades. The trigger might be a perceived slight, an injustice, financial pressure, changes in the home, business failure, and a host of other things. The trigger takes us back, immediately, to the unresolved painful emotions we experienced years before. In nanoseconds we relive the original experience and feel the emotions of it. So, when we react to the trigger event, we are not responding to it like we think we are, but to the unresolved event from years before. And, like the land mine, we explode with destructive force against innocent people who had nothing to do with our original problems.

Land mines in our lives can take several forms. For some, significant pressure can lead them to explode in wrath and rage. They may make harsh accusations and even threats. When the rage subsides and emotions settle, they will ask themselves, "What just happened? Why did I do that? I'm not even that upset with the guy; in fact, he is my friend."

For someone else, significant stress and pressure, particularly if it is at home, may lead them to seek relief in the wrong set of arms. But, feeling failure or lack of appreciation at work can be triggers for immoral behavior, too. Someone dwelling excessively on self-pitying emotions and thinking "I deserve to be treated better," is a prime candidate for an affair. There is a man or woman out there who is equally desperate for attention, and will readily grant you the understanding and affection you seek.

Land mine explosions are not limited to angry eruptions or adultery. They can include belittling humor, pornography, stealing, lying, and violence. A land mine explosion is any behavior that is foolish or sinful and is out of character for the person performing it. After their aberrant and unusual acting out, they wonder where the bad attitudes and behavior came from. Like the man walking in darkness, they do not know what made them stumble.

You cannot undo a land mine, but you can learn from it and even profit from it. Here are some suggestions for dealing with the land mine episodes in your life.

One, own the emotions and behavior. Yes, it may have been out of character, but we said it or did it. We are guilty and should admit it. Denying, minimizing, or dismissing the sinfulness and destructiveness of our actions will not erase them, but will simply re-bury the land mine, readying it with another deadly charge. "If we confess our sins, he is faithful and just and will forgive us our sins and purify us from all unrighteousness" (1 John 1:8). Openness and honesty are the beginning steps to shine light into the darkness of our hearts and purge the evil.

Two, take stock of what happened. What was the trigger that made us explode? Why were we so unstable and combustible? Have similar events happened in our past that we didn't address then? Is it possible that these past experiences are lying just under the surface of our heart and are too easily activated? Talking to a friend or even a counselor may help identify patterns in our life and behavior that will reveal unresolved issues.

Three, don't blame anyone else for our current or past problems. Parents who were neglectful, siblings who were abusive, or former employers who were unappreciative may explain some of our unstable tendencies, but simply blaming them will not relieve us of the problems. The problems are ours to deal with.

Four, make amends when possible and appropriate restitution to anyone we have hurt. Apologize, make repayment for anything we have damaged or taken, and seek reconciliation. A third party may be necessary to help with this.

Five, work on character. Continue walking in the path of righteousness. Seek God's will for all things in our lives. Pray for strength in areas of weakness. Do not leave the land mines unresolved. Left unattended they will eventually explode, and the damage they cause can be irreparable.

Through Christ we have been set free from the law of sin and death (Rom. 8:2). But, even though we have crossed from death to life in Christ, the heart continues to be a battleground where the old man of sin and the new man of righteousness struggle for control. We have to submit to the Spirit of Christ that now reigns in our hearts and is actively working to purge the sinful nature. "Therefore, do not let sin (a land mine) reign in your mortal body so that you obey its evil desires" (Rom. 8:12).

God is working to purge our lives of darkness and the foolishness, sin, and land mines that proliferate in it. We can submit our will to his, humbly and honestly admit sin, and seek God's work in our lives for character transformation, and the light of Christ will give us peace.

PRIDE & QUARRELS

> Pride only breeds quarrels, but wisdom is found in those who take advice.
>
> Proverbs 13:10

Two sets of opposites are contrasted in this verse: pride vs. advice and strife vs. wisdom. One attitude produces behavior that ushers in peace, the other produces behavior that shreds relationships.

Pride is "an exaggerated opinion of one's importance within society and a refusal to accept one's place within its structure under God ..." (Waltke, *Proverbs*, 1:560). Pride is foolishness, and the opposite of wisdom, because it runs counter to the order God has established, with himself as the sovereign and the rest of us as his subjects. Elevating ourselves disturbs God's ranking, creating chaos and disorder.

Quarreling is one manifestation of the disorder. Quarrels disturb what should be harmony in relationships between family, friends, and fellow worshipers. It prevents people from enjoying relaxation and bonding together. Quarrels also disturb periods of worship that should be observed with reverence for God and in communion with fellow worshipers.

Isaiah bemoaned worship in his day that was disrupted by pride and quarreling. "'Why have we fasted,' they say, 'and you have not seen it? Why have we humbled ourselves, and you have not noticed?'" (58:3a). Isaiah corrects the false notion about their own humility when he responds, "On the day of your fasting you do as you please and exploit all your workers. Your fasting ends in quarreling and strife and in striking each other with wicked fists" (Is. 58:3b-4). These worshipers refused to accept their place in the structure under God. They elevated themselves over their fellow worshipers and workers, abusing some and fighting others. Pride disrupted the family of God.

Remember the destructive pride of Pharaoh? In his elevated view of himself, he simply could not allow any counsel to penetrate his hard heart. He wouldn't listen to the word of God delivered by Moses, and even after nine plagues besieged the land, he still adamantly refused to let the Israelites go. Only after the tenth plague, when every family in Egypt wept at the loss of a first-born, did he finally say, "Go!" Even then, he changed his mind and tried to bring the Israelites back.

Pharaoh's pride bred quarrels and strife at every level of Egyptian society: between Egyptians and Hebrews, Hebrew slaves among each other, and the Hebrews against their own leader, Moses. And his pride led to such loss of life that "there was not a house without someone dead" (Ex. 12:30).

Arrogance and fighting leads to painful consequences, but the fallout is not limited to them alone. The destructive force of pride and quarreling affect even innocent and unsuspecting bystanders. How many innocent people perished for the sin of Pharaoh?

Let's bring this closer to home. Pride is not only the property of powerful leaders like kings, presidents, and business tycoons. Pride can infect any of us, and often does. Has pride ever kept us from forgiving a neighbor or even our own spouse? Has pride kept us from seeking the forgiveness we need for ourselves? Has pride prevented us from seeking wise counsel to help our marriage or improve our parenting skills? In our pride, have we ever looked with condescension upon a brother or sister with whom we disagreed, pleased with our own rightness and judgmental of their misguided views? Much of the discord that finds its way into our marriages, parent-child relationships, friendships, and church life may be credited to that sinister invader: arrogant pride.

Fortunately, there is good news. While pride only breeds quarrels, wisdom is found in those who take advice. Wisdom is life lived under the direction of God and his influence upon our hearts. That influence is exerted through scripture, experience, and the wise counsel of godly people. The challenge for us is to lay aside our assumptions about our own importance and rightness, and be willing to listen to the voice of God in the different ways it is mediated to us. Blessed is the man, Proverbs says, who listens to such counsel. He will find wisdom, he will enjoy richness of life, and he will receive the favor of God (Prov. 8:32-35).

LISTENING

> Even in laughter the heart may ache, and joy may end in grief.
>
> Proverbs 14:13

I lost my first baking contest to cardboard. I made my mother's specialty plum cake. I followed her recipe and her advice as I cut the plums, set them in the batter, heated the oven, and timed my masterpiece. I didn't get to sample my own cake until all of the entries were cut and everyone got to eat from each other's creations.

Everyone liked the plum cake and assurances abounded that I would win the contest. But then one more cake was produced. It was chocolate, and I have to admit that it looked delicious. Everyone gathered around the table as the chocolate masterpiece was cut, and it was at that moment I knew who won the contest.

There are different ways of determining the winner of any contest. For a cake baking contest, I thought it would be the taste of the entrée, and initially that was to be the determining factor. The rules changed in midstream and humor became the determining factor. It seems my fellow contestant simply applied chocolate icing to a heart-shaped box. He did so with such artistic flair that the cake truly did look amazingly delicious. And it was not until the hostess tried cutting into the dessert that she, and all of us, discovered the true nature of the enticing entrée: cardboard.

The laughter that followed won the day, and the contest was decided on the basis of creativity and humor. Taste was no longer a factor.

I think of this story when I read that "Even in laughter the heart may ache." Laughter can be like a coating of enticing chocolate: creamy, dark, and inviting. But it may mask a deep incongruity—there is no substance to the appeal. What looks tantalizing is really fake, fraudulent, and terribly disappointing. It isn't fluffy and tasty; it is cardboard.

How much laughter do we hear from people who are using the appearance of joy and levity to mask inner pain, guilt, and shame? How many people find it easier to force a fake laugh than to admit to their true, painful inner dispositions? Even in laughter, the heart may ache.

Laughter is good and healthy, but only when it is honest and genuine. Icing on a real cake is not only inviting; it is enjoyable when the inner substance is real cake. But when it is mere cardboard, it disappoints, and if you lose a contest because of it, it can even be annoying.

Listen to the laughter of others; listen for any signs that the laughter may be masking greater hurt. You may be able to help. And, let's listen to our own laughter. Let's learn to gauge our own hearts, lest our apparent joy end in grief—grief that could have been avoided.

God promises that one day all tears shall be dried. In that day, laughter will emanate from the depths of our hearts and reverberate with genuine joy and celebration. Until then, we continue to do the work of sorting through the content of the heart, turning our bruises and aches over to the heavenly father, who heals them with his presence in our lives.

WE CAN ENCOURAGE

> A cheerful look brings joy to the heart, and good news
> gives health to the bones.
>
> Proverbs 15:30

Scripture urges us to encourage others, but too often people and situations discourage us. You can bet we serve as someone else's source of discouragement.

Three things make it difficult to actively encourage other people. First is our own wounded spirit. Some children are subjected to a barrage of constant criticism, putdowns, and other forms of verbal abuse. Successes are ridiculed and accomplishments downplayed. Instead of developing a sense of self-esteem and feeling good about themselves, they doubt their own worth and value. What they don't see is that their woundedness is actually a powerful resource to help other wounded people who feel beaten and bashed. God has them placed in a unique position to be able to say, "I've been there. I understand." Those five words may be the most refreshing speech a hurt and lonely soul may hear.

Two, we lack knowledge of how to encourage. Knowledge comes from teaching and observing. In some families humor is used routinely to embarrass, especially those who are younger. It is often not meant to be malicious, but is intended as a form of humor. However, in such circumstances, we are not teaching our children to be encouragers.

It is imperative that we receive positive feedback from those close to us, especially in the formative years, for the benefit of our self-esteem. This doesn't mean that misbehavior is not corrected, for certainly it must be. But it does mean that the honest effort and positive accomplishments of children (or anyone) be recognized (Eph. 6:4). Receiving such affirmation creates a desire in us to encourage others and helps develop the insight and skills to be able to.

A negative cycle of belittling humor and painful speech can be broken when we take the encouragement verses of scripture seriously. Why does the Bible emphasize the importance of building others up so much? Because we need it and we need to learn how to encourage others. We can also break this cycle if we pay attention to how other people make us feel based on the way they speak to and treat us. What attracts us to certain personalities? What do we find offensive? If we are made to feel a certain way by how people treat us, we can be reasonably sure when we act in similar ways to others, they will be either encouraged or hurt. That insight can help us change to become more encouraging.

A third reason it is difficult to encourage others is that we may be envious. Envy is the resentment we feel toward someone for their success and accomplishment. Someone has said that we love genius, but only at a distance. We don't mind their bright light outshining ours if they are in another classroom. Or on another continent. If they are in our little orbit and we are regularly overshadowed by their brilliance, we can resent it. How will we respond? If we can admire their splendor and seek to learn from them, we can grow under their influence. But what if they are younger than us, have less training, or are a bit arrogant in their success? Will we be grateful for their contributions and humbly learn from them?

If we cannot appreciate and honor the accomplishments of other people, our heart becomes a battle ground for envy. If we can't be humble and gracious before the successful, then we must assert ourselves over them. We do that through gossip and malicious talk to reduce their esteem. We make disparaging comments. We critically evaluate their performance, typically offering negative feedback (often under the guise of constructive criticism). When envy is assailing our heart, we don't have much spirit left to encourage.

To counter an envious spirit, we must first realize that it is a core sin that births many other sins (James 3:16). After repenting of it, we can pray for a spirit of gratitude and a humble spirit to be able to encourage others rather than detract from them.

There are several things that work against being able to encourage others, but all of them can be overcome by the Spirit of God at work in our lives. A cheerful look or encouraging word refreshes both the giver and the receiver.

IS PEACE POSSIBLE?

> When a man's ways are pleasing to the LORD, he makes
> even his enemies live at peace with him.
> Proverbs 16:7

War rages all around us. Countries war with each other on the international scene and our country is often involved. War rages on the national scene as well. Fighting and violence erupt not only in our larger cities, but even in smaller towns regarded as peaceful. We hear too many stories of people opening fire on unsuspecting citizens. We can see war rage in the home, too. Family too often becomes the locus of verbal and physical abuse. Sadly, children learn how to be violent in the very realm where they are supposed to learn peace and love.

War is caused by greed, anger, and envy. These unwholesome attitudes drive nations, social groups, and families to hurt and abuse. One group acts in violence causing another group to respond in kind. As we know from history, violence can spread from cities to countries and even most of the world. We have seen wars where the victims of violence number in the tens of millions.

There is one other place where war rages, a place so basic that it is really the birthplace for the other wars we see on a larger scale. There could never be violence in a family, a nation, or the world unless there was first violence in this other place. That place is the human heart.

The Sage describes a scoundrel and villain as one whose heart is a boiling cauldron of unholy attitudes. He is one "who goes about with a corrupt mouth ... who plots evil with deceit in his heart —he always stirs up dissension" (Prov. 6:12-14). The turmoil the scoundrel creates in his outer world begins first in his own inner world.

This inner war that rages in the human heart is described further in Galatians 5:19-21: "The acts of the sinful nature are obvious: sexual immorality, impurity and debauchery; idolatry and witchcraft; hatred, discord, jealousy, fits of rage, selfish ambition, dissensions, factions and envy, drunkenness, orgies, and the like."

Paul pictures a soul that is at war with itself. Internal attitudes of hate and violence war against the very soul that gives them residence. The person whose heart is tortured with these emotions does violence against himself with innumerable weapons of spiritual destruction: low self-value, self-loathing and doubting God.

The heart is not big enough to contain this war. It soon erupts outside the person's own heart and life and rages against family members and friends. The war soon takes on the weapons of criticism, gossip, immorality, and drunkenness. The destruction at work in the unregenerate heart is now shared with other victims.

The scale for this progress of violence and destruction continues to press forward until it encompasses the whole world. Nations war against nations over every conceivable cause. Most of the reasons can be traced back to something Paul named over two thousand years ago: a sinful nature that "desires what is in conflict to the Spirit ..." (Gal. 5:17).

The realm of the Spirit is so far removed from the realm of the flesh or sinful nature as to constitute a totally alien reality to what most of us see and know in this world. Paul also describes this realm to us: "The fruit of the Spirit is love, joy, peace, patience, kindness, goodness, faithfulness, gentleness and self-control." (Gal. 5:19-20). These attitudes are alien to many of us because we so rarely see them manifested in the public arena. Greed and self-promotion get the headlines. They propel this world. They generate war at every level.

So, is peace possible? Yes. Definitely, yes. Every person that renounces the reign of the sinful nature in their heart and submits to the rule of God's Spirit undermines war at all levels. When a man's ways are pleasing to the Lord, he makes even his enemies live at peace with him. Peace, because it is endowed with God's nature, can trump hatred and violence. Do we believe that? Our answer may reveal just how energetically we are preaching and practicing the message of God's peace (Col. 1:20).

JUDGMENT OR MERCY?

> Pride goes before destruction, a haughty spirit before a fall.
>
> > Proverbs 16:18

Ron and Karen were blind to their own weakness and hypocrisy. They felt very comfortable acting as the judge and jury of their congregation as they ruled on doctrinal soundness, member behavior, and moral performance. Ron and Karen exuded confidence to the point of pride. It was inconceivable to them that they could be wrong in their judgments or in their own personal deportment.

One of Ron and Karen's chief problems was a poor memory. When Jeremy, a young man in the congregation, was arrested for possession of an illegal substance at a party, Ron and Karen turned their full attention to his case. They followed his arrest and court proceedings. They wondered if Jeremy showed enough remorse when he came back to church. Even his parents seemed a bit too casual about the whole problem. Ron and Karen didn't like what they saw and expressed their concern and dismay to a number of members, but managed to restrain their full displeasure. But when Jeremy was asked by someone to help pass the collection plate, Ron and Karen couldn't contain any longer.

"What is this church coming to? Here is a young criminal coming back to church before his sentence is even announced, and we welcome him back as if nothing happened? Shouldn't something be said at church? Shouldn't he have to make a statement of apology to all of us? When Simon the Sorcerer sinned publicly, wasn't he publicly condemned by the Apostle? Should we do any less? I mean, we still love the boy and that is why we are so concerned. If we treat his sin too lightly, other kids in the church might start taking drugs, too. We can't believe the church is doing this. Somebody needs to do something!"

Much of what Ron and Karen say is true. God does want confession for sin (1 John 1:8). Peter did severely castigate Simon. A bad example can lead others into bad behavior. Can anyone argue with these biblical principles?

Here is where Ron and Karen have a problem that is even more severe than that of Jeremy and his parents: they can be right in their judgment but totally wrong in their attitude and disposition. Playing the role of judge and jury for so long has deceived them into thinking that they are fit for that role by some kind of moral superiority. They simply cannot conceive that their judgment would be wrong. They cannot conceive that they could be wrong.

And they can't remember their own past.

Twenty years ago, in this same community, Ron and Karen's son was arrested for possession of an illegal drug. Further, he was arrested for drug use, underage drinking, and dealing. He was even guilty of repeat offenses. Over a period of several years and a couple of treatment programs, their son gained his sobriety, paid his debt to society, and began living cleanly. Today, he is in a healthy marriage and is involved in another church.

But Ron and Karen forget that. They also forget that the church, the same church they are attending now, forgave their son and encouraged him in his first steps of sobriety.

Members of the congregation are speechless that today Ron and Karen would be so harsh and judgmental toward another young man guilty of a lesser offense than was their own son. Can they not remember?

Of course they can, but they choose not to. To remember would require humility and admission of their own family's failings. Ron and Karen may not have the internal strength or moral integrity to make such an admission. Pride is so much easier. And a natural function of pride (not self-respect, but haughty arrogance) is that we sit in judgment of everyone around us. A haughty spirit makes us feel safe and secure. It insulates us from moral assessment by other people and steels us to our own moral failings.

That is why pride eventually leads to a fall. Haughty pride that sets us above others to judge and evaluate them also puts us in competition with God. The proud and haughty person is in essence trying to unseat God and do his job for him.

Does all this mean that we can never judge the attitudes or behavior of others? Of course not. We must recognize sin and name it (Rom. 1:18-32). We must call people to repentance, confession, baptism, and faithful living. But, we must remember four things as we minister to those in sin.

One, the Bible calls us to put off ungodly dispositions and actions from our own lives (Col. 3:5-9). The person who condemns sin in another while ignoring it in himself invites God's judgment upon himself (Rom. 2:3). His haughty spirit will lead to a fall before the throne of God.

Two, judgment must be done with a view toward restoration, reconciliation, and peace (James 5:19, 20). Even if the proud man's judgment against another sinner is true, his arrogant disposition hinders any opportunity for real healing and peace to follow. "Pride only breeds quarrels ..." (Prov. 13:10), not friendship.

Three, the Bible calls for us to exercise mercy. "Do not judge, or you too will be judged. For in the same way you judge others, you will be judged, and with the measure you use, it will be measured to you." (Matt. 7:1-2). How can Ron and Karen read these verses and not feel a twinge of guilt that the same mercy and kindness that was extended to their son they now deny to another's son? Oh, that they could hear these words from Jesus: "Shouldn't you have had mercy on your fellow servant just as I had on you?" (Matt. 18:33).

Finally, Proverbs is very clear about how God feels about pride: "The LORD detests all the proud of heart. Be sure of this: They will not go unpunished" (Prov. 16:5). In condemning another with a haughty spirit (even if the judgment itself is correct), the proud person threatens his own spiritual security.

Ron and Karen have enough biblical foundation to what they are doing to convince them and many of their close friends that they are right, always and without fail. Yet they can only maintain that posture by exercising an excessive degree of pride to mask their sin and keep their critics at bay. However, all they while they are inwardly hoping no one will have the temerity to ask, "Ah, what about your son? Remember twenty years ago? Can you not extend a little compassion to Jeremy and his family?" No, they cannot extend compassion. That is one of the pitfalls of pride, and one of the reasons it sets us up for a horrible fall.

BELIEF AIDS

Whoever gives heed to instruction prospers, and blessed is he who trusts in the Lord.

Proverbs 16:20

My faith in God was birthed in my family. My parents took us to Bible classes and worship. They believed in God and taught and modeled faith for us. Faith was so natural and simple for me I couldn't understand how anyone couldn't believe in God.

My faith was buttressed in college where I studied Bible and theology. One class in particular, Christian Evidences, gave further information and support to faith. We studied some of the great thinkers in apologetics (the defense of faith) and classical arguments for believing in God.

We also learned sophisticated terms and concepts that have been used by Christian philosophers to defend the existence of God and give Christians confidence in their faith. One of these concepts is known as the Teleological Argument. The Teleological Argument is based on observation of the world, where we can see design, such as order and purpose. From this design, we can reasonably conclude that a great designer planned the order and purpose in the universe. God is the great designer.

The Ontological Argument asserts that reason rather than observation is the basis for determining that God exists. The classic statement was made by St. Anselm in the eleventh century. He wrote, "God is that than which nothing greater can be conceived." I first studied that concept when I was about nineteen years old, and remember having such a difficult time trying to grasp it that I figured it had to be right, so God must exist!

The Cosmological Argument is also known at the First Cause or Uncaused Cause argument. It posits that nothing can cause itself. We can't cause ourselves; we can't make ourselves. So, our existence must be explained on the basis of something greater than us causing our existence. That something greater than us is God, also called the unmoved mover in this argument.

I don't know how thoroughly I processed these thoughts and concepts, but they did give me some confidence that belief was reasonable. Men a whole lot smarter than me conceived these complex arguments, and if they believed in God, then it was reasonable for me to believe, too. I was comfortable with my faith.

That comfort was shattered in my mid-twenties when I read about a man's explanation for not believing in God and I couldn't successfully counter his reasons. Does God exist? Is he the creator? Is faith reasonable? These questions and more overwhelmed me through the day and late into the night. My study, sleep, and calm were wracked by these disturbing questions that robbed me of peace. I dug out my old texts and studied the great philosophical arguments from my evidences class. These classic arguments satisfied the intellectual questions I had, but they couldn't quiet the doubts I felt at an emotional and spiritual level.

These kinds of questions are tough when you are a preacher! I turned to a respected professor and explained my dilemma. He gave me a list of books and articles to read, and encouraged me to stay in the struggle. Faith was reasonable, he assured me.

With his encouragement, I began a long study and search for myself. I am happy to say that the search and struggle were worth the effort. I do believe and am confident that faith in God and his redemptive plan in Jesus are reasonable. This belief forms the basis for my life, my family, and my work. I am still a minister of the Gospel and believe this work has eternal value.

What confirmed the value of faith for me? It wasn't the complicated and sometimes confusing teleological, ontological, and cosmological arguments. No, it was something that went beyond the intellect to the heart. While a number of factors confirmed the value of faith for me, one of the most convincing was the presence of good people in my life who faithfully modeled faith in their daily lives. Those who heed the instruction of God prosper, not necessarily in worldly terms, but in the quality of their personal lives and their relationships. Good people who love God encourage my faith more than anything else, and because of them, I have been one of the blessed because of trust in the Lord.

MONEY IN THE HAND

> Of what use is money in the hand of a fool, since he has no desire to get wisdom?
>
> Proverbs 17:16

When Ray received a $100,000 settlement for an injury sustained on the job, he thought he was rich. That was equal to three or four years of his pay at the time. Numerous needs and wants previously out of reach were now affordable. He bought his parents a new car. He bought a new truck. He picked up the tab when he partied with his buddies. In less than a year, Ray was broke again. Of what use was money in his hand?

The ability of money to bless or curse is determined by the character of the person who possesses it. Money can be used selfishly in an attempt to satiate lusts of the flesh, but all such attempts are vain because the nature of lust means it can never be satisfied. Or, money can be used generously to bless the lives of the owner and others. Blessing or curse;

the determining factor lies in the heart of the one who holds the money in his hand.

A fool in Proverbs is someone uncompromisingly committed to himself. His ideas, wants, and needs take precedent over anything and everyone else. He thinks he knows everything (Prov. 12:15), so he is not willing to listen to the advice of others (Prov. 23:9). Even when he is blatantly in the wrong he refuses any correction from others (Prov. 15:5) and holds tenaciously to his position (Prov. 26:11). The fool speaks caustically (Prov. 20:3) and acts inconsiderately (Prov. 29:11), hurting and alienating people around him.

A wise man in Proverbs is committed to the various communities he finds himself in, such as his family, neighborhood, workplace, and church. Wisdom is the building block for knowledge about life (Prov. 1:2) and for having a relationship with God (Prov. 1:7). Whereas foolishness rejects a sense of community responsibility and accountability, wisdom is developed and thrives in healthy connection with other people. Wisdom first develops at the feet of mom and dad (Prov.1:8) and receives further development from other mature, learned people God sends our way (Prov. 21:11). A man of wisdom thinks about his path in life (Prov. 14:8) and creates a joyous environment for himself and those around him.

Think of the different approaches these two people will have toward their use of money. How can money serve any practical use in the hand of a fool since his use of it will be selfish and exploitive? He lacks the internal mechanism to turn off the flow of pleasure seeking. So long as the money can flow, the pleasure will flow. Such was Ray's experience.

Even if the foolish man doesn't squander his money in mindless and decadent pursuits, there are other ways to render money worthless. Money can become an idol, causing us to sacrifice everything else of value at its altar. We may, in the pursuit of money, lose our spouse, children, and standing in the community. Even if our drive for money follows only legal means to acquire it, we may grow so distant from our family due to time away in financial pursuits that the natural affection of the heart grows dim, withers, and dies. Such a man may become rich, but if he is all alone, of what comfort is his money to him? Proverbs 23:4 cautions "Do not wear yourself out to get rich; have the wisdom to show restraint." Do not wear your family out, either.

In either case, the fool with money in his hand does not bless his community. His money either runs through his hands as he merrily enjoys what money can buy, or he acquires and hoards it selfishly, not sharing or blessing the lives of others with it, even his own family.

Since the wise man is more oriented to his family, friends, and church, his use of money will vary widely from the foolish man. Should he acquire extra money, he may pay off bills and fund a retirement account, but his use of his resources won't be exploitive or hurtful of others. Because a wise man lives with a constant awareness of God, all of his resources are at God's disposal. He honor's the Lord with his wealth (Prov. 3:9) and shares generously with the poor (Prov. 22:9), knowing that whatever he does in service to the needy is regarded as being done to God (Prov. 19:17; Matt. 25:40,45).

Money is useless in the hand of the fool because it doesn't serve any beneficial purpose for anyone. It isn't even useful for the fool who possesses it because he lacks the wisdom to use it with discretion, honor, and blessing. So give a discerning eye to your money, being mindful that your use of it provides a revealing glimpse into your heart.

SKI SLOPES & PRIDE

> Before his downfall a man's heart is proud, but humility comes before honor.
>
> Proverbs 18:12

My high school shut down every Friday after lunch and everyone went to the ski slopes near East Burke, VT for physical education. Ours was not the only school in the area to do that, as became apparent when I went to my first ski lesson. I was a freshman in high school towering above all the first, second, and third graders present for their first lesson, too.

Our instructor taught us the snow plow (also called the wedge). He showed us how to put more pressure on one leg to turn, then to straighten out and put pressure on the other leg to reverse direction. He even showed us proper falling techniques to avoid injury.

After our basic lessons, this high school student and his entourage of elementary school kids made two or three runs down the bunny slope together. Then it was time to move on from the T-bar to the chair for a run down a real hill.

I was seated next to a third grader. He looked up at me and asked how old I was. He thought fourteen was pretty old. He added that his mother was also old, about twenty-two. So in addition to being in class with third graders, I now got to enjoy conversation with them. But my real humbling experience was about to begin.

Our instructor took us to a short slope with a steep drop. "If you can manage this hill, snow plowing all the way down, you can handle some of the main slopes all the way down from the top of the mountain," he said.

The instructor went ahead, asking me to stay behind and send the elementary students down one at a time. He would stand at the bottom and yell instructions to them as they navigated their first slope. I appreciated the assignment because it restored some dignity to my position: I might be in my first ski lesson with kids much younger and shorter than me, but at least the teacher acknowledged my age and maturity! That dignity didn't last for long.

After all the youngsters had reached the bottom, the instructor yelled, "Okay, Warren, your turn." I got in position at the edge of the slope, bent my knees, had my poles at the side, and shoved off. Only a short way down I put pressure on my right ski and turned it inward, causing me to turn left (which I wanted to do). But I was going too fast already, put too much pressure on the ski, and lost balance. I fell over my ski, landed on my back, and "skied" all the way down the slope on my back, with my skis in the air over my head.

Before I could get up, ten first, second, and third graders gathered around me with obvious concern for my health and safety. I'm looking up at a sea of little faces when my third-grade friend with the aged mother asked, "Are you okay, Warren?"

I was until he asked.

What makes humility so tough is we don't like the conditions that produce it - failing, falling, and fumbling. We like to be on top of our game, showing well, standing above the crowd. That was my role when the instructor made me his temporary assistant. The descent from that lofty position to one of humble, "Uh, yeah, I'm okay kids, thanks," was swift.

Learning that humility comes before honor and recognition is a hard lesson. To achieve something worthy of respectful admiration from others takes years of sacrifice, discipline, and hard work. There are no short cuts. Speaking persuasively, building a house, presiding over a company, or re-building a car engine takes time, practice, and effort. If we won't willingly give up false pride for the lowly journey of growth and development, God may send a slope our way to teach us that humility comes before honor.

NEVER SATISFIED

> The fear of the Lord leads to life: Then one rests content, untouched by trouble.
>
> Proverbs 19:23

Robert E. Lee supposedly said: "Postal officials tell us that before Christmas, tons of letters are delivered to the post office to Santa Claus, but after Christmas, very few letters of thanks are written to him. From childhood onward, human beings seem to be characterized by thankless-ness" (21st CC Nov/Dec 2008, P.24).

I agree with him, if indeed he really said it. I've never written a thank you letter to Santa Claus. I do remember slipping downstairs early one Christmas morning and seeing a pile of gifts and saying, "Thank you, Santa." But I didn't write to him.

Special days like Christmas bring special gifts with them. But, how long after afterward does it take for us to begin thinking about what we would like next Christmas?

Financial fortunes are made every day in America. Some industries are booming and have not felt any of the financial reversals. I hope we have strong industries that can carry us until others are developed. Even in times of upheaval, we have strong expectations of what we would like, fortunes that can continue to be made, and abundant Christmas celebrations. I hope for that. But we should keep a few ideas in mind.

One, every blessing we have is from God. Every meal is a blessing from God, whether a plump turkey or a lean ear of corn. Every article of clothing is from God, whether a new three piece suit or hand-me-down jeans (Deut. 8:10-14; 18).

Two, gratitude is always a proper response to God, no matter how much or how little we actually have. "Enter his gates with thanksgiving and his courts with praise; give thanks to him and praise his name" (Ps. 100:4).

Three, even a little with the Lord is better than an abundance of material things without him. There are different kinds of proverbs within the book of Proverbs. One form is known as the "better than" proverb where two things are compared, and one is stated as being better than the other. Here are a couple of "better than" proverbs: "Better a little with the fear of the LORD than great wealth with turmoil" (Prov. 15:16). "Better a meal of vegetables where there is love than a fattened calf with hatred" (Prov. 15:17).

Each one of the these proverbs focuses on the importance of relationship with God, relationship with others, and the importance of spiritual values, over and above having things of this world. Perhaps the reason some of our brothers and sisters in impoverished regions can be very comfortable with their lack compared to the abundance we enjoy is that they are less focused on what to wear and drive, than in what is in the heart.

Four, at some point in life it is appropriate for us to say, "Lord, thank you for everything you have given me. I have enough." I don't know what that point is. Even as I say this I'm thinking about a sports jacket I would like and a hunting rifle that would be neat to own. Do I actually need them?

Have you ever had older people in your family who said, "Don't give us anything for Christmas, we have enough? Cheryl had a grandmother like that. We'd give her a present for Christmas, and the next year she might give it back to us. It was kind of annoying! It is also a good place to be in life. She was genuinely able to say about the things of this world, "I have enough. I'm satisfied. Thank you, Lord."

LIFE, PROSPERITY, & HONOR

> He who pursues righteousness and love finds life, prosperity and honor.
>
> Proverbs 21:21

I stumbled upon one of my greatest wildlife trophies while hunting for something else. On a hillside in Sunlight Basin outside of Cody, Wyoming, I found a large antler shed by a bull elk. I have since used it many times in talks and demonstrations for schools and churches.

Some of the greatest joys in life are serendipitous; that is, we experience them while engaged in another activity. Such joys are unexpected. In a sense, serendipitous joys find us, rather than us finding them.

Life, prosperity, and honor are in a sense serendipitous. We can work for a good life, material gain, and respect. But the greatest experiences of these blessings may come to us unexpectedly as we are engaged in the daily grind of life.

Part of the daily grind of life is to pursue righteousness and love. The idea of being righteous in the Old Testament was to walk in faithful, covenant relationship with God. It meant to depend on him in our walk: "Trust in the Lord with all your heart and lean not on your own understanding" (Prov. 3:5). At such times the pursuit of righteousness is more than a daily grind; it is war for our soul. Conflict will rage within us at times as we wrestle with God's command to forgive and reconcile versus our own inclination to resent and retaliate. Pursuing righteousness and leaning upon the Lord's understanding at such times means we subdue our personal inclination for what God calls us to do. We also wage such battles over respect vs. lust, contentment vs. greed, and holding our tongue vs. gossiping.

Love is also part of our daily grind. It is the chief attitude and behavior that governs our treatment of other people. From Leviticus 19:18 to 2 John 5, love has served as the bedrock of proper relationships with others. To love others is to seek their best interests (Phil. 2:4), to nurture their spiritual growth (Peck, *The Road Less Traveled*, 81), and to accept them unconditionally. This doesn't mean we approve of their lifestyle or behavior, but that we accept them where they are and nurture their spiritual growth at that point. That is difficult. How do we love a gossiper? A liar? Even if we are repulsed by their behavior, is our character mature enough to seek their best interests? Can we love a beautiful person without lusting for them? Can we love a rich person without craving a share of their wealth? Can we love a prominent person without playing on their position for some advancement of our own? Our own frail character will strain the integrity of our honest and pure affections for the beautiful, the well-off, and the well-placed. Love, like righteousness, thus becomes part of the daily grind, part of the war we must wage in our hearts to pursue what is truly worthwhile in life.

God promises that if we pursue these two qualities we will find our treasure. Like an elk antler lying on the side of the hillside, we will stumble upon pleasurable and significant experiences in life when we make the pursuit of higher goals our aim.

God promises life. Life is the flow of blood in our veins and breath in our lungs. But it is more than merely surviving; it is thriving. The word life is also a metaphor for enjoying what is good and worthwhile. The man who pursues righteousness and love will know what it is to really live. His relationships will be honest and dependable. He will have companions who stick closer than brothers (Prov. 18:24). His marriage will be a fountain of refreshing water that never runs dry or overflows its banks (Prov. 5:15-18). He will be respected in business and the community. Life for him will be good.

God also promises prosperity. The word for prosperity is also the word for righteousness. The NIV translators probably used prosperity because righteousness had already been used in the first part of the verse (Bland, *Proverbs*, 194). The Sage may be saying that the one who pursues righteousness will find it, and appreciate it for its own value. A relationship with God is reward enough in itself, and in that sense life is prosperous. In another passage, the Sage says love and faithfulness will win a man a good name in the sight of God and man (Prov. 3:3-5). Proverbs also offers hope for material prosperity to the person who works hard and lives right. The righteous man honors his commitments, works hard, and enjoys the fruit of honest profit (Prov. 28:19).

Finally, God promises honor. Honor is recognition for living well. People may seek honor by promoting themselves and shining the spotlight in their own direction. But that is attention, not honor. Honor is what other people give you because you have weathered the grind, fought the battles nobly, and rebounded from the defeats (through repentance and change). Honor is when your kids tell you "Thanks for being good parents," and when your neighbors mow your yard when you have been ill. Honor is when your boss says, "Take some extra time, we know how you work around here." Honor is when Jesus says, "Well done, good and faithful servant."

Life, prosperity, and honor are enjoyed by those who pursued something else—righteousness and love. Pursue doesn't mean a half-hearted attempt. It is a passionate quest (Longman, *Proverbs*, 396). It means to put our heart into the attempt. It is to give our all to live a good life. For those who will make the effort, God says he will reward them.

Finding a beautiful elk antler was serendipitous for me. It was a fortunate discovery experienced while seeking something else worthwhile. Life, prosperity, and honor come into our lives the same way as blessings from God.

SUGGESTIONS FOR STUDYING PROV-ERBS

HOW TO PREACH ONE-SENTENCE PROVERBS

The one-sentence proverbs from chapters 10:1 to 29:27 offer challenges to preaching because of their brevity and succinctness. They seem to lack sufficient material from which to develop a full length lesson. But, there are a few approaches to these proverbs that make them valuable material for sermons.

Behind every proverb is a story, and the single-statement is simply a summation of a drama lived out in real life. For example, the Sage provides the background story to the numerous sluggard proverbs. In 24:30-34 he describes an experience of observing the unattended farm of the sluggard. Weeds had overtaken the crops and the protective wall was crumbling. The Sage wrote, "I applied my heart to what I observed and learned a lesson from what I saw: A little sleep, a little slumber, a little folding of the hands to rest— and poverty will come on you like a bandit, and scarcity like an armed man" (vv.32-34). This brief statement of financial and social doom for the lazy man is a summation statement of a larger story that the wise man has studied with keen observation.

The approach of the Sage is to study the attitudes and behaviors of people and the eventual outcomes of their actions. He pays attention to cause and effect, noting how certain actions produce discernible results. He then summarizes what he observes in brief, tightly worded phrases that capture the essence of what he has observed and reflected upon. The result is a compact statement encapsulating a vital truth distilled from a much larger and complicated drama. The proverbs thus provoke our thinking, luring us into their story, and challenging us to imagine their application in the drama of our own lives.

There are several steps I have found helpful in using the sentence proverbs for sermons or classes. Even if we don't know the original context for a proverbial statement, we can catch the essence of it and imagine situations where it would apply. The steps are as follows:

1) Read, reflect and pray upon a particular proverb. Look for key words or ideas in the sentence being repeated in surrounding verses. Does this verse fit into a larger theme? What seems to be the main idea? What does it say about attitudes, behavior, or life?

2) Think of an Old Testament story that illustrates the truth of the proverb you are studying. Since there is a story behind every proverb, find one that seems to flesh out the truth of a particular proverb.

3) Think of a New Testament text or story that illustrates this truth as well. Many times a statement of Jesus or situation in his life complements the proverb.

4) Finally, think of a situation in your own life that exemplifies the message or statement you are studying. Ideally, you will spend enough time reflecting upon a proverb that you will think of situations in your own life where it applies. You may think of an instance in where you lived up to the expectation of the proverb, or you may think of a situation where you didn't. In either case, your own life experience validates the truth you are studying.

Here is an example of how a sermon may be developed from a one-sentence proverb. I'll use Proverbs 11:24: "One man gives freely, yet gains even more; another withholds unduly, but comes to poverty."

1) Study, reflection, prayer, and larger context.

This verse is part of a larger theme in the book about generosity and selfishness. Following verses discuss generosity, hoarding (selfishness), goodwill (the result of a generous spirit), and trusting in riches. This one verse opens up a wide array of possibilities for a sermon, and even at this early stage it is apparent that you will have to think about how to narrow the scope of the lesson.

2) An Old Testament story.

Possibilities could include Moses, who gave up life in the palace with its accompanying wealth to live among the impoverished Israelites. He did not give material things, but gave his very life to his people, and what he gained was not physical possessions or wealth, but much spiritual treasure (Ex. 2:11ff; Heb. 11:24-28).

Think also of Boaz. He graciously allowed the less fortunate to glean his fields after the initial harvest (as the law stipulated). He gave freely and God blessed him not only with an abundant harvest, but with a wife, Ruth.

These are two stories that exemplify the positive aspect of Proverbs 11:24. Negative examples can be considered, too. During David's sojourn in the wilderness, he requested aid from a local farmer. Instead of providing aid, the farmer, Nabal, offered insults and almost lost his life when David came after him in anger. Only the intervention of his wife, Abigail, spared him. But, even that was very short lived as he died shortly after. Nabal withheld and came to a fate worse than poverty (1 Sam. 25).

3) A New Testament story.

Numerous stories from Jesus' life and ministry would fit here. Think of the two brothers fighting over an inheritance (Luke 12:13ff), the rich man and Lazarus (Luke 16:19ff), and the rich young ruler (Luke 18:18ff). These stories all contain negative considerations of what it is to withhold blessings from others. Considered positively, think of Zacchaeus. As a tax collector, Zacchaeus earned his living by overcharging the citizens in his territory. Tax collectors were thought of as little more than legitimized thieves. They were hated by the people because of their abuse of power and how they amassed their fortunes by taking from others. But after his encounter with Jesus, Zacchaeus opened up his tight fist and began to share, pledging to make proper recompense for overcharging, and giving half of his possessions to the poor. This man overcame his tendency to withhold and began to give freely. What did he receive for his change of heart? Jesus said of him, "Today salvation has come to this house ..."

4) Personal story.

I remember my parents offering help to people on numerous occasions: to motorists stranded in the country, to an injured friend, and to neighbors needing help repairing their homes. Sometimes what was freely given was money; at other times, it was time and labor. I have seen my parents gain from their generosity. It may not have been financial gain, but appreciation and friendship.

In Proverbs, the man or woman who withholds is considered selfish and greedy. They do not receive God's approval, and will not be blessed for their behavior. God likes the righteous spirit of generosity and mercy. These are the attitudes and dispositions we want to pass on to our children, and Proverbs 11:24 was written to help us do that.

HOW TO PREACH THEMES IN PROVERBS

While the one-sentence proverbs can be, and often are, treated individually, you will notice as you read the book that the subject of a proverb tends to be repeated throughout the whole work. In fact, the Sage develops and provides extended treatment of a number of themes. Among them are:

- Wisdom (prudence, understanding, knowledge)
- Folly (mockery, simple, hating knowledge)
- Fear of the Lord
- Listening to instruction
- Speech
- Integrity
- Morality
- Righteousness
- Wickedness
- Money and more.

One way to preach individual verses on these topics is with the one-sentence method, but another approach is to collect the various verses on a given theme and study them together to see the message or messages that develop.

Glenn Pemberton used this approach in an excellent study of the fool. By looking at various verses together, he identified the following traits of foolish behavior.

First, a person may commit foolish actions without actually being a fool, at least not yet. Some examples of this would be speaking before listening (Prov. 18:13) and acting without self-discipline (Prov. 5:23). Such behavior is typical of children or untrained young adults. Someone who is insecure and looking for attention or acceptance may also act out in these ways. While the behavior is foolish, it does not mean the person is a fool

The second stage is for a person to consciously act foolish. This person's conduct is no longer just a lack of discipline, but is now intentional misbehavior. Consider a young person who is consistently disobedient to his parents (Prov. 15:5), purposely repeats foolish behavior (26:11), and even finds pleasure in it (15:21a). Once he begins to enjoy his foolish behavior, a young man may lack reason or motivation to turn from it. He is on well on the road to becoming foolish.

A person moves to the third level of becoming foolish when he positions himself beyond correction. That is, he insulates himself from the wisdom and counsel of others, especially from those who care for him and seek his best interests, such as parents, teachers, coaches, and Sunday school teachers. He places himself beyond correction because he chooses the path of least resistance (1:8ff.) and thinks he is always right (12:15), thus shutting out any wise input from others. By doing so, he demonstrates that he hates knowledge and wisdom (1:7 & 22). This posture makes it nearly impossible for him to see his own sins and folly.

The fourth and final stage in the development of a fool is collapse and rage. Decent people grow weary of the fool and distant themselves from him, leaving him alone to pursue his self-destructive behavior. The selfish pursuits of greed, sensuous pleasure, or shallow popularity take their toll, leaving the fool to wallow in disgrace and dishonor. When trouble comes into his life (broken relationships or punishment), he blames others, even God. "A man's own folly ruins his life, yet his heart rages against the Lord"

(Prov. 19:3). This man is in the advanced stages of folly. He consciously acts foolish, enjoys it, and in his mind is never at fault for the bad things that occur in his life. Since he can't see his own guilt and doesn't have the conscience to experience shame, he can't repent and change.

Pemberton says, "Becoming a fool requires no decision, no action—by anyone. A person who does not actively decide for wisdom will ultimately become a fool. In the same way, a parent (or community) who does not deliberately shape a child's character into wisdom will become the parent of a fool." Also, "Through their proverbs the sages challenge the reader to face their own character development" (Glenn Pemberton, "Fool's Life: Deformation of Character" in Restoration Quarterly.)

This is an excellent example of gathering together the various proverbs on a given theme and studying them together to see the message they convey.

Below are some other brief examples of what a thematic study might produce.

Friends:

Be careful (Prov. 12:26)

Be selective (Prov. 22:24-25)

Exercise wisdom (Prov.23:9)

Impure motives in friendship:

Wealth (Prov. 14:20)

Flattery (Prov. 5:3)

Power (Prov. 19:6)

Qualities of true friendship:

Pleasantness (Prov. 27:9)

Honesty (Prov. 27:5)

Tough love (Prov. 27:6)

Forgiveness (Prov. 17:9)

Loyalty (Prov.17:17, 27:10 and 18:24).

As you develop a thematic lesson, illustrate your message with other stories from scripture to show how the message of Proverbs fits into the larger biblical witness. Also, add stories from your personal life to show how they continue to bear upon contemporary life.

HOW TO PREACH EXTENDED SECTIONS IN PROVERBS

Another approach to preaching Proverbs is preaching extended sections of verses. Extended sections refers to extended discourses, such as occurs in chapters 1 through 9, or that appear in clusters in chapters 10 through 29. Though many of the verses in this latter section appear without a context and without any apparent connection to the verses preceding or following, there are occasions where repetition of words or key ideas create a cluster of verses that are joined together and may be treated as a group. Proverbs 27:14-19 is an example of apparently disparate verses that have a thread that binds them together and provide a powerful lesson.

Proverbs 27:14-19 is connected by similar subject and content matter. All of the verses are concerned with relationships between individuals, and at least two of the relationships described are what we would call dysfunctional today. In Proverbs wisdom and character are not developed in isolation but in relationships with other people, even if the relationships are sometimes strained and challenging. As this passage will demonstrate, dysfunctional relationships have the potential to develop wisdom and build character in those who approach the problems in a godly manner.

In verse 14 a man is disturbed by a neighbor who blesses him loudly in the morning. A good neighbor is one who avoids harming his neighbor (3:29) and brings him blessing (17:17). This neighbor, though pretending to be friendly with his greeting, is not being a blessing. He is rude and insincere.

In verse 15 a man is disturbed by his wife's quarrelsome behavior. The wise wife builds her home (14:1), a reference to care and nurture. The environment she creates is a peaceful one where every member of the family is cherished. But the quarrelsome wife is critical and argumentative, setting her husband and family on edge. Instead of protecting the home, she attacks it and disrupts it, threatening to destroy it. Her husband fails in his attempts restrain her behavior (v.16). Instead of the home being a place of peace and security, it is turbulent and chaotic.

Verses 14 and 15 present two challenging relationships, one between a man and his neighbor and another between a man and his wife. Both the neighbor and the spouse are rude and inconsiderate and make the man's life miserable. It is easy to imagine ourselves in such situations, and desiring to get out. But, the Sage does not allow the man an easy exit. Instead, he uses the dysfunction of these two relationships to mature and shape the man.

In verse 17 the Sage writes, "As iron sharpens iron, so one man sharpens another." This verse is typically used to describe friendships that are pleasant and affirming, such as two friends that encourage each other and walk together through tough times. But, this verse actually appears in a context of anger, feuding, and chaos. Rather than being descriptive of relationships that are mutually encouraging and helpful, it is used of relationships that are chaotic and painful. The Sage seems to be saying that it is in the context of relationships that are stressful and trying that one grows and matures.

The metaphor of Proverbs 27:17 supports this idea. Two pieces of iron or metal rubbed together produce friction and heat. Rubbing steel together is abrasive and it wears on the edges. Yet it is in this abrasive action that the edges are honed and sharpened. Likewise, it is in the abrasive nature of relationships that we often find our most growth. Friendly relationships are more desirable, but, at least on occasion, the friction of distressful relationships, though not enjoyable or fulfilling, can be beneficial.

Proverbs 27:18 then says, "He who tends a fig tree will eat its fruit, and he who looks after his master will be honored." This verse employs two metaphors for the years of nurture and care it may take for a relationship to pass through periods of chaos and disorder before it begins to sweeten and provide joy to those who are in it. Raising fruit to the point of harvest can take years of nurture and care before one can enjoy the sweet produce. A faithful servant who for years labors without recognition or appreciation may one day earn the attention and favor of his master. In the same way, people who nurture relationships as a gardener does the fruit tree and a servant does the master may one day enjoy a harvest of peace and unity in the relationship. So, verse 18 encourages members of dysfunctional relationships to stay engaged and face the conflict wisely and maturely.

Verse 19 provides a conclusion to this extended collection: "As water reflects a face, so a man's heart reflects the man." The meaning of the metaphor of water is found in the second part of the verse. As the reflective quality of water allows a person to view their own face, so the face of another person can provide reflection as well.

Bruce Waltke says the idea of seeing our reflection has two possibilities. One, through contemplating our own lives and behavior, we may gain insight into the content of our heart. What thoughts dominate our mind? Are we frequently angry? Vengeful? Do we demonstrate appreciation to the people around us? The answers to such questions can reveal much about the state of our heart and character.

A second way to understand this metaphor is that we can see ourselves reflected in the responses other people make to us. Are people often short with us? Do they avoid our company? Are they impatient with us? If these things happen only occasionally, we may assume the other person has a problem or is having a bad day. But, if they happen with regularity and by a number of people, the problem may not be with everyone else, but with us. In the negative responses of other people toward us, we can see the reflection of our own character defects. One writer calls the interaction between the various participants in Proverbs 27 the reciprocity of relationship (Roland Murphy, *Proverbs, Word Biblical Commentary*, 209).

In the first option, we look into our own hearts. In the second option, we look at the behavior of other people toward us. Dave Bland refers to these two options as introspection and interaction (Bland, "Iron Sharpens Iron," *Leaven*). While both options are viable, the appeal of interaction is that through the interplay of relationships the participants can gain greater understanding and clarity of thought about themselves and others.

Wisdom "is a community effort" (Longman, *Proverbs*, 481). In community we experience conflict, and in the working toward resolution, we not only improve the health of the community, but we expose the flaws of our own character as well, and in the light of exposure is found hope for our own growth and development. So what appeared to be a random assortment of verses in Proverbs 27 is actually a cluster of verses that share the thread of conflict, resolution, and character development. Careful reading of the biblical text and the use of good commentaries will reveal other verses in Proverbs that have a thread or threads running through them that bind them together and lend themselves to be treated as an extended section.

SCRIPTURE INDEX

Proverbs 1:7   36, 37, 224

Proverbs 2:7-8   85
Proverbs 2:11   224

Proverbs 3:1-2   41, 64, 129
Proverbs 3:5   45, 229, 231
Proverbs 3:6   200
Proverbs 3:11, 12   87
Proverbs 3:29   43, 195
Proverbs 3:34   82

Proverbs 4:3-4   45, 72
Proverbs 4:23   128

Proverbs 5:3, 8   28
Proverbs 5:15   23-24
Proverbs 5:15-18   25, 115
Proverbs 5:23   237

Proverbs 6:23   119
Proverbs 6:25   30

Proverbs 8:5   107

Proverbs 8:30-31   89

Proverbs 9:1-5   97
Proverbs 9:13-18   98

Proverbs 10:3-4   102
Proverbs 10:4   99, 135
Proverbs 10:7   73, 121
Proverbs 10:9-10   152
Proverbs 10:11   152
Proverbs 10:14   48, 152
Proverbs 10:19   78
Proverbs 10:20   151
Proverbs 10:28   137
Proverbs 10:32   152, 153, 170

Proverbs 11:9   47, 195
Proverbs 11:10   49
Proverbs 11:11   155
Proverbs 11:23   178
Proverbs 11:24   234-236
Proverbs 11:29   75

Proverbs 12:2   103
Proverbs 12:11   111
Proverbs 12:13   157
Proverbs 12:15   188, 224
Proverbs 12:18   50, 77, 160
Proverbs 12:26   180

Proverbs 13:10   211, 220
Proverbs 13:11   103
Proverbs 13:14   51
Proverbs 13:18   105
Proverbs 13:24   51, 53
Proverbs 13:20   53

Proverbs 14:1	36
Proverbs 14:8	108, 224
Proverbs 14:10	240
Proverbs 14:13	213
Proverbs 14:18	107
Proverbs 15:10	109
Proverbs 15:29	83
Proverbs 15:30	182, 214, 183-184
Proverbs 15:31	185
Proverbs 15:33	91
Proverbs 16:7	216
Proverbs 16:18	218
Proverbs 16:20	221
Proverbs 16:21	49
Proverbs 16:24	50, 159
Proverbs 16:26	55
Proverbs 16:28	164, 195
Proverbs 16:31	128
Proverbs 17:1	78
Proverbs 17:10	122
Proverbs 17:12	188
Proverbs 17:16	223
Proverbs 18:4a	201
Proverbs 18:8	162
Proverbs 18:12	225
Proverbs 18:13	57, 173, 237
Proverbs 18:21	47, 160
Proverbs 18:24	175, 230
Proverbs 19:11	145, 189
Proverbs 19:18	59
Proverbs 19:20	193

Proverbs 19:23   227

Proverbs 20:7   125
Proverbs 20:21   104
Proverbs 20:29   127
Proverbs 20:30   193

Proverbs 21:9   33
Proverbs 21:17   76
Proverbs 21:21   229
Proverbs 21:23   164

Proverbs 22:6   131
Proverbs 22:15   61, 193

Proverbs 23:22   63
Proverbs 23:24   143
Proverbs 23:31-32   117

Proverbs 24:10-12   139
Proverbs 24:27   111-112
Proverbs 24:32   133

Proverbs 25:1   205
Proverbs 25:11   161, 166
Proverbs 25:17   176
Proverbs 25:21   148

Proverbs 26:20-21   168
Proverbs 26:24   169

Proverbs 27:5   131, 192
Proverbs 27:6   191
Proverbs 27:7   113
Proverbs 27:9   195
Proverbs 27:12   116

Proverbs 27:14-19   239-242
Proverbs 27:14   195
Proverbs 27:16   114
Proverbs 27:17   196, 198, 240
Proverbs 27:18   198, 240
Proverbs 27:19   241

Proverbs 28:19   231

Proverbs 29:7   93
Proverbs 29:11   141
Proverbs 29:15   65
Proverbs 29:17   65, 69
Proverbs 29:22   165

Proverbs 31   35-37, 37-39
Proverbs 31:30   35

SUBJECT INDEX

Abortion	202
Adultery/Affair	28-30
Alcoholism	186
Amis, Martin, *Koba the Dread: Laughter and the Twenty Million*	177
Anderson, Herbert & Edward Foley, *Mighty Stories, Dangerous Rituals*	173
Anger	177, 209
Arguing	168-70, 211-13
Bidermann, Gotlob Herbert, *In Deadly Combat: A German Soldier's Memoir of the Eastern Front*	148
Bland, Dave, *Proverbs,* College Press NIV Commentary	136, 163, 167, 180, 189, 231
—, "Iron Sharpens Iron," *Leaven* (8:2) 2000	200, 242
Character	66, 136, 155, 177, 201, 210
Choices	41-42
Communication	71-73, 78
Compassion	147-149
Contentment	227-29
Cowardice	139-41
Criticism	131
Defensiveness	141-43
DeWit Hyde, William, *The Five Great Philosophies of Life*	138
Dinesen, Isak, *Sorrow-Acre Winter's Tales*	94
Discipline	87-89, 105-7, 109-11, 113-15
Of children	50-53, 59-69
Dobson, James	
Parenting Isn't for Cowards	67
When God Doesn't Make Sense	84
Drunkenness	115-17

Encouragement   50, 184, 214-16
Envy   215
Failure   72, 81-83
Faith   221-23
Faust, Shelley, *Is That You Lord Blog*   50
Fear of the Lord,   35-37
Fool, Development of   237-238
Fool/Foolishness   61-63, 97-99, 107-9, 123, 135,
                                       151-53, 154, 155-57, 187-89, 224
Fox, Michael, *Proverbs*, Anchor Bible Commentary   86
Forgiving   145-47, 189-90
Friendship   175-77, 179-82, 191-94,
                                                   196-200, 230, 238-39
          Qualities of,   195
Funerals   143-44
Farming   101-3
Gallagher, Kathy, *When His Secret Sin Breaks Your Heart*   201
Goals   111-13
Gossip   162-64, 168-70
Grizzly Bear   197-99
Happiness   137-39
Holidays   183
Humility   91-93
Influence   53-55, 127-28, 131-34
Ingram, Nathan, *Christ at the Coffee Shop*   57-58
Instruction, of children   79
Integrity   53-55, 124-28
Judgment   218-21
Justice   139-41
Larson, Martin, *Jefferson: Magnificent Populist*   206
Laziness   101-3
Listening   173-15, 188, 213-14
          to our children   57-58,
          children to parents   63-65
Longman, Tremper, *Proverbs*, Baker Commentary   105, 162, 166, 184, 231, 242
Love   82-83, 230
Lust   30
Marriage
          Adultery in,   28-30
          Differences/divorce,   33-35
          Romance in,   30-33
          Sex in marriage,   23-28
McCartney, Bill, *Blind Spots*   202

McCreesh, Thomas. "Wisdom as Wife: Proverbs 31:10-31," *Revue Biblique* 92 (1985) 38

McNeal, Reggie, *A Work of Heart*   187

Mentoring   53-55, 119-20, 131-32

Mercy   218-221

Money   101-4, 223-225, 227-229

Motivation   55

Murphy, Roland. *Proverbs*, Word Biblical Commentary   154, 241

Neighbor, rude   196

Parents

       Respect for,   63-65

Patton, John, *Is Human Forgiveness Possible*   147

Peace   216-18

       In the home   69

Peck, M. Scott, *The Road Less Traveled*   230

Pemberton, Glenn, "Fool's Life: Deformation of Character" in *Restoration Quarterly*
                                                                    237-238

Perdue, Leo G., *Proverbs*, Interpretation   153

Plantinga, Cornelius, *Not the Way it is Supposed to Be: A Breviary of Sin*   140

Prayer 83-85

Pride   194, 211-13, 218-21, 225-27

Proverbs

       How to read   11-13

       Who wrote the proverbs   15-17

       Character-consequence   135-37

       How to Study and Preach   233-42

Rebuke   122-24, 188, 191-94

Respect   128-30

Righteousness   49, 53-55, 110,
                                                   124-26, 157-59, 178-79

Daniel-Rops, *Jesus and His Times*   92

Rosemond, John, *A Family of Value*   68

Shawchuck, Norman and Roger Heuser, *Managing the Congregation*   147

Simple   107-9

Smedes, Lewis B., *Forgive & Forget: Healing the Hurts We Don't Deserve*   146

Smick, Elmer B., Theological Wordbook of hte OT, 1:151   195

Solomon   205-7

Spanking   51-53

Speech, see Words

Storytelling   45-47

Submission to God   200-01

Teaching   49-51-52

Thinking   79, 108

Trust   42-45

Van Leeuwen, Raymond C. *Proverbs*, New Interpreter's Bible   140
Waltke, Bruce. *Book of Proverbs*, NICOT, 2004   90, 102, 151, 153-54, 179
                                                        180, 196, 199, 211, 241
Whybray, R.N., *The Book of Proverbs*, Cambridge Bible Commentary   53
Wicked   49, 154-59, 179
Wisdom   53-55, 83, 97-99, 123, 135,
                                                        151-54, 205-7, 212, 224
          How Proverbs produces,   17-20
          Order in Life,   20-22
Wives
          Noble character   35-39
          Relationship with husband   25-28
Woods, Serena, *Grace is for Sinners*, 2009   83
Words   151-66
          Words children should never hear,   47-49
          Words children should hear,   49-51
          Words, appropriate,   166-67, 170-71
Work   99-103